NEW YORK BREWERIES

NEW YORK BREWERIES

LEW BRYSON

STACKPOLE
BOOKS

Published by
STACKPOLE BOOKS
5067 Ritter Road
Mechanicsburg, PA 17055
www.stackpolebooks.com

The author and publisher encourage all readers to visit the breweries and sample their beers, but recommend that those who consume alcoholic beverages travel with a nondrinking driver.

Printed in the United States of America

10 9 8 7 6 5 4 3 2 1

First Edition

Cover design by Caroline Stover

Labels and logos used with permission of the breweries.

Library of Congress Cataloging-in-Publication Data

Bryson, Lew.
    New York breweries / by Lew Bryson.
       p.   cm.
    Includes index.
    ISBN 0-8117-2817-X (pbk.)
    1. Bars (Drinking establishments)–New York (State)–Guidebooks. 2. Microbreweries–New York (State)–Guidebooks. 3. Breweries–New York (State)–Guidebooks. I. Title.
TX950.57.N7 B79   2003
647.95747–dc21

                                  2002153841

*This book is dedicated to the memory
of two of my favorite New Yorkers:*

F. X. Matt II,
*who always had time to talk to a librarian
who wanted to write about beer,*

and

Curt Childs,
*who raised the love of my life and
never questioned my career choice.
At least, not to my face.*

*I miss them both, and I am deeply in their debt.
This one's for you, gentlemen.*

Contents

FOREWORD

It was in the small airport of Idaho Falls that I discovered Lew Bryson and I shared a similar taste for exploration—make that beer exploration. We had arrived simultaneously at the invite of Anheuser-Busch for a writers' round-table conference and a tour of the massive A-B maltings.

We had both been studying the Grand Tetons on the descent. Knowing we had a few hours to kill until the welcome dinner, we headed over to the car rental desk like it was the only thing to do. We pointed the car in the direction of the mountains and found a gem, Otto Bros. Brewing, just over the border in Wyoming. And we made it back for dinner—at least in time for the main course!

Since I have known him, Lew Bryson has hunted down brewery after brewery, sharing his boundless enthusiasm for the task with his readers. Brewers are happy to have Lew visit, too. His infectious laugh announces his arrival; his calling card is a guarantee that he will "get it right."

In his first book, Bryson performed a valuable service to beer lovers—both resident and visiting—in Pennsylvania. Now he's providing the same service to those in New York State.

From the tip of Long Island, to the bowels of the city, to the Canadian border, Bryson has personally gathered the information that makes this guide such a valuable resource.

New York bears some resemblance to Pennsylvania, brewerywise: Both states have a rich brewing history, both have seen pioneer microbreweries emerge, followed by brewpubs and brewery restaurants; and both boast about the same number of breweries today, roughly fifty.

Bryson traces the heyday of New York State brewing, when Brooklyn was the nation's brewing capital—most of the breweries indeed moved to Pennsylvania—to the modern-day opening of the Belgian-style Brewery Ommegang near Cooperstown, once the heart of hops-growing country.

Old giants such as Matt Brewing in Utica and High Falls (the former Genesee) in Rochester still thrive; regional craft breweries have become established; and brewpubs offer rich and diverse experiences. Whether you're exploring the Adirondacks, roaming the city streets, or shuffling off to Buffalo, Lew Bryson's guide is a must for the beer lover's back pocket, or at least the glove box.

Tony Forder
Editor and copublisher, *Ale Street News*

ACKNOWLEDGMENTS

I had a lot of help with this book, and it's a good thing: I *needed* it! First thanks go to Kyle Weaver, my editor at Stackpole Books, who always knew we had a series here.

My thanks also go to my longtime publishers: Tony Forder at *Ale Street News* and John Hansell at *Malt Advocate,* two of the very first people who paid me for writing. We've seen a lot together, guys. Special thanks to Tony for the Foreword.

For giving me two thoughtful interviews way back in 1994, my thanks to Steve Hindy of Brooklyn Brewing and the late F. X. Matt II of Matt Brewing: my first brewer interviews as a writer.

Many thanks to the people who taught me about beer. To Dr. Paul Thibault, who first put a good beer in my hand, and the late Wilhelm Lauzus, who put that beer in Paul's hand and so many more in mine. Again to John Hansell, who opened my eyes to how little I knew about beer after ten years of learning about it. To Michael Jackson, who taught me about dealing with editors (I'm one of his) and handling questions you don't want to answer.

To the people who supply me with excellent beer: Tom Peters of Monk's Cafe in Philadelphia, Ray Deter of d.b.a, the owners and staff of the Incredible Walkable Triumvirate of Syracuse (the Blue Tusk, Clark's Alehouse, and Awful Al's), and the folks at MacGregor's and Beers of the World in Rochester.

There are some great beer people on the Internet, like the No Bull Inn gang, Bob-O, RP, and Mikey: You keep me humble and laughing. There's Paris Lundis at the best brewery and bar locating website on the net: www.pubcrawler.com. Thanks for all the great bars I've found at your site (and you're welcome for all the New York ones I've added!). I don't know what I'd do without the phone number and address finding capabilities of the www.Google.com search engine site. And to the people on the USENET newsgroups, the geeks at rec.food.drink.beer and the freaks at alt.beer: Thanks for your contentious support.

Thanks to some of the friendliest beer geeks in New York City for their friendly, boozy tutelage: Andy Ager, Phil Clarke, Bill Coleman, Steve Snyder, and Dave Witzel. And to my old friend Dan Raspler, who shared his NYC apartment. Thanks also to the Salt City Homebrewers in Syracuse for giving me such a warm welcome when I crashed your meeting.

My thanks to almost all the brewers of New York. Thanks first to Bill Newman, who started things on such a good foot, and apologies from all of us for not drinking more beer. Thanks to Matthew Reich, who gave it a serious try before Manhattan was ready. Thanks to Marc and Tim at Middle Ages, fellow lovers of Ringwood. To the Bethels, who run the friendliest neighborhood non-brewpub I've ever seen. To Mark and Pete at Blue Point: You *are* cocky, but the beer sure is good. To Phil Markowski, who always takes much more time to talk to me than I deserve. To Joe Rogers, who's completely obsessive about his beer and other things (get that muskie out of the freezer!). To Rob Davis, a wide-open guy who makes real good beer. To Nat Collins, who has always brewed great beer when people let him. To Don and Wendy at Ommegang, who made me see the evil of chain restaurants. To Goose Gossage, who saved all my Albany notes! And to Neill Acer, who told me to shut up and drink.

Special thanks go to Tim Herzog of Flying Bison, who led me and my uncle Don on a marathon pub crawl in Buffalo, pointing out closed breweries, architectural sights, and Buffalo landmarks as we went.

Thanks to my relatives, especially the upstate in-laws. To my mother-in-law, Claire Childs, and John and Gayle Childs (thanks for the Buffalo suggestions, John), who hosted me on a number of research trips. To my brother-in-law Chris Childs, his wife, K. D., and the kids, who hosted me for a really fun week. To my father, Lew, for unfailing map support and for stellar driving on that Buffalo pub crawl while the electrical system in the car went haywire. To my uncle, Don Harnish, who comes along to keep me from drinking alone and is great company. To my mother, Ruth, for proofing the manuscript.

Most of all, thanks go to my family. My children, Thomas and Nora, spent a lot of days without me and cheerfully got by on kisses and promises. My wife, Catherine, makes all of this possible. She supports me, she encourages me, she believes in me. I can never thank her enough.

To all of you, Cheers!

INTRODUCTION

Welcome to New York and its breweries! After a long time, the Empire State is again home to numerous breweries, though it's a far cry from the glory days of beermaking one hundred years ago. Almost every New York town had a brewery then; some, like Buffalo and Brooklyn, had twenty or more. Some of the architectural relics of these breweries are still to be found, huge and often ornate memorials to the thirst of swarms of immigrants who wanted only to have a cold beer after their day's long labors.

New York has grown a new crop of breweries. We're up to fifty-four, counting the solid presence of survivors like Matt's and High Falls (formerly known as Genesee) and the big Anheuser-Busch brewery in Baldwinsville, with still more on the way. This is reflected in the resurgence of different styles of beer in America and the rise of what have been called microbreweries or craft breweries. To understand where these new breweries came from, we need to take a look at our country's history, during which American brewing went from a vibrant, broad industry to a fossilized oligopoly of brewers making one style of beer, take it or leave it. What happened?

The Rise and Fall of American Brewing

The most popular alcoholic drink in early America was cider, followed closely by rum. Americans drank a lot of these beverages and a lot of alcohol in general. Per capita annual consumption of alcohol was over ten gallons by the 1840s. That's gallons of pure alcohol, not gallons of rum at 40 percent alcohol or cider at 7 percent. Americans drank pretty much all the time.

When Americans did drink beer, they mostly drank imported British ales. And when Americans began brewing, they mimicked the English by producing similar unfiltered ales. Cider was still the most popular drink through Andrew Jackson's presidency, but things changed rapidly in the 1840s.

There were three complementing components to this change. German-style lager beers are believed to have been first brewed in America in Philadelphia, in 1840, by a brewer named John Wagner. This refreshing beer became very popular with laborers because it could be drunk quickly to quench a thirst.

Paradoxically, the temperance movements that swept the nation in the 1840s accelerated the rise of lager beer. Temperance had strong effects on many suppliers, retailers, and drinkers. One of its major "successes" was wiping out America's cider-producing orchards almost entirely. The 1840s saw fields of stumps on many farms. This movement was particularly rampant in upstate New York, and woodcut illustrations of the devastated orchards are a bemusing legacy. The demand for drink did not go away, of course, and lager brewers picked up the shifting market.

The third thing that drove lager's popularity was the rise in immigration to America after the squashed European rebellions of 1848. Germans and other beer-drinking Europeans came to America by the thousands, and they wanted their beer. America was happy to supply it.

New York had its hand in all this, with plenty of breweries pumping out beer, ales, and lagers. You may have heard one bit of New York brewing history sung by a Vassar College woman:

> And so you see, for old V.C.
> Our love shall never fail.
> Full well we know
> That all we owe
> To Matthew Vassar's ale!

Successful Poughkeepsie brewer Matthew Vassar endowed Vassar College, America's first privately endowed college for women, in 1861. Vassar had built his business to become a major regional brewer and had strong ideas about sharing his success with the community, an ideal that many New York brewers stick to today.

New York's contribution was not limited to the famous breweries of the state's history. The Susquehanna Valley, south of Cooperstown, was once the nation's largest producer of hops. The Busch family had a large hops farm and mansion on the western shore of Otsego Lake; the *Chief Uncas* tourboat, which plies the lake, was their little pleasure boat.

There were over two thousand breweries in America at the turn of the century, mostly small local breweries producing almost every style of beer, although lager was a clear favorite. The temperance movements, however, had not gone away.

The Great Killer of breweries in America was the little social experiment called Prohibition (1920–33). By 1939, after this fanaticism had run its course and the industry had briefly boomed and settled down, only about five hundred breweries remained.

Everyone knows that people didn't stop drinking during Prohibition, but the quality of the beer they drank was dramatically affected. Some drank "needle beer" (near beer injected with alcohol) or low-grade homebrew, made with anything they could get their hands on. They used cake yeast and the malt syrup that brewers were making to survive. Other beer generally available during Prohibition was low-quality and relatively weak, made from cheap ingredients with large amounts of corn or rice.

Illicit brewers used the high-gravity system: Brew very strong beer, and then water it down. This saved time and money, as did greatly shortened aging times. Federal enforcement agents knew that hops were a commodity really used only for brewing; brewers, therefore, lowered the amount of hops they used to avoid suspicion. For fourteen years people drank literally anything that was called beer.

These changes brought on some long-term effects. The corn and rice and high-gravity brewing produced a distinctly lighter-bodied beer with an identifiable nonbarley taste. Low hopping rates made for a sweeter beer. Over Prohibition's fourteen years, people got used to light lager beer. The process continued over the next three decades as big brewers came to dominate the market.

The rise of big breweries and the decline of small breweries can be traced to several important developments. World War II brought a need to get lots of beer to troops abroad. Huge contracts went to the brewers who were big enough to fill them. Hops and malt for home-front brewing were considered largely nonessential. F. X. Matt once told me about going out with his father on Sunday afternoons during the war, trying to talk farmers into growing hops along the borders of their fields.

Improvements in packaging made buying beer for home consumption easier, and refrigerated transportation enabled brewers to ship beer long distances to reach more customers. These improvements required large capital investment possible only for successful, growing breweries.

Mass market advertising during broadcast sporting events got the national breweries in front of everyone. The advertising further convinced Americans that light lagers were the only type of beer out there. Advertising was expensive, but effective. The big breweries got bigger, and small ones went out of business.

Why did the rise of big national brewers necessarily mean that American beer would become all the same type of light lager? Simple

Adirondack Pub and Brewery, Lake George ③⓪
Anheuser-Busch, Baldwinsville Brewery ⑨
Barker Brewing Company, Fredonia ①
Big House Brewing Company, Albany ②⑦
Big House Grill, Albany ②⑦
Black Forest Brew Haus, Farmingdale ①⑦
Blue Point Brewing Company, Patchogue ①⑨
Bootleggers, Plattsburgh ③②
Brewery Ommegang, Cooperstown ①④
Brickhouse Brewery and Restaurant, Patchogue ①⑨
Brooklyn Brewery, Brooklyn ①⑥
Brotherhood Winery, Washingtonville ②③
Buffalo Brewpub, Williamsville ②
Chelsea Brewing Company, New York City ②①
C. H. Evans Brewing Company at the Albany Pump
    Station, Albany ②⑦
Cooper's Cave Ale Company, Ltd., Glens Falls ③⓪
Cooperstown Brewing Company, Milford ①④
Custom Brewcrafters, Inc., Honeoye Falls ⑤
Davidson Brothers Restaurant and Brewery, Glens
    Falls ③⓪
The Distillery, Rochester ④
Eddie's Brewery and Grill, Orchard Park ②
Ellicottville Brewing Company, Ellicottville ③
Empire Brewing Company, Rochester ④
Empire Brewing Company, Syracuse ①⓪
Flying Bison Brewing Company, Buffalo ②
Gentleman Jim's, Poughkeepsie ②④
Gilded Otter Brewing Company, New Paltz ②⑥
Great Adirondack Brewing Company, Lake Placid ③①
Heartland Brewery and Chophouse, New York City ②①
Heartland Brewery, Midtown, New York City ②①
Heartland Brewery, Union Square, New York City ②①
High Falls Brewing Company, Rochester ④

Hyde Park Brewing Company, Hyde Park ②⑤
Ithaca Beer Company, Ithaca ⑧
John Harvard's Brew House, Lake Grove ①⑧
Lake Placid Craft Brewing Company, Plattsburgh ③②
Lake Placid Pub and Brewery, Lake Placid ③①
Malt River Brewing Company, Latham ②⑦
Market Street Brewing Company and Restaurant,
    Corning ⑥
Matt Brewing Company, Utica ①③
Mendocino Brewing Company, Saratoga Springs ②⑨
Middle Ages Brewing Company, Ltd., Syracuse ①⓪
Original Saratoga Springs Pub and Brewery, Saratoga
    Springs ②⑨
Pearl Street Grill and Brewery, Buffalo ②
Ramapo Valley Brewery, Suffern ②②
Red Lion Brewing Company, Watertown ①②
Rohrbach Brewing Company, Rochester ④
Sackets Harbor Brewing Company, Sackets Harbor ①①
Southampton Publick House, Southampton ②⓪
Syracuse Suds Factory, Syracuse ①⓪
Troy Pub and Brewery, Troy ②⑧
Typhoon Brewery, New York City ②①
Wagner Brewing Company, Lodi ⑦
Yankee Brewing Company, Staten Island ①⑤

reasons, really: Making it all the same is cheaper and easier. Success breeds imitation. Image is easier to market than flavor. A large national brand has to appeal to a broad audience of consumers.

This led to the situation in the 1970s in which one dominant style of beer was made by fewer than forty breweries. People who wanted anything else had to seek out the increasingly rare exceptions made by smaller brewers or buy pricey imports of unknown age and freshness. The varieties of beer styles were unknown to most Americans.

This is the real key to understanding the craft-brewing revolution. These beers are not better made than Budweiser; in fact, Budweiser is more consistent than many American craft-brewed beers. What craft-brewed beers offered was variety.

The American Brewing Revolution
How did microbreweries get started? Fritz Maytag bought the Anchor Brewery in San Francisco on a whim in the mid-1960s. He had heard it was going out of business and knew it brewed his favorite beer. Fritz was an heir to the Maytag appliance fortune and could afford to indulge his whims. But he got hooked on brewing, and Anchor led the return of beer variety in America. Fritz brewed Anchor's trademark "steam" beer, an ale and lager hybrid; he brewed the mightily hoppy Liberty Ale; and he brewed the strong, malty barley wine he called Old Foghorn. Things were off and . . . well, things were off and walking in the United States.

Next came the microbreweries. Ambitious homebrewers, maverick megabrewers, and military or businesspeople who had been to Europe and wanted to have the same kinds of beer they drank there started these small breweries, cobbling them together like Frankenstein's monster from whatever pieces of equipment they could find. The beer was anything but uniform—sometimes excellent, sometimes awful—but even so, it found a receptive market.

The revolution started in the West and grew very slowly. New Albion, the first new brewery in America since World War II, opened in 1976. Five years later, Bill Newman started his brewery in an old mattress factory in Albany, brewing his great amber beer. F. X. Matt Brewing started making Saranac 1888 (today's Saranac Amber) in 1987. They were prescient, they were good, but they were also too soon. Newman finally gave up on brewing, and Saranac was a loss for Matt's for years.

Things started popping in the mid-1990s, and dozens of small breweries opened. Wall Street and the money people caught wind of this and blew the little fire into a blaze with the focus of their hot attention for possible profit. New York reached a total of over sixty breweries in 1998.

Then the long-anticipated shakeout hit the industry, and the press has gleefully reported several times since then that microbrewing is dead. Most of the larger micros had troubles, and some of the under-capitalized ones went under. The tragic events of September 11 hit the industry hard as people reevaluated their lifestyles. Some were hit harder than others. Brooklyn Brewing's Steve Hindy told me, "We lost about fifteen accounts in Manhattan." Lost? "They're just . . . gone," he said. "Windows on the World was the biggest."

Has the hammer fallen? Will microbrewing last, or was it just a passing fad? In my opinion, the genie won't go back in the bottle. Brew-pubs are established in their communities, and more are still opening. Matt's continues to thrive on the Saranac line, and the Pale Ale stub-bornly outsells the Lager and the Light. The state's smaller microbrew-eries are doing well; a number of them were having their best years ever and were planning expansions as I finished this manuscript.

People have discovered the many different ways beer can taste. No one thinks all wine comes in gallon jugs anymore, and everyone knows there are more types than red and white. Beer is on that same path.

How I Came to Love All Beer

My beer-drinking career has been reflective of America's beer revolu-tion. I started with beers from big breweries, some that are no longer around. I had my first full beer as a freshman in college. When I was a kid, my father often let me have sips of his beer with dinner. That was Duke Ale, from Duquesne Brewing of Pittsburgh, one of Pennsylva-nia's many defunct breweries. But I'd never had a beer of my own until Tim Turecek, a guy from Binghamton who lived on my dorm floor, handed me a Genny Cream, a 16-ounce solidly brown and green returnable, dripping with condensation. I drank it, and it was good.

I drank a lot more of them over the next three years. Genny Cream, Prior's Double Dark, Stroh's, and Rolling Rock were my sta-ples, along with Rheingold and National Premium when the money was tight. Then one night in my senior year at Franklin & Marshall College, I met my medieval history professor for drinks, a special treat for a few legal-age students.

The bar was the Lauzus Hotel, in Lancaster, Pennsylvaina. Run by old Wilhelm Lauzus, an ex-German Navy man, the bar carried over 125 different beers in 1981, not too shabby at all in those days. I had no clue and grabbed my usual Stroh's. My professor laughed and slapped it out of my hand. He pulled a German beer, an Altenmünster, out of the cooler and popped the swingtop. "Try this," he said, and changed my life.

It was big, full in the mouth, and touched by a strange bitterness that I'd never tasted before. That bitterness made another sip the most natural thing in the world, like pepper on potatoes. I've been looking for beers outside the American mainstream ever since. It's increasingly easy to find that kind of beer in New York, where breweries are turning out everything from whopping Imperial stouts to crisp, bitter pilsners to rippingly hoppy India pale ales to bubbly, spicy hefe-weizens.

Is that all I drink, beers like that? Well, no. When I mow my lawn, or when I'm grilling up a batch of spiedies on a hot afternoon, sometimes I want a cold glass of something dashingly refreshing and fizzy. Then I might reach into the back of the fridge and pull out a secretly stashed bottle of Saranac Light. Don't tell the beer geeks; they might not renew my membership card.

My family and I have enjoyed traveling to New York's breweries and sampling these beers at the source. I met a bunch of new people and made a lot of friends. Beer traveling is a great way to have fun, and this book will serve as a guide for your travels in New York. Hoist one for me!

How to Use This Book
This book is a compendium of information about New York's breweries. It also lists some of the interesting attractions and best bars in New York. It offers facts and opinions about brewing and beer-related subjects.

It does not present a comprehensive history of any brewery, nor is it one of the ubiquitous books that try to rate every single beer produced by every single brewery. It is not a conglomeration of beer jargon—Original Gravities, International Bittering Unit levels, Apparent Attenuations, and so on. And it's not about homebrewing. There are too many of these kinds of books anyway.

It is a travel guide about breweries and New York, two subjects dear to my heart. Sharing information has been a central part of the success of the rise of microbreweries in the United States. I've been sharing what I know for over twenty years, and this book and its companion volume, *Pennsylvania Breweries*, represent my latest efforts to spread the good word.

The book is organized in alternating parts. The meat of the book, the brewery information, is presented in eight sections. The first section begins with a general description of the state's three large mainstream breweries, The Big Guys. Each of the seven geographical sections—Long Island, Manhattan, Hudson Valley, Capital District, Adirondacks, Finger Lakes/Glacial Region, and the Great Lakes—is prefaced with a description of the area for those unfamiliar with it. The "A word about . . ." sections are intended as instructional interludes on topics you may be curious about. There should be something there for almost everyone, whether novice, dabbler, or fanatic.

The history and character, highlights, my observations, and other information about the company are presented in a narrative section for each brewery or brewpub. A brewpub sells beer to be enjoyed on location, whereas a brewery sells its beer primarily off-premises. Matt's and High Falls are regional breweries; Anheuser-Busch is national. If any beers have won Great American Beer Festival (GABF), Real Ale Festival (RAF), or TAP NY awards, those are noted, but not every brewery enters these competitions. Potential annual capacity in barrels, as listed for each brewery, is a function of the fermenting tank capacity and the average time to mature a beer. Lagers take longer, so on two identical systems with the same fermenter setup, an all-lager brewery would have significantly lower annual capacity than an all-ale brewery.

The other area beer sites I've listed for most breweries may include miltitaps, historic bars, or restaurants with good beer selections. Whenever possible, I visited these bars and had at least one beer there. A few of these descriptions are based on recommendations from brewers or beer geeks I know personally.

The Big Guys

N ew York has three big breweries that dwarf the other breweries in this book, all three located upstate. There are two home-grown, regional breweries—Matt in Utica and High Falls in Rochester—and an arm of the world's largest brewer, Anheuser-Busch, in Baldwinsville.

I'm ambivalent about Anheuser-Busch; any lover of small breweries is. They're huge, and they continue to grow in America's market and in worldwide markets, at the expense of other breweries. They are a company that is sensitive to perceived threats, and have used their market power to punish other breweries.

Yet they are also extremely successful and insanely quality-oriented. I've been to Anheuser-Busch's Elk Mountain hop farm and Idaho Falls maltings as a guest of the company, and I was terrifically impressed by what I saw. They have forced the rest of the market to consider freshness dating with their "Born On" dates—a marketing ploy that leverages their matchless distribution network and the advantages of twelve national breweries, but a good thing nonetheless. They have over one hundred highly skilled brewers. And I admit to a certain pride that the world's largest brewer is American.

I have been called an Anheuser-Busch apologist by some beer geeks. It's not so. I seek the truth about Anheuser-Busch, and with all the fog created by angry microbrewers and homebrewers who seek an easy target, and by the company's own publicists, it's not always easy to find. I will say that whenever I've spoken to Anheuser-Busch technical people, they have always given me honest, complete answers to all my questions. I'll leave it at that.

As for the other two, they are regional breweries, a strange, caught-in-the-middle class. Some call them fossils, some call them smokestack breweries, some call them beer factories. They somehow survived Prohibition, World War II, and three decades of brewery wars between 1950 and 1980. They are gritty survivors, working with old plants, a fiercely loyal but aging customer base, and sheer guts.

Matt Brewing has been known as F. X. Matt Brewing, West End Brewing, and the Utica Club Brewery. But it's always been the same brewery, right there in Utica. The brewery is famous upstate for the Schultz and Dooley "talking stein" television commercials for its Utica Club beer and beloved by collectors of breweriana for producing a line of character steins (I have an Officer Suds stein on my shelf). The commercials are classics: the tall German stein, Schultz, and the small Irish stein, Dooley, with many sidekicks like Bubbles La Brew and the Moon Man stein, with all the voices done by Jonathan Winters.

These days, the steins are actually doing better than Utica Club. Utica Club is in a planned decline, a heavily discounted brand that relies on a steadily graying market. Matt's has managed to reinvent itself as a craft brewer. It is all about the Saranac brand these days, though the contract brewing that kept the company alive in the 1980s and 1990s is still important. Matt's is known as the Cadillac of contract brewers—it's where brewers would most like to have their beer brewed.

I first visited the brewery back in 1987 and have been back a number of times. It's one of the best brewery tours anywhere, with its Victorian appointments and spotless brewhouse. F. X. Matt II, the man who saved the brewery from closure in the 1980s, recently died, a death that was mourned in many places. In a long tradition of German brewmasters, he was a firm, patriarchal man, but also quick with a smile and a font of stories about brewing history.

High Falls also recently changed its name and its owners. It was long known as the Genesee Brewery. The change is recent and snatched the brewery from the scrap heap. The new management has latched on to several big contract brewing jobs, and the brewery is working hard.

High Falls is still home to the Genesee line of beers, a "mini-mainstream" line of American-style light-bodied lagers. Upstate kept these brands alive for years, though Genesee Cream Ale enjoyed a strong surge in the East in the late 1970s and early 1980s.

In the 1990s, Genesee created the J. W. Dundee's, HighFalls, and Michael Shea lines of beers; the beers were labeled as coming from, for example, "Michael Shea's Brewing, Rochester," and many people had no idea they were from Genesee. J. W. Dundee's Honey Brown Lager hit big in the early 1990s, supported by a hilarious "Beer God" advertising campaign. One well-known billboard had the Beer God, a rough-carved stone idol, shouting, "You in '63 Impala! Pull over now, sell car, buy more Honey Brown!"

Laughs weren't enough, though, and the brewery hit rough times. I'm happy to say it looks like it's back in good shape, with vigorous leadership at the helm and big plans for the future. It even plans to start tours soon. That's good news for the beer lover, because this is a very cool, very big brewery.

These big breweries are a part of this book as much as the smallest, hippest brewpub. It's all about beer, folks. The idea that only small breweries can make good beer is ridiculous. Anheuser-Busch's quality control is at a level most craft brewers wish they could achieve, even if they don't care for Anheuser-Busch's beers. Similarly, the idea that only small breweries can make interesting beer is neatly disposed of by the incredibly varied and delicious Saranac line.

Besides, it just warms my heart to see the two old breweries making it in a market dominated by giants like Anheuser-Busch. And those guys aren't so bad either. Fred Matt told me that his production guys talk to the A-B production guys up at Baldwinsville all the time. "They help each other out," he said. "They're good guys." Nice to see that under the corporate colors, everyone's still a brewer—and an upstater.

Anheuser-Busch Companies, Inc. Baldwinsville Brewery

2885 Belgium Road, Baldwinsville, NY 13027
www.budweiser.com (all Anheuser-Busch website links are collected
at www.anheuser-busch.com/misc/links.html, a fascinating page)

Anheuser-Busch is the world's largest brewer, with approximately 49 percent of the U.S. market and 8 percent of the world's market. The brewery in Baldwinsville is only one of the company's twelve breweries in the United States, a diversified production plan that allows Anheuser-Busch to deliver beer across the country, as fresh as possible. The Baldwinsville brewery does not give tours, and it doesn't even have a gift shop or hospitality center; it is purely a production facility.

So why did I bother to include this brewery in a travel guide? Well, it is a brewery, and it's in New York; that would be enough for me. But there is another reason: The truth needs to be told about Anheuser-Busch (A-B).

The truth? Yes, truth, because there's a lot of silliness out there. Because Bud Light and Budweiser are the world's two largest-selling beers, A-B is often the whipping boy of the microbrewers. A-B has taken its share of shots at the micros as well, to be sure, but that's business.

The truth is, A-B has over one hundred highly trained and qualified brewmasters, who are fanatical about quality in ingredients and process. I've met some of them. They're nice guys, but just between you and me, they're nuts. One of them talked to me for an hour about yeast; it was like he couldn't stop himself. Because A-B is so huge, and so profitable, they can afford to do their own research on barley strains (they have a barley research institute), and malting (they have three of their own maltings), and hops (they have several hop farms), and rice (they have two rice mills), and yeast (they have . . . well, you get the picture).

Why so much research, why so much fanaticism? Trace it back to the true founder of the business, Adolphus Busch. After marrying Bavarian Brewery owner Eberhard Anheuser's daughter, Adolphus bought into the business in 1865. He took it from a penny-ante operation to a strong regional brewery. Part of the reason for this success was his superb salesmanship abilities. Adolphus was reputed to use every trick in the book, and some unpublished ones to boot.

Beers brewed: Budweiser (GABF Gold, 1995–96; Silver, 1993; Bronze, 1989, 1994), Bud Light (GABF Gold, 2000; Silver, 1995; Bronze, 1991–92, 1996), Bud Dry (GABF Gold, 1989; Silver, 1990), Bud Ice, Bud Ice Light, Busch (GABF Gold, 1988–89; Silver, 1997), Busch Light (GABF Silver, 1992), Busch Ice, Natural Light, Natural Ice, Hurricane, Tequiza, Doc Otis Hard Lemon, Michelob Golden Draft, Michelob Golden Draft Light, Michelob (GABF Gold, 2001), Michelob Light (GABF Gold, 1992; Silver, 1989), Michelob Amber Bock (GABF Gold, 1998; Bronze, 2000; honorable mention, 1999), O'Doul's (GABF Silver, 1993–96; Bronze, 1999), Red Wolf (GABF Gold, 1995; Bronze, 1997), and Bacardi Silver. (Anheuser-Busch has won more GABF medals (44 as of 2001) than any other brewery.)

But another large component was his obsession with quality. Adolphus traveled widely in Europe and America, sampling beers, studying brewing processes, and evaluating malts and hops. He wrote long letters with detailed instructions on purchasing the finest malt and how to best use it to make excellent beer. "You cannot make a fine beer with inferior malt," he said in one letter I've seen.

This obsession continues today. A-B buys only the finest hops they can find; I've talked to independent hops brokers who confirm it. Their maltings are top-notch operations, and their rice operations are so high-quality that the company is actually able to export rice to Japan. They buy the best equipment and maintain it perfectly.

That's why I laugh when earnest beer geeks say, "If Anheuser-Busch wanted to, with their talent and equipment and quality control they could make the best beer in the world." As far as A-B is concerned, they already do make the best beer in the world. It's called Budweiser.

They don't actually make that much Budweiser at Baldwinsville. They make a lot of different beers; plant manager Stephen McCormick said his facility was kind of the "utility infielder" of A-B. It makes all the odd packages: plastic bottles of Bacardi Silver, "aseptic" bottlings of Michelob Golden Draft, oversize bottles of Hurricane malt liquor, and "bowling pin" bottles of Bud. "Very popular in Mississippi," McCormick noted of the bowling pin bottles.

The Pick: I'm tempted to be ornery and pick Bacardi Silver, because it would really tick off the geekerie and because it does taste pretty good in a tall glass with ice and a slice of orange. But I'm going to be serious and say Michelob. I dissed Michelob for a long time; just didn't like it, even though the old heavy bottles were very cool. Then I had it on draft, and that's a different story. Good body, soft malty flavor, and some actual hop character. H. L. Mencken used to praise this beer, and I'm starting to get an idea why.

Directions to Anheuser-Busch Companies, Inc.: Baldwinsville Brewery

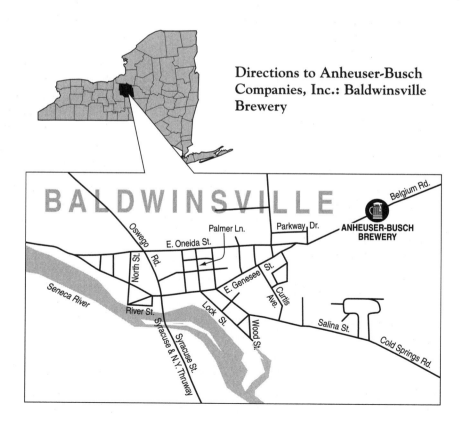

The four big brewkettles, the massive mash-tuns, the aerators (an Anheuser-Busch innovation in which the wort trickles down against blasts of warm air to remove sulfites), and the "chip tanks" (more on that shortly) are all controlled from a slickly automated command center. I walked all over the brewery, from the rail siding where six to eight railcars of malt come in every day, to the brewhouse where about 23 batches of beer are made every day, to the packaging hall where almost 270,000 cases of beer are bottled every day, to the loading dock where better than 200 truckloads of beer go out every day. I was blown away.

The "chip tanks" are the lagering tanks, where the famous beechwood aging takes place. I've seen it; I've held the beechwood. Thin strips of beechwood, about 18 inches long and 1.5 inches wide, are boiled numerous times, and then spread in the bottom of the chip tanks by hand. They provide a settling place for the yeast in the beer. The chips are used three times, and then dumped.

This is "beechwood aging." The theory is that without the chips, the yeast would be crushed. A-B brewers have told me they've done batches without the beechwood, and they could taste the difference. I believed them, because this *has* to be an expensive process, with lots of labor involved in purchasing, processing, and handling the chips themselves (they come from Tennessee and south Missouri, by the way). A-B wouldn't do something that expensive if there wasn't a good reason.

The chip tanks are huge, with specialized equipment you won't find anywhere else. They're expensive and exacting, all in the service of consistency of product. This is the heart of A-B's story and of their success. They do things their way, they are unafraid to spend on fanatical stretches of quality, and they plan for the future. I have a lot of respect for that.

I wish you could tour the facility; it's astonishing. Even so, it's worth a trip out from Syracuse just to see the size of the place from the road, and to enjoy the small-town charm of B'ville.

Opened: 1983. The brewery opened in 1976 as a Schlitz brewery; Anheuser-Busch was established in 1851.

Type: National brewery.

Owner: Anheuser-Busch Companies, Inc., Patrick T. Stokes, president and CEO. Plant manager, Stephen A. McCormick.

Brewer: Mark P. Sammartino.

System: 4 × 1,000 barrel Pfaudler brewkettles (approximately 930 barrel brew size each), 8.6 million barrels annual capacity.

Production: 7.8 million barrels in 2001; B-ville usually runs at or near capacity, but there was a month-long slowdown in 2001 for a large modernization program. Anheuser-Bush produced 99.5 million barrels nationwide in 2001. Isn't that *astounding?*

Tours: No tours at this facility.

Take-out beer: None.

Parking arrangements: None.

Lodging in the area: Microtel Inn and Suites, 131 Downer Street, 315-635-9556. See Syracuse listings, pages 204 and 205.

Area attractions: If you have a doll collector or a young girl in your family, you definitely want to make a stop at the **Goetz Dolls** factory, the American division of the German-based Götz Doll company (8257 Loop Road in the Radisson Corporate Park, 315-635-1055). This is where the American Girls series of dolls is made, and you can find lots of play and collectible dolls and accessories at the visitors center and store.

    Paper Mill Island, between the Seneca River and Erie Canal in the heart of town, was the first "brownlands" industrial site to be reclaimed in New York. Once a rusting eyesore of abandoned buildings and chemical contamination, Paper Mill Island is now a park, with walking trails and the Budweiser Amphitheater, generously funded by the Anheuser-Busch Companies. You can find a listing of events at the Amphitheater on the Baldwinsville Chamber of Commerce website: www.baldwinsvillechamber.com.

    The Beaver Lake Nature Center (8477 E. Mud Lake Road, 315-638-2519) is a major migration stop for ducks and geese, and offers miles of trails and boardwalks through wetlands, lakes, and meadows. Cross-country skiing is allowed in the winter.

    Also see page 205.

Other area beer sites: Various people at the brewery suggested the following as good places for a beer in B-ville: **Blue Water Grill,** 2 Oswego Street, 315-638-3342; **Lock 24 Seafood Restaurant,** 33 Water Street, 315-635-2794; **Lake Effect,** 7 Syracuse Street, 315-638-5015. See also pages 205–207.

High Falls Brewing Company

445 St. Paul Street, Rochester, NY 14605
585-263-9350
www.highfalls.com

If you're not from Rochester, you might have missed it, but there is no Genesee brewery anymore. Oh, there's still a huge brewery on the edge of the gorge where the Genesee River roars over the High Falls, and it still pumps out Genesee beer (and Koch's, and 12 Horse, and Honey Brown). But it's not the Genesee brewery anymore. As of December 17, 2000, it became High Falls Brewing.

This is significant stuff to me. My first full beer was a 16-ounce returnable of Genny Cream, ice cold and dripping with condensation. The first keg I ever bought was a half of Genny Cream for my twenty-first birthday. We put it in a garbage can, packed it full of snow, and drank it for three days. I was in a swing band for two years, and I always had two stubby bottles of Genny Cream waiting for the breaks.

I've got a history with this brewery, you see. Not so long a one as the Wehle family, who founded it back in 1878, but I've got my whole beer-drinking life in it. So it pained me to watch things at Genesee go from bad to worse in the last years of the twentieth century. Genesee was riding a wave on J. W. Dundee's Honey Brown Lager, a darker, slightly heavier beer that was selling like mad. Then it hit a wall. High Falls brand manager Shawn O'Donnell blames it on a lack of marketing support. "The old company didn't invest in marketing as much as they could have," he said.

The same thing was happening to the other brands, declining sales leading to lower ad spending, a classic declining spiral that killed off almost every other regional brewery in the nation. In today's market, regional breweries must spend, and spend big, to support mainstream brands that go up against the major brands. It's a fact of life. Genesee tried to duck that fact by leaning heavily on local

Beers brewed: All beers brewed on the premises. Year-round: Genesee Beer, Genesee Light, Genesee Cream Ale (GABF Gold, 1990, 1991; Silver, 1987, 1988, 1993, 1994; Bronze, 1995), Genesee Ice, Genesee NA, 12 Horse Ale (GABF Silver, 1988), J. W. Dundee's Original Honey Brown Lager, Michael Shea's Irish Amber (GABF Bronze, 1995), Koch's Golden Anniversary (GABF Gold, 1987), Kipling Light.

support. Unfortunately, they eroded the local support by discounting prices. Cheap beer sounds good, but when you actually look at it on the shelf, you think, gee, this stuff is lots cheaper . . . it must not be any good. That's a bad image for a beer, particularly one you're going to serve to friends and family.

Keeping Genesee open was getting to be more and more difficult for the Wehle family, and they lost heart. When Ted Wehle, who was running the brewery, died in 2000, they decided to sell it or just close it down. No strong suitors came forth, and it looked bad. Then Tom Hubbard, who was acting CEO at the time, started work on an employee buyout. With a firm commitment from the city of Rochester to keep the brewery open (the city was bleeding jobs from declines at Xerox, Kodak, and Bausch & Lomb) and money from private investors, Hubbard pulled it off, making a deal for the brewing assets of Genesee Corporation to create a privately held company, the High Falls Brewing Company.

The Pick: Dude, like, check out the *medals!* Genny Cream has won more medals than any beer in GABF history except the legendary Alaskan Smoked Porter. It's also a great drinking beer in the slightly sweet cream ale style, and easy on the wallet. I drank a lot of Genny Cream in my day, in college, when I played in bands. Yup, me and Genny, we go way back. Throw off your old prejudices and give the girl another try. It's smooth, it's a little sweet, but it never sticks in your throat. It's a winner.

What changed? High Falls is completely focused on brewing, unlike the Genesee Corporation's diversification into real estate and foods. The company has a new logo, with the falls front and center. Genesee got a new brand identity, with similar packaging for all four brands: Genesee Beer, Light, Cream, and Ice. In a move that pleased a lot of us hard-liners, Genesee's premium beer, 12 Horse Ale, was brought back, and it's being ale-brewed again. Advertising and marketing budgets were boosted and given a new look.

"You will see increased marketing support for all the brands," Shawn promised. "And you'll see a completely different set of ads. It won't be a guy sitting in a canoe in the middle of a pond, fishing. It's going to be young people rafting, biking, being active." Sounds like Genny's out of the 1950s at last.

"But it all comes back to Genny Cream," Shawn said, naming the brewery's strongest brand. "It always had a bad reputation in Rochester and Syracuse, but move away from here, and it's huge. We wanted to see how good our brands are, so we did a bunch of taste tests." He laughed. "When you take the label off a bottle of Genny Cream, it's amazing how well the beer does in taste tests."

The brewery's running near capacity at this point, thanks to major contract brewing business. Genesee made Sam Adams brands for years

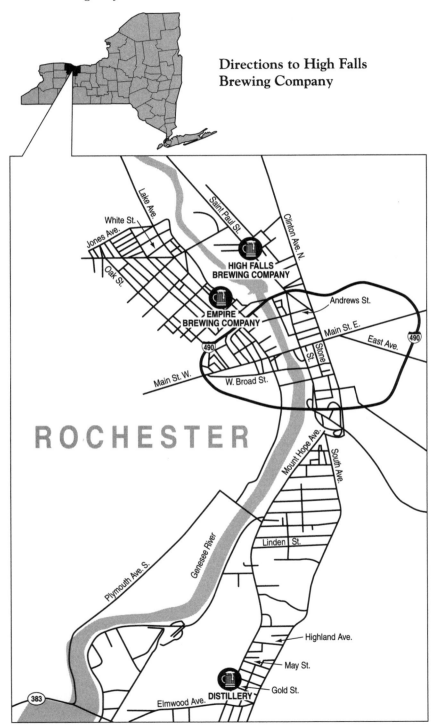

Directions to High Falls Brewing Company

(they've always made the Double Bock), and High Falls kept that going without a hitch; they're also making Mike's Hard Lemonade and Smirnoff Ice. "Tom does not love the contract brewing," Shawn allowed, "but he's not going to walk away from it." It does keep things busy, and it keeps people employed.

They've also got some big plans for the future. "We're in the process of developing three new projects for 2003," Shawn told me, but that's all he'd say. "We're really not saying anything right now on that." We'll just have to wait. But that's okay. I've been with these guys for over twenty years. I'm willing to wait and see what they've got.

Opened: Genesee Brewing was founded in 1878 by the Wehle family. High Falls acquired the brewery in December 2000.

Type: Regional brewery.

Owners: Employee- and investor-owned company, Samuel Thomas Hubbard, CEO.

Brewer: Gary Geminn.

System: 900 bbl. brewhouse.

Production: No figures released.

Tours: None at present; check website for future availability.

Take-out beer: None.

Parking: On-site lot.

Lodging in the area: 428 Mt. Vernon, 428 Mt. Vernon Avenue (585-271-0792); Crowne Plaza Rochester, 70 State Street (585-546-3450); Strathallan, 550 East Avenue (585-461-5010).

Area attractions: Have a little fun at *Seabreeze Park and Raging Rivers Water Park* (4600 Culver Road, 585-323-1900, www.seabreeze.com), a lakeside amusement park with flume rides and a real midway. How about fun museums? *The Strong Museum* (1 Manhattan Square, 585-263-2702) has a popular exhibit that puts children on television in "Sesame Street," a carousel, a collection of toys and dolls, and interactive science exhibits. Rochester is Kodak Town, and the *George Eastman House and International Museum of Photography and Film* (900 East Avenue, 585-271-3361) present an interesting look at the life of this private man who completely revolutionized photography, as well as a premiere museum of photography. *Maplewood Park* (Lake Avenue) is a huge public rose garden; phone for conditions: 585-647-2379. Been to Wegman's Supermarkets? Want to go to a *really* big one? Rochester is home to Wegman's and the Marketplace *Wegman's* has to be seen and experienced (650 Hylan Drive, 800-WEG-MANS). Naturally, it's open twenty-four hours—it's a Wegman's.

In case you didn't notice when you were at Monty's Krown (see below), Monroe Avenue is Rochester's Bohemia, with tattoo shops, whole-foods stores, alternative bookstores, and so on, fun for shopping and people-watching.

Other area beer sites: *Empire Brewing* is just at the other end of the Pont du Rennes footbridge. But we're talking about bars, and if you talk bars in Rochester, you must talk about **MacGregor's.** These places are fantastic, some of the best in New York, and Rochester has two of them; three if you count the one out at 7408 Pittsford Palmyra Road in Perinton (585-425-7260). The original is at 381 Gregory Street (585-271-3592) and is my favorite, a purely wonderful bar with tons of good beer and people who know how to serve it. The big new one out at 300 Jefferson Road in Henrietta (585-427-8410) has more taps, and good atmosphere too. I can't recommend either one enough; great bars, great beer. Get great food with great beer at **Dinosaur Bar-B-Que** (99 Court Street, 585-325-7090), the second Dinosaur, and similar to the original in Syracuse. You can see and smell the pit here, which is cool, and it overlooks the rush of the Genesee, which is beyond cool, but . . . the beer in Syracuse is better. The **Elmwood Inn** (1256 Mount Hope Avenue, 585-271-5195) is in a nice quiet part of town, just down the street from **The Distillery** (see page 217), and features a square bar with thirty-five taps, among which you'll find some decent beers.

In all my gushing over MacGregor's, don't overlook some excellent smaller bars. **The Old Toad** (277 Alexander Street, 585-232-2626) is very British, right down to the "Washrooms" signs to the bathrooms and the staff's accents. The Old Toad provides steady employment for foreign students with British, Scottish, or Australian passports. They have four (!) handpumps, snugs, and a relatively small but very select tap selection. Just up the street, on the corner with East Avenue, is **Monty's Korner** (355 East Avenue, 585-263-7650). A more sophisticated kind of place, with lots of glass and a high ceiling decorated with flags, the Korner has sixteen taps and one handpump, with no mainstream beers at all, just pure craft beer and imports. Impressive, and a great place for conversation.

Out on the eastern side of town is the other Monty's, **Monty's Krown** (formerly the Rose and Crown, 875 Monroe Avenue, 585-271-7050). This place is a lot more funky than the Korner, and has a blatant "No Bud—Don't ask!" sign behind the bar. If you don't trust bars that are too polished, this is your home, and with twelve great taps and a handpump, you won't be giving up much. There is live music; call for schedules. The last bar, **Jeremiah's Tavern** (1104 Monroe Avenue, 585-461-1313), surprised me the first time I went in, and that's a little embarrassing. I saw the place—it's a neighborhood tappie, motorcycles sitting out front, and packed at 6:00—and I figured, waste of my time here. Boy, was I wrong. This place gets "local beer" better than any other Rochester bar I've mentioned. They've got two Custom Brewcrafters beers on (their own: Anniversary Amber and Frog Grog Ale), they've got Rohrbach's Amber and Lager on, and they've got *four* Genesee beers on tap! Hail Jeremiah's, I say. Belly up to the bar and become part of this crowd.

I would be terriby remiss if I didn't let know about **Beers of the World** (3000 S. Winton Rd., Henrietta, 585-427-2852). This is not a bar, but a beer store, a beer supermarket. I've spents hours and hundreds of dollars in here, browsing the exceptional assortment of beers. You'll find a huge selection of German beers (check out the Weltenberger Kloster line), Eastern European beers (buy any porter from Poland: trust me), Belgians, Latin American, British, and the best of America's speciality brewers (one of the few places in New York with New Glarus Belgian Red, a superbly rich cherry ale). Prices are decent, the keg selection is great, and there is also an extensive selection of beer-related merchandise: glasses, books, coasters, shirts, openers, homebrewing supplies, and so on. One of the very best beer stores in America.

Matt Brewing Company

811 Edward Street, Utica, NY 13502
315-624-2480
www.saranac.com

Saranac is an Iroquois word meaning "cluster of stars." When the Matt family decided to stake the entire future of their century-old brewery on their high-end Saranac brand, "cluster of stars" was hardly an apt name. Their mainstream Matt's Premium and Utica Club brands, steadily declining in sales, still outsold Saranac 1888 Lager by about fifty to one. A more fitting picture might have been "cloudy night."

That was in 1992. The old regional brewery had been through some tough times, and things weren't getting a lot better. In 1989, the Matt family-owned trust that owned the brewery had decided it was time to sell out. But the founder's namesake, F. X. Matt II, wasn't ready to say die. "I have a stock answer when I'm asked why I fought for the brewery," he told me in 1994. "Family pride, stubbornness, and stupidity!"

F. X. talked some relatives into buying the brewery from the trust and got his son Fred to do the marketing. Most importantly, he lured his brother Nick away from his job as president of Vicks Health Care to take over as brewery president. The team was in place, and the fight for survival had begun.

The one thing the Matts didn't lack was energy. "We must have tried hundreds of ideas in the next three years," said Nick. "They weren't all bad ideas, but they didn't work." Sales of their mainstream brands continued to drop. Something radical was needed, and it happened in 1992. The family decided to stake everything on the Saranac brand, which at that time made up less than 1 percent of the brewery's sales. A friend in the industry asked F. X. if it was true that he'd bet all his barrels on one product. "I didn't have any barrels left to bet," he replied.

The first thing they did was to rename the brand Saranac Amber, a more forward-looking name than Saranac 1888. One of the hardest decisions was to replace their entire sales force. "We were a mainstream beer company trying to sell a specialty product," Nick explained. "The people out selling the beer were used to selling mainstream beer. It takes a whole different feel." It was also tough to kill the Matt's Premium brand, a brand with the family name on it. But seeing brewery after brewery follow their mainstream brands into decline convinced the Matts that it had to be done.

Beers brewed: All beers brewed on the premises. Year-round: Saranac Traditional Lager, Saranac Pilsener (GABF Silver, 1995), Saranac Adirondack Amber (GABF Gold, 1991; Silver, 1987; Bronze, 1989), Saranac Pale Ale (GABF Bronze, 1995), Saranac Black Forest, Saranac Black & Tan, Saranac Light, Utica Club, Utica Club Light, Maximus Super, Jed's Hard Lemonade, Jed's Hard Pink Lemonade. Seasonals: Matt's brings out new seasonals every year; sometimes they return, and sometimes they don't. Their Twelve Beers package for the holidays always has something new and is eagerly awaited by fans. Here's the most complete list I can come up with: Saranac Belgian White, Saranac Caramel Porter, Saranac Chocolate Amber, Saranac ESB, Saranac IPA, Saranac Kolsch, Saranac Maple Porter, Saranac Mocha Stout, Saranac Mountain Berry Ale (a descendant of Saranac Wild Berry Wheat), Saranac Nut Brown Ale, Saranac Octoberfest, Saranac Scotch Ale, Saranac Season's Best, Saranac Single Malt, Saranac Stout, Saranac Summer Wheat, and Saranac Winter Wassail. There are also the excellent Saranac sodas: root beer, diet root beer (one of the best diet sodas I've ever laid lip to, even at 35 calories per bottle), ginger beer, and orange cream.

Nick's expertise in the Vicks drugstore business delivered an idea that would shape the new character of the brewery: line extension. The year 1993 saw the introduction of Saranac Gold, now known as Saranac Pilsener, followed by the Black & Tan and Pale Ale. When the seasonal Mountain Berry Ale joined those four, the brewery released its first Adirondack Trail Mix cases and six-packs, with some of each beer. They were a hit and gave people a chance to try all the beers.

The success of this expansion gave birth to a burgeoning line of Saranacs, up to twenty-five at my last count. It's fun for the brewers, it's fun for the marketers, and it's a lot of fun for us drinkers. Even with all those Saranacs, and including the fairly mainstream Saranac Traditional Lager, the Saranac Pale Ale remains the biggest seller, with its solid English hop aroma and bitterness.

This is a very cool tour, from the Victorian "living room" reception area through the spotless brewhouse and lagering cellars to the clanging, clashing bottling line. You'll particularly appreciate the end of the tour, where one of the most beautiful tasting rooms in American brewing awaits you. Dark wood dominates, but the big windows lighten up the room's Victorian beauty. Sit and sip your Saranac, or sidle on over to the bar and hook your foot up on the rail.

The Pick: There are a lot of beers here, and I'm going to pick three. First, Adirondack Amber is the original Saranac 1888, and I've rediscovered its beauty lately. Get a big schooner of this on draft, close your eyes, and marvel at the hoppy freshness. Second, Saranac Black & Tan forthrightly defines this premix "style" for me. I still remember my very first bottle, on the shores of Keuka Lake. I sipped, and then I sputtered, "Black & Tan? Where's the Tan?!" The Saranac Stout in this blend comes through in spades: black, roasty, and bitter, great stuff. Finally, kudos to Matt's for Saranac Light, a reduced-calorie, all-malt beer that has flavor. I have to admit that this has become a regular in my summer fridge for grilling sessions.

I love this story. It has all the elements: heritage, risk, bold action, hard work, vindication, and a big helping of great beer. It pleases me to no end that Saranac has indeed become a cluster of stars for the Matt Brewery.

Opened: 1888.
Type: Regional brewery.
Owner: Nicholas O. Matt, president.
Brewer: Jim Kuhr.
System: 500-barrel Central Copperworks brewhouse, 1 million barrels annual capacity.
Production: Approximately 300,000 barrels in 2001.

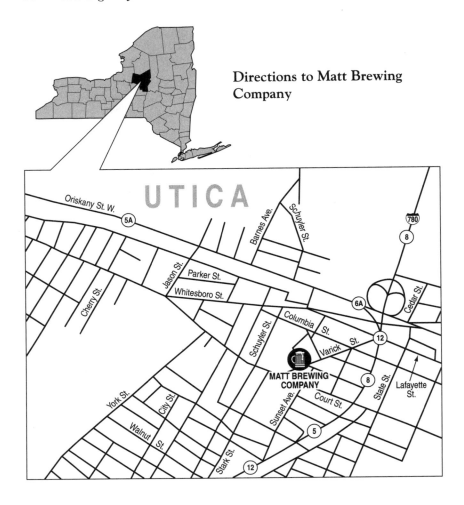

Directions to Matt Brewing Company

Tours: Thursday through Saturday, 11 A.M., 1 P.M., and 3 P.M., September through May. Monday through Saturday, as needed, from 11 A.M. through 4 P.M., June through August.

Take-out beer: Six-packs and cases.

Extras: There is live music in the brewery courtyard on "Saranac Thursdays" from mid-June through the end of August.

Special considerations: Kids welcome. The tour is not handicapped-accessible.

Parking: Off-street lot adjacent to tour center.

Lodging in the area: The Hotel Utica (102 Lafayette Sreet, 877-339-7829) is a newly refurbished grand hotel, part of the National Trust for Historic Preservation's Historic Hotels list; Rosemont

Inn B&B, 1423 Genesee Street, 315-792-8852; Red Roof Inn, 20 Weaver Street, 315-724-7128.

Area attractions: *The Munson-William-Proctor Art Institute* (310 Genesee Street, 315-797-0000) has a deep collection of American art. It also presents performances; call for schedules. Two exits west on the thruway is the *Turning Stone Casino and Resort* (Exit 33, 5218 Patrick Road, 315-361-7711) with golf, casino gambling, and high-stakes bingo. *The Children's Museum* (311 Main Street, 315-724-6129) is very interactive. The Dinorama is a favorite, with a full-size baby brachiosaurus in a simulated environment. There are a number of locomotives outside, always popular with children, and there is a car with a transparent "skin" so children can see what's under all that sheet metal. An excellent museum.

Other area beer sites: Utica's seen some turnover in bars lately, and a lot of the places I used to visit are gone. You might find some new places just poking around, but here are some sure bets. *Cavallo's Cigar Bar & Restaurant* is a great place to relax with your favorite Maduro-wrapped beauty, in the comfortable bar or on the outdoor deck (40 Genesee Street, 315-735-1578). There's a big bar with a big happy hour at *Babe's Macaroni Bar & Grill,* just over the bridge at 80 North Genesee (315-735-0777). It's a good place to try Saranac: Babe's has all the currently available brands on draft or in bottles, plus the Saranac sodas. In good weather, Babe's puts tables right out on the grass; it's a nice spot at twilight. Check out the odd but rewarding combo of Polish food and top-flight live jazz and blues at *Tiny's Grill* (1014 State Street, 315-732-9497). And there should be beer by the time this is printed at *The Wineseller,* right next door to the brewery on Edward Street. This is an outlet for the Brotherhood Winery of Washingtonville and also sells other New York products: cheese, maple syrup, and crafts. I assume they will also be selling the beer Nat Collins will be making for them (see page 77).

Micros, Brewpubs, and Craft Brewers

My young son, Thomas, sometimes accompanies me on brewery tours. Much to my delight as a writer, he's fascinated by words and what they mean and how people use them. I've explained to him that much of what people say is said because they don't want to say something more blunt or honest. Code words, euphemisms, and evasions are part of our everyday speech. Here's a little secret of the beer world: "Microbrewery" is just another code word.

When the new brewing movement started in America in the 1970s, no one knew what to call these little breweries. "Brewery pub," "boutique brewery," and "microbrewery" were all used. By the early 1980s, two words had settled into general use: microbrewery and brewpub. At the time, the industry's pundits defined a brewpub as a brewery that sold most of its beer in an in-house taproom. They defined a microbrewery as a brewery that produced under 15,000 barrels a year. These terms gained legal recognition in some states, as deals were struck to allow the new businesses to start up and as tax rates were determined. The federal government acknowledged the special nature of small breweries in the early 1990s, granting a substantial tax break to those with an annual production under 50,000 barrels.

Eventually the industry itself came up with a whole set of labels. "Brewpub" continued to be used for breweries that sold the large majority of their beer on premises by the glass. "Microbrewery" was for packaging breweries whose production was less than 50,000 barrels. "Regional" brewery applied to smaller breweries established before 1970 that did not distribute to all of America. Nationally distributing giants like Anheuser-Busch, Miller, Coors, and Stroh were dubbed "national brewers" or "megabrewers." But the growth of some successful microbreweries has made even 50,000 barrels an uncomfortable fit. Boston Beer Company, the contract brewery responsible for the Samuel Adams line of beers, sells more than 1 million barrels annually, and Sierra Nevada Brewing Company, an early microbrewery that produces all its own beer, is pushing 600,000 barrels. Clearly these are no longer microbreweries, yet their beer is exactly the same as it was. To be called a microbrewery has a cachet to it that most microbrewers don't want to surrender. What to call them?

Some propose the blanket term "craft brewery." This implies that the beer is somehow crafted rather than produced in a factory. Craft breweries are different, the brewers explain, because the beer is made in single batches, not in several that are then combined in one huge tank or blended after fermentation to ensure consistency.

Putting a label on a brewery these days is not as easy as putting a label on a bottle. For example, what do you call a place like Matt, a regional brewery that brews the very mainstream Utica Club, a dying line that is dwarfed by the company's powerfully delicious and varied Saranac line of beers? Brooklyn Brewery has their bottled beers brewed up at Matt's, but they also put a lot of beer out of their own brewery in Brooklyn. Then there's Custom Brewcrafters in Honeoye Falls, where they almost exclusively make beers for other people . . . and then sell those beers in their own tasting room as well. These breweries aren't readily pigeonholed.

The fact is, microbrewery has always been a code word, and so has craft brewery. They both mean the same thing. They describe a brewery that makes beer in an authentic manner—using ingredients and techniques appropriate to a given style of beer or brewing—and that brews beers other than mainstream American-style lager. What do I think such places should be called? How about breweries?

The distinctions are really all nonsense. Brewery size has nothing to do with the quality of a beer. Guinness Stout, the beer to which most microbrewers hopefully compare their own dry stouts, is brewed by a globe-girdling gargantuan of a brewer. Blending is likewise a nonissue. It goes on at microbreweries across the country.

In this book, I have bowed to convention and called the Matt and High Falls breweries *regionals*, and used the words *brewpub, microbrewery*, and *craft brewery*. Brewpub is the best of these terms. A brewery where beer is taken directly from the conditioning tanks to serving tanks and sold from a tap on premises truly deserves a unique name. But if I had my way, the others would all be called simply breweries. To differentiate a brewery based on the kind of beer it makes seems to be missing the point. Categorizing them by size penalizes the ones that succeed and outgrow the class. Call them breweries, and then let the beer do the talking.

Suburbia by the Sea
Long Island

Long Island is just too convenient a division of New York to ignore. It is a very different place, different from any other area you'll find in the state, or perhaps anywhere. Visiting Long Island requires an adjustment in your thinking. I can only imagine that living there does the same.

Long Island is physically separated from the rest of the state by water on all sides, linked only by eight bridges, two tunnels, and regular ferry lines. And it is a *long* island, 110 miles from Montauk Point to the eastern approaches of the Verrazano Narrows Bridge. The *Verrazano?* That's right. Take a look at the map: Brooklyn and Queens are both on Long Island. I know several New York natives who had never realized that.

Long Island also represents almost all of New York's saltwater coastline. Here's where you'll find the surviving fishing fleets, Fire Island National Seashore and Jones Beach State Park, and ferries to Block Island and Martha's Vineyard. You're never more than ten miles from the water on Long Island, whether it's the relatively sheltered waters of Long Island Sound, the safe harbors of the Great and Little Peconic Bays, or the long reaches of the Atlantic Ocean. Talk to Long Islanders, particularly those in Suffolk County, and it seems as if everyone or his cousin has a boat. The annual Blessing of the Fleet at Montauk Harbor in June is a popular event.

Until you get out as far as Patchogue and Port Jefferson, Long Island is heavily settled. Over two million people live on the island, and about half of them are in Nassau County, which is one-quarter the size of the eastern county, Suffolk. The only successful breweries on the island are all in the less densely populated Suffolk, an anomaly neither I nor any of the Long Island brewers could figure out, though

20

Mark Burford at Blue Point suspects it may be because breweries in Nassau County were pushed too hard for a quick return by NYC-based investors.

The population density has a chicken-or-egg relationship with Long Island's highways, with urban planner Robert Moses as the farmer. Moses' incredible power as the unelected city parks commissioner was wielded as effectively—and ruthlessly—on Long Island as it was in the boroughs of New York City. Robert Caro's Pulitzer Prize–winning biography of Moses, *The Power Broker*, is a thought-provoking portrait of a man who shaped New York, city and state, for better and for worse.

Moses' career really began on Long Island in the 1920s, where he saw the wild and unaccessible openness at Jones Beach and determined that he would make it a playground for the people of New York. The people he approved of, that is: The bridges on the route were too low to allow bus passage. Moses wanted only people who were well-off enough to have a car.

Jones Beach is still quite an attraction, though it is generally packed cheek to cheek in the high season. Moses put in bathhouses, pools, baseball fields, a boardwalk, picnic areas, and a restaurant. The beach itself is grand, over five miles of white sand. Try to visit in the shoulder seasons, early summer and early fall.

The other well-known beach on Long Island is Fire Island National Seashore, a long (32 miles), skinny barrier island with only minimal highway access. There is a park at either end, Smith Point County Park at the east and Robert Moses State Park at the west, which have parking lots, but otherwise the resort communities on Fire Island are reached by a number of ferries. Day-trippers are welcome in Ocean Beach and Ocean Bay Park, reached by the ferry from Bay Shore (631-665-3600). Fire Island is famously hospitable to gay men and women; Cherry Grove is a popular spot, reached by the Sayville ferry (631-589-8980).

Robert Moses was largely responsible for Long Island's set of highways. Three highways run the length of the island: the Long Island Expressway down the middle; the combination of the Belt Parkway, Southern State Parkway, and the Sunrise Expressway along the southern side; and the Northern State Parkway along the Sound. With a combination of service roads and connector roads, you can quickly get to any spot on the island . . . except, of course, when there's traffic. Usually, there's traffic, and it gets really heavy in the summer as people crush into the island to hit the beaches.

If that scares you off, don't let it. The traffic is heavy, and the prices are higher (as always happens on islands), but you'll find there is a beauty here that can't be overlooked. There may be sprawl, but there are plentiful trees and lakes to break it up. Hit the beaches even slightly off peak season, and you'll be almost alone. The prices may be higher, but the standards are a bit higher, too, and you can still find plenty of nonchain, family-owned stores to shop in and independent restaurants where you can enjoy delicious seafood.

Part of what drove the rapid expansion of Long Island's population was the aircraft industry that developed there. Long Island was a natural spot for trans-Atlantic attempts in the early days of aviation, and both the first flight across the Atlantic (1919) and Lindbergh's famous solo flight in 1927 started from there. Curtis, Sikorsky, Fairchild, Grumman, Republic—some of the most glowing names in American aviation were on Long Island, and over half of America's World War II fighters were built here.

You can relive that at the brand new Cradle of Aviation museum (www.cradleofaviation.org, 516-572-4111), in Garden City, where there are numerous examples of Long Island's most famous aircraft on display, including a P-47 Thunderbolt, an F6F Hellcat, an F-14 Tomcat, a Lunar Exploration Module, and various bizarre experimental aircraft. There's also an IMAX theater and a bunch of other exhibits on the history of Long Island aviation.

You'll find roadside produce stands as you drive east. There are still a surprising number of farms in Suffolk County, raising vegetables and fruits of all types. The farming runs more to viniculture on the North Fork, where there are over twenty wineries, most of which are open for daily tours and tastings. Pindar Vineyards is the largest, at 300 acres (Route 25, near Peconic, 631-734-6200), but other, smaller vineyards are fun to visit. There are also three wineries on the South Fork. The Long Island Wineries website, www.liwines.com, is a great place to get information on these wineries.

Then there are The Hamptons, on the South Fork. This is where the rich of New York go to enjoy their money, in the elegantly simple little towns and elegantly extravagant estates. It's not really about tourism, but there are things for the tourist. The public beaches near Montauk Point State Park are beautiful and not as crowded as other Long Island beaches. Town beaches in the South Fork may have stiff parking fees, and legal parking is strictly enforced. There are rental shops for bicycles (a great way to see the pancake-flat South Fork), canoes and kayaks, and windsurfing boards for the more adventurous.

If you go east till you run out of land, you'll get to Montauk. This flat, windswept, and wild area is home to the nation's oldest cattle ranch, Deep Hollow Ranch, started in 1658; Montauk Point State Park; and the Montauk Lighthouse (631-668-2544). The lighthouse is functioning but is also a museum, and you can climb it for the tremendous view.

That's Long Island, from Verrazano to Montauk. If you've never been here, you'll be surprised and impressed by the beauty, taken aback by the traffic and sprawl, and soothed by the nearness of the ocean. Take the time to meet the people, too. They're as much an attraction as anything on the island. They have their own accent, their own values, their own attitudes, and they vary from point to point. Get to know them, and you'll be glad you did. You might even want to buy them a beer.

Black Forest Brew Haus

2015 New Highway, Farmingdale, NY 11735
631-391-9500
www.blackforestbrewhaus.com

"The homebrew guys think this is boring," Joe Schineller said, laughing, as he showed me the Biering Fooding 10-hectoliter system he uses at the Black Forest Brew House. At first glance, it's hard to see why: This is a full bells and whistles brewhouse, a dream system for any pro brewer. But it's all automated, so all the brewer has to do for actual production is watch readouts, push buttons, and turn an occasional valve. There's no stirring the mash, raking the bed, adding the hops, all that hands-on stuff that's so romantic—to watch.

But the brewhouse, the fermenting capacity, and the serving system allow Joe to brew the way most brewpub brewers wish they could. All his beers (except the wheat beers) are fully decocted, all the lagers get a full seven weeks at 0°C/32°F to properly age, they're all naturally carbonated, and

Beers brewed: Year-round: German Pilsner, German Amber-Oktoberfest (GABF Gold, 1999), German Porter (fall–winter) alternates with Munich Dunkles (spring–summer). Seasonals: Dortmunder Lager, Hefe-weizen, Altbier, Kölsch, Blue Star Rauchbier, Weizenbock, Kraeusen Lager, Maibock, Vienna, Bock, Dunkelweiss.

they're served from "beer bags," 10-hectoliter plastic-foil bags that keep air off the beer by collapsing under air pressure as the beer is served, pushed by pumps rather than gas pressure.

All this costs more, which is typical of lager brewing. The extra costs largely disappear at the bigger production levels (and much shorter lagering times) you see at the megabrewers, but at brewpub level it's a real factor. Happily, there is no pressure at Black Forest to shorten lagering times to save a couple bucks, perhaps because of the influence of the German brewery that is a major investor in the brewpub.

Black Forest is loosely affiliated with the Privatbrauerei Hoepfner, in Karlsruhe, Germany. Dr. Friedrich Hoepfner owns about 20 percent of the place. The German brewery provides recipes, it sells malt to Black Forest (Hoepfner is one of the rare breweries that still maintains its own maltings), and Dr. Hoepfner comes over to inspect a few times a year. It also used to provide brewers; Joe Schineller is the first non-German brewer. The Black Forest idea was originally going to be a franchise, but this is the only one—an idea that got lost.

Still, Karlsruhe's loss is Farmingdale's gain. The beautiful German influence and top-grade equipment—and Joe's skill—show through in beers like the Dortmunder and the Pilsner. These beers are clean as fresh-fallen snow and brimming with malt complexity: not heavy, but nuanced, if you feel like taking the time. If not, they're great quaffers as well, and a superb object lesson in the differences between these two similar types of beer.

Black Forest is a study in dark wood and German *gasthaus* comfort, although the deck is more German-American in design and size. The brewpub avoids the way some German-themed places go overboard with Teutonic tendencies: The menu has German dishes but plenty of American food as well, and the staff doesn't have to suit up in lederhosen. There are German bands occasionally, but most of the music is supplied by dueling pianos doing pop classics and by live bands.

Because, after all, what most people love about German culture is the beer. And when the beer's this good, you can almost forgive them for being blind to Bach, and Schiller, and Mann, and Klee. So *Prost, Kamerad!* Hoist your mug and enjoy some Long Island–brewed German beer.

The Pick: This was tough, because I'm a sucker for a good lager, and Black Forest has a bunch of them. But Joe hit me right between the eyes with his Dortmunder, which is brewed precisely to style and beautifully differentiated from his Pilsner. The Dort is about 5.5 percent ABV and wonderfully balanced twixt malt and hop. I took a growler home, and by the time it was gone, we were all wishing I had picked up a few more. An all-day quaffer.

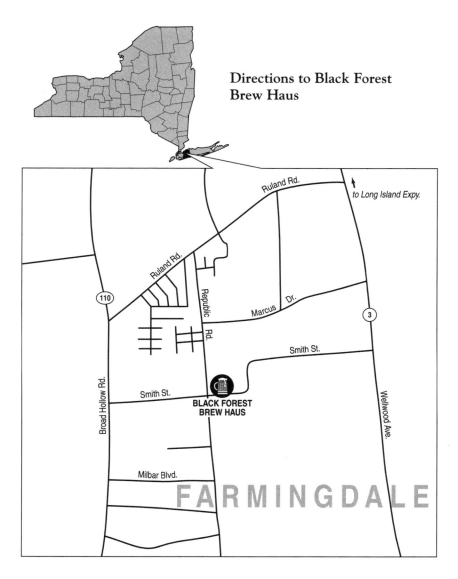

Directions to Black Forest Brew Haus

Opened: August 1998.

Type: Brewpub.

Owners: Todd Waite, Dr. Friedrich Hoepfner.

Brewer: Joe Schineller.

System: 10-hectoliter Beering-Fooding brewhouse, 750 barrels annual capacity.

Production: 700 barrels in 2001.

Brewpub hours: Sunday through Thursday, 11:30 A.M. to 11:30 P.M.; Friday and Saturday, 11:30 A.M. to 1:00 A.M.

Tours: Monday through Friday by request during daytime hours; scheduled tours are preferred.

Take-out beer: Growlers and 50-liter kegs (about 85 percent of a half keg).

Food: German-themed menu with American classics. If your doctor's not looking, try the loaded potato pancakes: crisp-fried latkes filled with sour cream and topped with cheddar and bacon. The Brew Haus's five wraps are popular, or you can cut straight to the carnivore's delight: six different steaks ranging up to the 22-ounce forest cut ribeye. But don't overlook the German dishes, like smoked pork chops, Wiener schnitzel, a variety of wurst, and the classic sauerbraten.

Extras: The Brew Haus features a live piano player Thursday nights and the popular "dueling pianos" on Fridays from 9 P.M. You can watch the games on a big-screen TV or one of the smaller TVs scattered about the place. There is also a happy hour buffet with two-for-one-beers on Thursday and Fridays from 3 P.M. to 6 P.M. During nice weather, you can enjoy your German-style beers in the German-style beer garden on the deck, where you'll enjoy live music, including a monthly (or bimonthly) oompah band; call for schedule.

Special considerations: Cigars allowed. Kids welcome. Vegetarian foods available. Handicapped-accessible.

Parking: Large on-premise lot.

Lodging in the area: Whitman Motor Lodge, 295 East Jericho Turnpike, Huntington Station, 631-271-2800; Melville Marriott, 1350 Old Walt Whitman Road, Melville, 631-423-1600; Rodeway Inn, 333 South Service Road, Plainview, 516-694-6500.

Area attractions: *Adventureland Amusement Park* is right around the corner (2245 Route 110, Farmingdale, 631-694-6868) with about thirty rides for little and big kids. *Jones Beach* is not far, as described above (516-785-1600). *The American Airpower Museum* is at the Republic Airport (7150 Republic Airport, East Farmingdale, 631-293-6398) and actually flies its B-25 Mitchell, P-40 Warhawk, and other aircraft. Call for flight schedules. *Old Bethpage Village* (Round Swamp Road, Bethpage, 516-572-8401) is a restored area set in the 1800s, with the usual blacksmith, hatmaker, all that crafty stuff, but get this: They also play "base ball" by the old rules—in fact, by two different sets of old rules, 1867 rules and 1887 style. The players are encouraged to take on the character of the colorful players of the age and to not scream when the ball hits their bare hands. You've got to see it to believe it.

Other area beer sites: *The Croxley Ale Houses* (129 New Hyde Park Road, Franklin Square, 516-326-9542; and 7–9 South Park Avenue, Rockville Center, 516-764-0470) are all about English ales and British food (don't worry, it's only fish and chips). The same people own **Waterzooi Belgian Bistro,** the one beer place every brewer on Long Island mentioned (850 Franklin Avenue, Garden City, 516-877-2177). With twenty-three draft Belgians and over one hundred bottled, you can see why—and that doesn't even take the great food into account.

Joe also wanted me to mention **KEDCO Brewing Supply,** the homebrew store at 564 Smith Street in Farmingdale (516-454-7800). It has a full supply of homebrew stuff and does regular brewing demos (there might be samples on tap, too).

John Harvard's Brew House

2093 Smithhaven Plaza, Lake Grove, NY 11755
631-979-2739
www.johnharvards.com

"John Harvard's Brew House is a chain!"

You'll sometimes hear that from the more exercised of the geek-erie, with the strong implication that if it's a chain, it can't be good. Balderdash. I am not a big fan of chain restaurants; I'm convinced they are a sign that the Apocalypse is near. It is the increasing blandification of America that has fired me on a quixotic crusade against chains.

But John Harvard's pleases me. John Harvard's has what so many chains do not: individual variety. On top of that, the John Harvard's in Lake Grove has D. J. Swanson at the brewkettle, and that won them the 2002 F. X. Matt Cup as the best craft brewery in New York. Chain brewpub? So what!

Grenville Byford and Gary Gut started the first Brew House on Harvard Square in Cambridge, Massachusetts, in 1992. Although there have been some failures, the chain is still strong, and the idea embodied in the company slogan, "Honest food, real beer," has proven attractive to people on Long Island.

The corporate history tells the tale of the young John Harvard watching William Shakespeare brew beer in Southwark, England. We are told that Shakespeare wrote, in addition to his plays and sonnets, a book of brewing recipes that John Harvard brought with him to America in 1637. The story is that the book was found in 1992 and is claimed as inspiration for the brewpub's beers. You can decide for yourself how "honest and real" the story is.

Don't doubt the sincerity of the slogan, though. The menu is innovative and eclectic, with a number of regional influences. The desserts are excessive, just the way you want them. A few local specialties may show up, but the food varies little from pub to pub. That, I'm not crazy about, but we are talking about chain brewpubs, not chain restaurants, so let's have a look at the beer.

The pubs have very similar brewing equipment with which they brew the same core beers. Each location has a handpump for serving cask-conditioned versions of some of the beers. The Brew Houses exchange recipes and information, a practice the brewers find very helpful. If a brewer runs into a problem, chances are someone else has had the same problem and can offer a solution, or at least some ideas. Brewers also formulate some of their own beers, and they are encouraged to tweak the core beers toward local tastes.

D. J. Swanson, an unassuming guy with a quick, quirky grin and lots of beer passion, hadn't been brewing in Long Island for long when he won the Matt Cup, and it was only a month later that I visited him at the freestanding brewpub in the parking lot at the Smithhaven Plaza. But he's putting his stamp on the place quickly, pointing out that the corporate heads back in Cambridge, including head brewer Tim Morse, give him plenty of freedom within pretty wide parameters. If this is a chain, John Harvard's has found the right way to run one.

I must confess that when I try to work up a good head of righteous beer geek indignation over this chain brewpub idea, it never lasts longer than stopping by for a pint at the Brew House. Would restaurant critics

Beers brewed: All beers brewed on the premises. Year-round: John Harvard's Pale Ale, Long Island Light Lager. Seasonals: Vienna Lager, May Gold Ale, Red Raspberry Ale, Munich Dark, Pinstripe Porter, Imperial Stout, Golden Barleywine, Old Willy IPA, West Coast IPA, Nut Brown Ale, Irish Stout, Espresso Stout, Cream Stout, Bock, Buckhead Scotch Ale, Scottish Ale, Hefeweizen, Kristallweizen, Pumpkin Spice Ale, Oktoberfest, Holiday Red Ale. *Winner, 2002 F. X. Matt Cup.*

The Pick: Let me make one thing clear: Visiting every brewery in New York still did not make me a Yankees fan. Some things are just genetic. But I do like D. J.'s Pinstripe Porter, a very drinkable porter that's not too heavy, not too roasty, and not too stoutlike. Differentiation is good. There's a light coffee-and-cream character here that I love, and a delicate layering of alefruit throughout. Well brewed, an elbow bender.

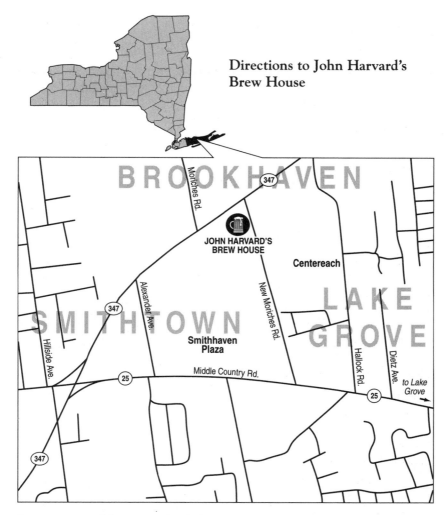

Directions to John Harvard's Brew House

hate McDonald's so much if they served exciting, healthier fare with more flavors than just fat, sugar, and salt? It's a deep philosophical problem, and I intend to ponder it over my next pint of D. J.'s Pinstripe Porter.

Opened: July 1997.
Type: Brewpub.
Owners: Grenville Byford, Gary Gut.
Brewer: D. J. Swanson.
System: 14-barrel Pub Brewing Systems brewhouse, 2,400 barrels annual capacity.
Production: 2,200 barrels in 2001.

Brewpub hours: Seven days a week, 11:30 A.M. to 1 A.M.

Tours: Anytime during restaurant hours.

Take-out beer: Half-gallon growlers.

Food: John Harvard's menu features upscale pub fare, including Asian crispadillas, chicken pot pie, catch-of-the-day salad, calamari, and a few local specials.

Extras: Live music; call for schedule.

Special considerations: Cigars not allowed. Kids welcome. Vegetarian food available. Handicapped-accessible.

Parking: Large mall lot.

Lodging in the area: Wyndham Wind Watch Hotel & Hamlet Golf Club, 1717 Vanderbilt Motor Parkway, Hauppauge, 631-232-9800, golf course on site, fee to play; Holiday Inn Express, 3131 Nesconset Highway, Centereach, 631-471-8000. Also see page 34.

Area attractions: You're in the suburbs, right? Walk over to the **Smithhaven Plaza Mall** and do some shopping. Walk in the other direction, and there's **Sports Plus** across the street (110 New Moriches Road, Lake Grove, 631-737-8881). Get it working with a rock-climbing wall, full-size skating rink, forty-eight bowling lanes, bumper cars, a boatload of arcade video games, and cutting-edge virtual-reality sports experiences.

Other area beer sites: See page 27.

Blue Point
Brewing Company

161 River Avenue, Patchogue, NY 11772
631-475-6944
www.bluepointbrewing.com

"The owner wanted to raise trout on the spent grain from the brewery. We filled the spent-grain hoppers with water and dumped the trout right in. But it was summer on Long Island, and trout need cold water. So he goes out and buys an ice machine, and we spent half our time throwing ice on the trout! It was a disaster, but I could see that the demand was there, even for their beer. Pete and I figured, we could do this."

Mark Burford has some great stories about how he and Pete Cotter came to open Blue Point Brewing. That one's about working at Cobblestone Winery & Brewery, a Long Island outfit that didn't make it, as a winery or brewery, or a fish hatchery. He doesn't have the standard "good beer epiphany" story because his dad always drank beer like Beck's and Guinness, and as Mark says, "You can never go backward with beer." He does have some West Coast brewing stories.

"I was in the navy, in San Diego. I kept getting in trouble because I'd get a weekend pass and head upstate and go beerhunting. Sierra Nevada, Anchor, St. Stan's—wow, I'd always get back a day late and be in trouble. Anyway, some guy opened a brewery near San Diego, the Bolt Brewery, in an old railroad car. It was a great idea, but he was too far from anywhere. I hung around all the time and pestered him about brewing."

While Mark was getting in trouble and learning about brewing, Pete was traveling around the world, trying beers everywhere. "Then I came home," he said, "and when I had American beer again, I was, like, what the hell's going on here?" That jives with Mark's reason for opening the brewery. "I didn't have a choice. It was a calling; I had to." The two guys were locals and old friends. They had met in Patchogue at Fadely's Deli and Pub in the 1970s ("We, ah, might've been underage," Pete admitted), and stayed in touch till they started Blue Point.

"We heard they were auctioning off the Wild Goose brewhouse, so we drove down to Cambridge [Maryland] and bought it. We took the bricks too, because we didn't have money to buy new bricks. We only had half the slab poured for the brewery at the time. We got the other half poured when we raised more money."

But my favorite Blue Point story is the one Mark told about sweating out the BATF inspection. Literally. They didn't have the money to finish all the BATF requirements on plumbing, wiring, and so forth, but they had enough done to brew, and make some beer to sell so they could finish the brewery. All they had to do was get certified. Mark tells the story well.

Beers brewed: All 12-ounce bottled beers are contract-brewed at Clipper City Brewing in Baltimore for now; Blue Point was buying a bottling line as I wrote this. Year-round: Toasted Lager, Pale Ale, Oatmeal Stout Robust Porter E.S.B. Seasonals: Pilsner, Summer Ale, Winter Ale, Octoberfest, Double Blond, Old Howling Bastard Barleywine. Toasted Lager, Summer Ale, Winter Ale, and Pale Ale are available in 12-ounce bottles.

The Pick: Aw, mom, do I *hafta?* It's rare that I come across such a uniformly excellent line from a brewery; no missteps on this tap dance. I'll cut it to two, reluctantly. The Oatmeal Stout is just flawless, full, rich, but not heavy, with a surprisingly alluring finish. If you like hops, really like *hops* and not just their bitterness, the E.S.B. is chock full of hop flavor and aroma—huge amounts of citrus, grassy, spicy flavors lying on a smooth malt base. This is the beer Blue Point sends out cask-conditioned to accounts that know how to handle it, and I'll bet it's fantastic.

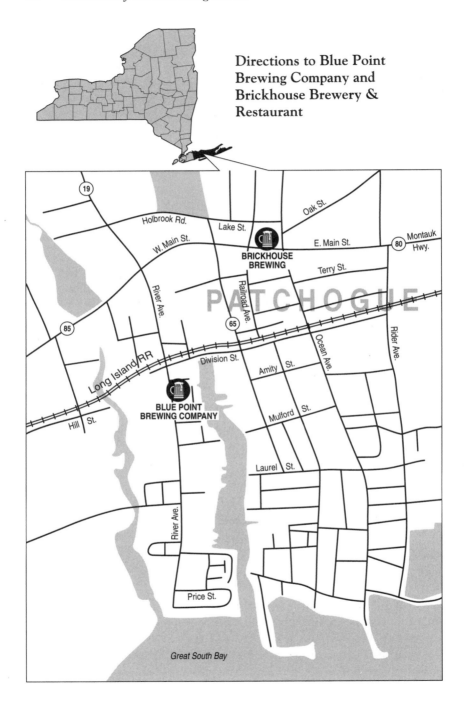

Directions to Blue Point Brewing Company and Brickhouse Brewery & Restaurant

"It was a hot Long Island day. The guy made his inspection, and then he's got to go over the inspection with us before he leaves. The whole time he's inspecting, Pete and I are slamming ice-cold water, so we're insulated. We had the meeting in a room with the heat on and no windows. We're sitting there, almost hypothermic from the water, and he's sweating. He asked us if we had anything to drink, we told him we were sorry, but we didn't even have tap water yet. He sweated like crazy for about ten minutes, then he just started signing everything and got the hell out of there."

I'm happy to say that it all was worth it. There's a sign in Blue Point's tasting room that sums it up pretty well for me: "We're cocky, but the beer's really good." No sense in being modest when there's nothing to be modest about. From the flagship Toasted Lager to the huge and complex Old Howling Bastard Barleywine, these beers are both flawless and interesting, assertive but not over the top, a truly excellent product line.

It only seems fitting to let Mark have the last word. To wrap up the interview, I asked him why Blue Point made these particular beers; were they aiming at a particular market? Nothing of the sort. "It's personal taste," he said. "We're not 'creating brands.' We're brewing beers for exploration." A good idea for a brewer in this old seafaring town.

Opened: November 1998.

Type: Brewery.

Owners: Mark Burford, Peter Cotter.

Brewers: Mark Burford, Tom Keegan.

System: 25-barrel Peter Austin direct-fire brewhouse (ex-Wild Goose brewery), 5,000 barrels annual capacity.

Production: 4,000 barrels in 2001.

Tours: Blue Point has open tasting room hours Thursday and Friday, 3 P.M. to 7 P.M., and Saturday, noon to 7 P.M. They love to give walka-rounds of the brewery at that time and generally "share some air" with their customers.

Take-out beer: Six-packs, single oversize bottles (750-milliliter), half-gallon and 2-liter growlers, half and sixth kegs.

Extras: Surprise, a micro with live music! Blue Point actually has occasional blues shows booked for the brewery and will be sponsoring an annual blues festival. Call or check the website for scheduling.

Special considerations: Cigars not allowed. Kids welcome. Handicapped-accessible.

Parking: On-street or in lot in rear.

Lodging in the area: The Inn at Medford, 2695 Route 112, Medford, 631-654-3000; The Great South Bay Inn, 160 South Country Road, Bellport, 631-286-8588; Econo Lodge, 3055 Veterans Memorial Highway, Ronkonkoma, 631-588-6800.

Area attractions: Patchogue's **Main Street** is a nice walk, with some shops for browsing. They also have a **Swezey's Department Store,** a family-owned independent Long Island chain (225 West Main Street, 631-475-0280). You can catch a **Long Island Ducks** baseball game at Citibank Park in Central Islip (3 Court House Drive, Central Islip, 631-940-DUCK), but you might want to call ahead; the Ducks have broken the Atlantic League annual attendance record twice already. **The Long Island Maritime Museum** is not far away, in West Sayville (86 West Avenue, 631-HISTORY, www.limaritime.org). They're right on the water and host a lot of events, winding up the year with a boat burning on Halloween. That's my kind of museum. They also have an extensive collection of models, seafaring artwork, and exhibits on the oyster industry.

Other area beer sites: I've been to a lot of bars in my line of work, and to plenty more in my off hours—a purely amateur pursuit of tapside camaraderie—but I have to say that I've *never* seen a bar like **Fadely's Deli & Pub** in Patchogue (440 West Main Street, 631-758-8882). The sign's out of date: There is no deli, just one jar of pickles under the bar, and Mr. Fadely doesn't own the place anymore. They have only seven taps, but all of them are exceptional, including three taps of Blue Point that couldn't be fresher. It's a weird place, with only three chairs and a tiny 8-foot-long bar, but the locals sure were friendly. **The Sage Cafe** (4 Montauk Highway, Blue Point, 631-363-9562) was recommended by most brewers on Long Island. Go for the great beer, the great food, or the StoryJam, an open-mike storytelling night the third Tuesday of every month.

Brickhouse Brewery and Restaurant

67 West Main Street, Patchogue, NY 11772
516-447-BEER
www.brickhousebrewery.com

When you walk in the front door at the Brickhouse Brewery, take a good look at the gleaming 10-barrel Bohemian Brewing system in the front window. Like any Bohemian system, it's gorgeous: beautiful, functional curves and shiny copper-cladding. But take a particular look at this one, because I once helped polish that baby. Just wanted you to know the lengths I'll go to for the story.

Patchogue (pronounced "patch-hog") is a fairly quiet seaside town situated between the social heights of the Hamptons and the cheek-by-jowl sprawl of Nassau county. The Brickhouse itself is in a 150-year-old brick building in the center of town, a former general store and one of the older buildings on Long Island. The building's foundation is ship's ballast, a reminder of the days when Long Island was a fishing and trading center.

Upstairs is Shand's Loft (Shand's was the name of the general store), sometimes used as private dining space and tricked out with a great display of breweriana. Down in the main bar, you'll find dark wood fronted by a streetside window-wall and centered around a rectangular bar.

If you're visiting during the summer, you're in for two special treats. First is the beergarden out back, where you'll be greenly insulated from traffic by thick, lush vines of hops strung around the grassy garden. Second, you can relax out there is a stunning glass of Summer Buzz, a walloping honey-wheat ale (brewed with local honey) that weighs in around 8% ABV.

Beers brewed: All beers brewed on the premises. Year-round: Main Street Light Golden Ale, Hurricane Kitty Pale Ale, Brickhouse Boys' Red, The Paul Brown, Old Porchdog Porter. Main seasonals: Blitzen Ale, Summer Buzz Honey Wheat.

The Pick: This is easy. The Summer Buzz is an arresting beer, an 8.1 percent honey-powered headknocker, and the Hurricane Kitty Pale Ale is whackingly hoppy ("not soothing, but it sure is interesting," my notes say), but the beer that won me hands-down was the Old Porchdog Porter. Smooth, rich, medium-bodied, nice chocolate flavors without the stoutlike roastiness too many porters display. No complaints, this is great beer.

The owners, who are known as the Brickhouse Boys, have created a very successful space for live music here, with major performers coming through on a regular basis. That's part of why the Main Street Light beer is the pub's best-seller. A lot of people come for the music and don't even know it's a brewpub.

Music is the heart of the "Live after 5" shows that the Brickhouse puts on out on Main Street every other Friday in the summer. Local merchants are in on the event. They shut down two blocks of Main Street and live bands play out there for a roaring good time. Brickhouse sells beer on the sidewalk at one end, the boys from Blue Point sell beer at the other end, and everyone has a great time. The two breweries get along fine, and they should—Brickhouse's brewer is Mark Burford, one of the partners at Blue Point.

But if you're coming for the beer first, head on in and drop anchor at the bar. Ask AnneMarie (one of the friendliest brewpub bartenders I've ever come across) for a pint of Old Porchdog Porter. Check out the brewboard for beer info, maybe wander out back to the hop-draped garden. And don't forget to check out that polish job!

Opened: June 1996.

Type: Brewpub.

Owners: Dave Knapp, Tom Keegen, Bill Murray, George Hoage.

Brewer: Mark Burford, Tim Woods, assistant brewer.

System: Bohemian Brewing 10-barrel brewhouse, 1,200 barrels annual capacity.

Production: 500 barrels in 2001.

Brewpub hours: Seven days a week, 11:30 A.M. till 2 A.M.

Tours: By appointment.

Take-out beer: Half-gallon growlers and half kegs.

Food: Pretty typical American pub fare, with some nice surprises, like the three shrimp appetizers (coconut, stuffed, and classic cocktail), the twin sausages with apple-kraut and horseradish mustard, linguini fra diavolo, and sauerbraten. There are innovative seafood and pasta specials every day, and a regular menu of steaks and grilled seafood.

Extras: Live entertainment Wednesday through Saturday evening. Call for schedule or check the website. Open-mike night Wednesday with Ed Travers. Darts. Satellite dish for all kinds of sports: four games at once on five TVs plus a large-screen projection TV. Upstairs dining room and bar for private parties up to one hundred people. Summertime dining in a very nice hop garden out back, the hoppiest hop garden I've ever seen in an American brewpub. Over the summer, Brickhouse and Blue Point jointly sponsor a block party in the Main Street block by Brickhouse every other Friday. The street's blocked off, there's live music, and plenty of great beer. Lucky Patchogue!

Special considerations: Cigars allowed. Kids welcome. Vegetarian food available, but limited. Handicapped-accessible on first floor.

Parking: Plenty of street parking.

Southampton Publick House

40 Bowden Square, Southampton, NY, 11968
631-283-2800
www.publick.com

To get to the Publick House, you have to go to The Hamptons. It's got to be dealt with. There is a bizarre concentration of money out here on the South Fork of Long Island. It's the place where New Yorkers move when they've really, really made it. A resident recently proclaimed that there were two kinds of people in the world: those who are part of The Hamptons' social scene, and those who wished they were part of The Hamptons' social scene. As a friend of mine, spirits writer Gary Regan, responded, could we possibly form a third group?

It was probably inevitable, then, that the Southampton Publick House wound up with the man who is arguably the most celebrated brewer on the East Coast, a celebrity brewer the equal of Rogue Ale's John Meier. Phil Markowski probably won't like my saying that, because he's almost as publicity-shy as John Meier, but fame is a burden that doesn't ask the famous for permission.

Phil started as a homebrewer, like many brewers. "My coworkers were all doing it," he explained. "I had to. I was buying imports, the best beers I could get, and I just had to know more about beer. Then, after a while, I fantasized about how cool it would be to go pro." New England homebrew guru Pat Baker hooked him up with the people at New England Brewing in 1989. Phil was between jobs (as an electrical engineer), and he "jumped at the opportunity."

That's where I met Phil in 1992, on an impromptu tour that he's been gracious enough to claim he recalls. Once he found out how enthusiastic we were about beer, he took his time explaining things, broke out beers and snacks, and entertained us with brewing stories. It was the high point of a great beer exploration trip.

New England Brewing was a great education for Phil, but he told me ten years later, "I like the brewpub routine better. It's got variety." It sure does; just look at that list of beers. Phil brewed all kinds of beers while feeling out his regulars. "I've found they will go for lagers and Belgian styles," he said. "They don't like hoppy beers, and they don't like extreme flavors. That's okay. Hops aren't necessary for me. I like them, but you have to work with your customers."

That doesn't mean you can't have fun. Phil's brewed a number of experimental beers and less common styles (he had a Baltic porter on when I visited) and won medals for a number of them. He also does what he calls his Beer Cellar Reserve bottlings, a small amount of hand-bottled specialty beers that are kept and aged. Don't look for them in local beer stores; they're available only at the bar for consumption on the premises. I'm working my way through some that Phil gave me, and they've been extremely enjoyable; whatever else you do at Southampton, get some of these.

Beers brewed: All beers brewed on the premises. Year-round: Montauk Light, Golden Lager, Pale Ale, and Secret Ale. Seasonals vary widely according to Phil's whim (you may find anything, in other words) and have included Southampton Saison (GABF Silver, 1998), Porter, Baltic Porter, Pumpkin Ale, French Country Christmas Ale, Bohemian Pilsner, Belgian-style Quaddruple, Sullivan's Irish Ale, English Special Bitter, Southampton May Bock, 80 Shilling Scottish Ale, Black Raspberry Wheat Ale, Southampton Bavarian Wheat, Burton Ale, Belgian Amber Ale, Oatmeal Stout, Old Willy Winter Warmer, Oyster Stout, New Year Old Ale, Herb's Barleywine, Southampton Old Ale (GABF Gold and RAF Gold, 2001), Biere De Garde, Belgian Double Wit, Double Ice Bock (GABF Gold, 2000), and Grand Cru Strong Ale (RAF Gold, 2001). These last six have been part of Phil's Beer Cellar Reserve offerings, hand-bottled specialty beers available for consumption at the bar only.

Oh, and eat, too! The food is excellent and well varied, with some seriously good seafood. You can enjoy it in the more quiet dining room or right in the pub's exceptionally comfortable bar, with its atmosphere of a shore home's enclosed porch. With the high gated hedge and porch entry, you could even tell yourself that it is someone's home, and you've been invited to be part of the social scene in The Hamptons. . . .

Or maybe not. But you are invited to share the beers of an innovative brewer with a touch of genius to his art. And in my book, *this* book, that's even better.

Opened: June 1996.
Type: Brewpub.
Owners: The Sullivan brothers.
Brewer: Phil Markowski.

The Pick: The Saison is a slam-dunk for The Pick: The yeast produces amazing spicy flavors in a beer that is not overly sweet, overly tart, or overly dry, an exemplary balance. This is a great "all-afternoon" beer for the Publick House's cool, casual bar. I'd also mention the May Bock, with its smooth, full body and clean malt finish. As I wrote in my tasting notes, "Not much more you could ask for from a maibock."

Directions to Southampton Publick House

System: 15-barrel DME brewhouse, 1,500 barrels annual capacity.

Production: 1,200 barrels in 2001.

Brewpub hours: Seven days a week, 11:30 A.M. to 1 A.M.

Tours: No scheduled tours, for insurance reasons.

Take-out beer: Half-gallon growlers.

Food: The Publick House has an American menu; that is, it's reflective of America's diversity. There's plenty of seafood, of course, and the seared tuna with wasabi and teriyaki glaze is a favorite appetizer. Tackle the bone-in rib steak or jerk-roasted Atlantic salmon, or relax at the bar with a big brewery burger or a variety of wraps. The emphasis is on preparation, and the food is exceptional. Vegetarians take note: Phil Markowski is a long-time vegetarian, so there's always something good here for you, and the kitchen is happy to adjust dishes for vegans.

Extras: There are six TVs in the bar, and they're always tuned to sports; it gets especially fanatical during football season.

Special considerations: Cigars allowed. Kids welcome. Vegetarian food available. Handicapped-accessible.

Parking: Ample street parking.

Lodging in the area: Southampton Inn, 91 Hill Street, 631-283-6500; The 1708 House B&B, 126 Main Street, 631-287-1708; The Capri, 281 County Road 39A, 631-283-4220; Evergreen on Pine B&B, 89 Pine Street, 631-283-0564.

Area attractions: The best attraction in Southampton might just be the town itself. Southampton is closer to New England than it is to the rest of New York, and it shows; the town looks very New England, with everything squared away just so. Even the windows on the firehall have lace curtains. There are some high-end shops and boutiques on **Main Street** and **Job's Lane.** You can tour a whaling captain's home, an 1890s saloon, and even an outhouse or two at the **Southampton Historical Museum** (17 Meeting House Lane, 631-283-2494). There are a dozen restored buildings in all, and the outhouses are original.

Other area beer sites: *The Hansom House* is an indescribably funky establishment with live music (call for schedule) and a decent draft selection (256 Elm Street, 631-283-9772).

Beer Traveling

First things first: "Beer traveling" is not about driving drunk from brewpub to brewpub. Beer outings are similar to the wine trips celebrated in glossy travel and food magazines; they're pleasant combinations of carefree travel and the semimystical enjoyment of a potion in its birthplace. To be sure, the vineyards of France may be more hypnotically beautiful than, say, the streets of Troy, but you won't get any special-make hot dogs with famous Zippy sauce in the Rhone Valley, either. Life's a series of trade-offs.

Beer traveling is sometimes the only way to taste limited-release brews or brewpub beers. Beer is usually fresher at bars and distributors near the source. And the beer you'll get at the brewery itself is sublimely fresh, beer like you'll never have it anywhere else—the supreme quaff. You'll also get a chance to see the brewing operations and maybe talk to the brewer.

One of the things a beer enthusiast has to deal with is the perception that beer drinkers are second-class citizens compared with wine and single-malt scotch connoisseurs. Announcing plans for a vacation in the Napa Valley or a couple weeks on Scotland's Whisky Trail might arouse envious glances. A vacation built around brewery tours, on the other hand, might generate only mild confusion or pity. Microbreweries sell T-shirts and baseball caps, and beer geeks wear them. I've never seen a Beringer "Wine Rules!" T-shirt or a Chandon gimme cap. Beer-related souvenirs are plastic "beverage wrenches" and decorated pint glasses. Wine paraphernalia tends to be of a higher order: corkscrews, foil cutters, tasting glasses.

How do you as a beer enthusiast deal with this problem of perception? Simple: Revel in it. The first time my family went on a long camping trip with an experienced camper friend, we were concerned about wearing wrinkled clothes and sneakers all the time. Our guide had one reply to all our worries: "Hey, you're campers! Enjoy it!" It worked for us; it will work for you: "Hey, I'm traveling to breweries!" How bad can that be?

When you're planning a beer outing, you need to think about your approach. If you want to visit just one brewery, or perhaps tour the closely packed brewpubs and bars in Syracuse, you can first settle in at a nearby hotel. Get your walking shoes ready, and you're set to work your way through the brewery offerings. If you plan to visit several breweries in different towns, it is essential that you travel with a non-drinking driver.

You should know that the beer at brewpubs and microbreweries is sometimes stronger than mainstream beer. Often brewers will tell you the alcohol content of their beers. Pay attention to it. Keep in mind that most mainstream beers are between 4.5 and 5.0 percent ABV, and judge your limits accordingly. Of course, you might want to do your figuring before you start sampling.

About that sampling: You'll want to stay as clear-headed as possible, both during the day so you can enjoy the beer, and the morning after, so you can enjoy life. The best thing to do is drink water. Every pro I know swears by it. If you drink a pint of water for every two pints of beer you drink (one to one's even better), you'll enjoy the beer more during the day. Drinking that much water slows down your beer consumption, which is a good thing. Drinking that much water also helps keep away the *katzenjammers*, as the Germans call the evil spirits that cause hangovers. There is, however, no substitute for the simple strategy of drinking moderate amounts of beer in the first place.

Beer traveling is about enjoying beer and discovering the places where it is at its best. You could make a simple whirlwind tour of breweries, but I'd suggest you do other things too. Beer is only part of life, after all. I've always enjoyed trips to breweries more when we mixed in other attractions.

The Big Hop
New York City

New York City is so big in so many ways. Where do you start? It is richly historic, one of the oldest cities in America, dating from the famed "purchase" of Manhattan island for $24 in 1624. Washington's famous inaugural address was delivered here, architecture and invention thrived here, and the world's famous have lived and visited here.

It is strongly cosmopolitan, a melting pot since the earliest days of immigration through the Ellis Island period and into today, when it is still home to numerous strong ethnic neighborhoods. As one group has arrived, established itself, become acclimated and successful, and then moved out to the suburbs, another comes in to replace it.

It is incredibly wealthy, with the financial clout of Wall Street, the New York Stock Exchange, the NASDAQ, the major banks in the city, and the numerous corporate headquarters and wealthy individuals that call the city their home. The world looks to New York as its financial center.

It is wonderfully creative, home to theater, art, dance, music, letters, and scholarship. American broadcast media takes its direction from New York as much as anywhere else, the *New York Times* is the paper of record, Howard Stern and Don Imus are in New York.

It is a powerhouse of sports teams. The New York Yankees, baseball's winningest franchise, calls the city home, as do the scrappy New York Mets, and some of the game's greatest have played here. Football, ice hockey, basketball—New York fans are rabid fans, and they revel in their teams' glories and despair in their defeats.

It is simply huge. New York encompasses 314 square miles, largely on a cluster of islands, and is home to over seven million people in five boroughs: Manhattan, Queens, Brooklyn, the Bronx, and Staten

Island. The breweries, by the way, are in Manhattan, Brooklyn, and Staten Island.

It is deeply symbolic. The Statue of Liberty stands in New York Harbor, a beacon to all the world's oppressed, an icon of American freedom. New York is synonymous with freedom, hard work, and success to people the world over who have never been to America.

It was this symbolism, this concentration of the American character and wealth, that led to New York's being targeted in the national tragedy of September 11, 2001. The horror of the World Trade Center disaster was numbing. Large parts of Manhattan were cut off, and it seemed everyone knew someone who died. The city mourned.

But then it sprang back. It committed to clearing the debris, all of it. It carried on with business. Wall Street regained its bustle, companies took up temporary quarters, and the city, battered but defiant, went back to work. The hardest thing to bear is the truncated skyline, the reminder of that day. But plans are being discussed to rebuild, to memorialize, and the city lives on.

I feel it is futile to even attempt to cover what to see in New York. Whole libraries of guidebooks have been written on this city; there is a book just on its bars (Tim Harper's *Good Beer Guide to New York,* an excellent if somewhat dated guide). I couldn't do justice to 1 percent of the attractions. I urge you to get a good guidebook—there are many, too many to even recommend one—to plan your trip . . . then plan three more, and you'll see what I mean. There's a lifetime's worth to see and do in New York.

Likewise, a smattering of lodging suggestions seems pointless. Prices are high in Manhattan, and there are hundreds of hotels. You'll probably do a better job finding a place that will suit your needs than I can.

However, I can give you the beer attractions in the areas near the breweries, and that will be plenty to occupy you. It's what I know best, after all. I advise you to make use of the subway and bus system to get around: Driving is insane in Manhattan, though it's doable in Brooklyn. A daily Metro "Funcard" is only $4, and it's a real deal.

But my best advice is to use the help of a New York City bar pro: Bill Coleman. This pleasantly mad beer maven has a New York Beer Alert! website at hbd.org/mbas/beer.html. Bill tries to keep his favorite beer bars (and it's a great list) updated on tap availabilities. Take a look; it's informative and fun.

Final note: Your favorite bar might not be here. I didn't get to all the bars in New York. I've just picked some of my favorites and the best recommendations of friends who have earned my respect.

Brooklyn

Brooklyn is a great place to walk around, and you can even drive here with the hope of finding a parking space.

Mugs Alehouse (125 Bedford Avenue, between 10th and 11th Sreets, 718-384-8494) is practically the house tap for Brooklyn Brewery. It's about a two-minute walk from the brewery, and they usually have six taps of Brooklyn beer on, along with twenty-five other great taps and a ton of hard-to-find bottled beers. The bartenders are beer-savvy, the jukebox is exceptional (look for the beer-drinking songs), the food's good and cheap, the beers come in very reasonably priced 20-ounce imperial pints, the bathroom's immaculate, and there's an excellent spirits selection. One of the best beer bars in New York. The state, that is. *The Gate* (321 5th Avenue, 718-768-4329) is another funky little multitap, with a nice tree-shaded outside drinking area and a cool dark bar. Although the twenty-four-tap selection is outstanding, they just like beer here, they're not insane about it, and that's nice. Nice playground across the street, too. Walk north on 5th, and you'll find *Bierkraft* (191 5th Avenue, 718-230-7600), an excellent retail beer store that also has a ton of neat gourmet foods; lots of cheese. The owners are homebrewers, so you can get as geeky as you'd like. Be sure to check out the Eastern European imports; there are a lot here. The other beer store in Brooklyn (and between the two of them, you needn't go elsewhere) is *American Beer Distributing,* at 256 Court Street in the Cobble Hill section (718-875-0226, www.americanbeerbuzz.baweb.com). It not only has the best selection in the five boroughs, it also has lots of beer glassware and T-shirts, a huge selection of gourmet sodas and bottled waters, and plenty of keg beer.

Sparky's Ale House (481 Court Street, 718-624-5516) is in a nice neighborhood, has a homey atmosphere, and does four sampler drafts for $5, a great deal to taste the variety of beers here. When the weather's cool, Sparky's has up to four casks of real ale going. *The Brazen Head* (228 Atlantic Avenue, 718-448-0430) is named for Dublin's oldest bar, but it's not just another Guinness hole. This smart, sophisticated place has fifteen excellent taps, a ton of single malts, and a lot of ambulances going by outside. It's one of the more polished beer bars. *The Waterfront Ale House* (155 Atlantic Avenue, 718-522-3794) is a Brooklyn beer bar institution, the earliest multitap in Brooklyn. The taps are still hot, with some beers you won't see elsewhere, and there's great food, with a good selection of hot sauces to put on it; beware the house hot sauce! *Brooklyn Alehouse* (103 Berry Street, 718-302-9811) and *Teddy's Bar* (96 Berry Street, 718-384-9787) both come recommended from the gang at Brooklyn Brewing, and that's good enough for me. Not quite in Brooklyn, but definitely worth the trip, is **Bohemian Hall** (29-19 24th Avenue, Astoria (Queens), 718-274-4925, www.bohemianhall.com), the city's last open-air beer garden; and it's a real garden, too, with big trees, not just a cramped space with no view in back of a bar. Czech and German beers meet Czech and German food, the prices are right, and you may find you don't want to leave. Do call ahead to be sure it's open; the hours can be irregular.

Midtown Manhattan

The Ginger Man (11 East 36th Sreet at Madison Avenue, 212-532-3740) is one of Manhattan's three best beer bars. It's a constant struggle among the three—Ginger Man, d.b.a, and Blind Tiger—to see who's the best, and I'm not getting in it. When I'm at the Ginger Man, I'm real happy: lots of excellent taps, well-kept casks (and if they're not, just tell them; they actually listen to customers and will pull a bad cask), big bottled selection including plenty of Belgians, and a deep selection of single malts. Food's good, too. **The Collins Bar** (735 8th Avenue, 212-541-4206) is beautifully divey-looking, but it's friendly and has frequent specials on its carefully chosen ten taps. Check the whisky selection and the jukebox for some welcome variety. Not far away is **St. Andrew's** (120 West 44th, off 6th Avenue, 212-840-8413), a stand-up place—really, there are no bar stools—with an immense selection of single malts (over 140) that completely overshadows the thirty great taps of beer. Great place, good people, and excellent conversation. A couple doors down is **Virgil's Barbecue** (152 West 44th Street, 212-921-9494), where you will find a couple good beers (Brooklyn Pilsner and the like) and some great barbecue; get the barbecued lamb with cornbread and barbecue beans. There is a **Waterfront Ale House** in Manhattan, too (540 2nd Street, 212-696-4104), and it's just as good as the Brooklyn bar.

If you're looking for German beers, head over to **Hallo Berlin** (402 West 51st Street, off 9th Avenue, 212-541-6248) or the **Hallo Berlin Beer Hall** (626 10th Avenue at 44th Street, 212-977-1944), both with great German food. The beer and spirits selection at the Beer Hall is bigger, and there is outdoor seating. British beers? Hit the **Manchester Pub** (920 2nd Avenue, 212-223-7484) for a snug little bar with a good selection of British, Belgian, and German beers in bottles, and about sixteen taps of good beers, including Fuller's ESB. If you want Irish, New York's full of Irish pubs. I'll pass on Garrett Oliver's recommendation of **Maggie's Place** (21 East 47th Street at Madison Avenue, 212-753-5757) as "the best jar of Guinness in the city." It was an excellent pint, and the place is polished and neat as a pin, very Irish.

Downtown Manhattan

Let's start with the two other "best in Manhattan" claimants for beer selection. **The Blind Tiger Ale House** (518 Hudson Street at West 10th Street, 212-675-3848) has a beautiful tap selection and plenty of single malts and tequila, and it's a natural and fun place to hang, a surprisingly attractive place given its name. The other, **d.b.a.** (41st Avenue at 2nd Street, 212-475-5097) goes out of its way to get the first of the most unusual draft and bottled beers (partner Ray Deter told me he finds them "on Beer Mountain") and sports a great malt selection and a pretty wide bourbon selection. There's a patio out back for nice weather. Note: d.b.a. does not serve food, but there's good takeout available in the neighborhood, and the bar has no problem with deliveries.

Brewsky's and **Burp Castle** are flip sides at the same address (41 East Seventh Street, 212-420-0671 and 212-982-4576, respectively). Brewsky's is a dive with excellent beer and no pretension whatsoever, where geeks come to drink beer and talk beer with other geeks. Burp Castle is a bit gimmicky, with its "Brewist Order" monks and Gregorian chant, but the beer selection, particularly that of bottled Belgians, is impressive. Speaking of Belgians, you'll want to visit either (or both) **Cafe des Bruxelles** (118 Greenwich Avenue, 212-206-1830) or **Vol de Nuit** (West 4th Street and 6th Avenue, 212-979-2616), where you can get delicious Belgian food to go with your Belgian beers. Get delicious German food to go with your German beer at **Zum Schneider** (107 Avenue C, near 7th Street, 212-598-1098); good German drafts and bottles here.

Finally, **McSorley's Ale House** (15 East 7th Street, 212-473-9148) has a line out the door many times, doesn't serve really great beer (though it's better than some), and is somewhat dingy. But you really have to go. McSorley's is New York's oldest bar, and the history has to be breathed to be appreciated. Go in the afternoon to avoid the crowds, and be prepared to order two (small) beers at a time; that's how it works here.

Yankee Brewing Company

201 Arlington Avenue, Staten Island, NY 10303
718-447-5411
www.yankeebrewingcompany.com

Sal Pennacchio gets the award for microbrewing grit. "When did this all get started?" I asked him as we walked around his Yankee Brewing operation. "I started homebrewing twenty-one years ago," he replied, "and by 1984 I was ready to open a brewery. I just didn't know how to raise the money." It's a long, tortured story, but Sal is brewing at last.

Sal got beer writer Michael Jackson's first book. "I opened that and saw all those beers, then I looked at the crap on the shelves in the stores. If I wanted to drink those book beers, I'd have to make them. So I learned to homebrew. I liked the brewing, and I liked sharing beers and knowledge. It's all interesting, the history, the different glassware for different beers, even the math in the brewing."

Sal liked it so much he opened a homebrew shop in his house. "I started the guys at Long Valley [brewpub in New Jersey]," he remembers proudly. "I sold malt to Garrett Oliver." All this activity led to a half-page article in the *New York Times* in 1984 on homebrewing and Sal's involvement in it. He brewed, he planned, he schemed for six years. In 1990, Sal said, "I made the decision. I mortgaged the house and started contract brewing at Point Brewery in Wisconsin."

Sal made his New York Harbor Ale, and he was happy with it. Contracting wasn't ideal, but the beer was good. Then he had a chance to get more control over the brewing and reduce shipping costs. A microbrewery in Hoboken approached Sal about brewing his beer there. "I pulled out of Point and changed all my labeling and packaging to reflect the change," Sal recalled bitterly. "I bought thousands of labels, six-packs, cases."

Beers brewed: All beers brewed on the premises. Year-round: New York Harbor Light, New York Harbor Ale, New York Harbor Porter. Seasonals: Winter WheatFest, New York Harbor Octoberfest, New York Harbor Peach Wheat, "and some surprises," Sal promises.

The Pick: I'll pick the Harbor Light kölsch, since that's the only new Yankee brew I've had. I had the Ale back when it was being contract-brewed, but that memory fades in the face of the kölsch. It's snappy, a little grainy, and not overdone in the ester department. It compares well to Shiner Summer Stock, one of the best American kölsches out there. Don't overlook it because of the "light" moniker.

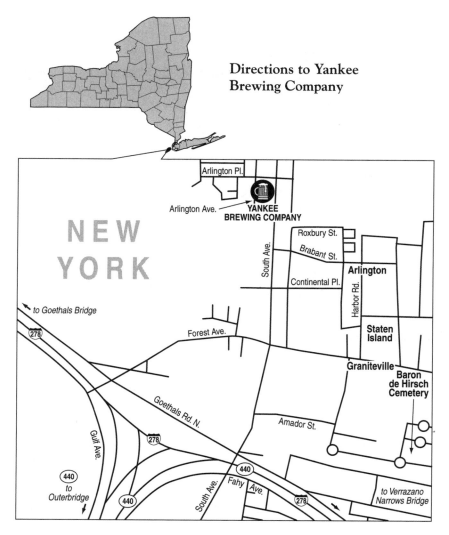

Directions to Yankee
Brewing Company

All for naught: The brewery in Hoboken went under four months after it started brewing Sal's beer. "It almost killed me," Sal said. "I was making real beer!" He figured he'd had his shot and got a job and worked on some personal problems he'd been neglecting. Sal was out of the beer biz and getting his life in order.

But people kept telling him they wanted his beer. Finally, enough people had asked him about it that he looked into raising money. Money was there this time, and in May 2001, Sal started to put things together. He got hold of the 20-barrel HDP brewhouse out of Mountain Valley, lined up space on Staten Island, and started making plans. September 11 put the brakes on a bit, but in the spring of 2002, Old World Brewing was back on track.

Old World Brewing? That's the name Sal had been using ever since the homebrew shop. "But what does it say," Sal thought. After more thought, he decided that start-up was a great time for a name change and picked Yankee Brewing Company. "I'm a big fan," he admitted. "And 'Yankee' says East Coast. Besides, the team's not a beer." The Staten Island Yankees farm team didn't mind; they put Sal's New York Harbor beers in their ballpark.

So Sal is going out and hitting the streets with his selling shoes on, while experienced brewer Dan Carter mans the kettle. "It's good beer," Sal said. "Really good beer, and people want it." I hope it works this time for Sal; I've got my fingers crossed.

Opened: Began contract brewing as Old World Brewing in 1990; opened Staten Island brewery in May 2001; changed name to Yankee Brewing in June 2002.

Type: Brewery.

Owners: Sal Pennacchio, Stephen DeMaria.

Brewer: Dan Carter.

System: 20-barrel HDP brewhouse, 3,800 barrels annual capacity.

Production: Not available.

Tours: Saturday, 1 P.M. to 3 P.M., but not in summer or on holidays, because "I need a day off!" Sal said. Call ahead for tours.

Take-out beer: Six-packs, cases, half, quarter, and sixth kegs.

Special considerations: Kids welcome. Handicapped-accessible.

Parking: Street parking. Don't use the lot unless you ask someone in the brewery first.

Area attractions: *The Staten Island Ferry* (718-390-5253) is a famous trip through New York Harbor; what better way to celebrate touring the brewery and trying Sal's New York Harbor Ale? It's free, it's passengers only, and it's twenty-four hours a day. *Historic Richmond Town* is 100 acres of restored buildings (mostly moved from elsewhere on the island), a re-creation of three centuries of Staten Island life, beginning with the Dutch settlement. The streets are alive with guides and craftspeople in period dress. There are craft demonstrations, a gift shop, and visitors center (441 Clarke Avenue, 718-351-1611). Richmond Town is open Wednesday to Sunday; hours vary seasonally.

Other area beer sites: Staten Island? According to the folks at **Killmeyer's Old Bavarian Inn** (4256 Arthur Kill Road, at Sharrots Road, 718-984-1202), it's *Spaten* Island! Killmeyer's is a somewhat rambling blend of German *gasthaus*-style restaurant, old New York–style bar, and modern hangout. There's a good selection of German drafts (which you can have delivered to your table in a 3-liter wooden barrel) and specialty spirits, and Sal's New York Harbor beers. You can also get a delicious, really reasonable German lunch. There are a lot of German places in New York City; this is one of the best. As you might expect at a place called **Adobe Blues** (63 Lafayette Avenue, 718-720-2583), there's live blues and a southwestern theme, down to the adobe exterior, rail fence, cacti, and the rattler-looking king snake in the terrarium behind the bar. The food's great Tex-Mex, and though there's only five taps (all good), they've got a great bottle selection, described as "178 beers, 32 countries, 22 styles." They also have over fifty tequilas and mezcals.

Brooklyn Brewery

119 North 11th Street, Brooklyn, NY 11211
718-486-7422
www.brooklynbrewery.com

I like to think that Steve Hindy got the idea to open the Brooklyn Brewery while under fire. Gunfire, that is. "I was a journalist for fifteen years," he told me. "I was in the Middle East from 1979 to 1984, covering things like the civil war in Lebanon and the Iran-Iraq war. I was sitting in the stands when Anwar Sadat was assassinated." It was time to duck and cover and, it occurs to me, a perfect time to think to oneself, "I have got to look into another line of work."

Oddly enough, Steve had learned to homebrew in the Middle East. "When Saudi Arabia went dry in 1953," Steve said, "ARAMCO issued pamphlets to its employees with instructions on making wine, beer, liquor. . . . I learned homebrewing from some American diplomats on Middle East stations."

He did get out of the Middle East and moved back to New York, where he got to know his neighbor, Tom Potter. "I was brewing beer," he said, "Tom was drinking it, and I started pitching the idea of doing it for a living. Tom's got an MBA, and he was skeptical. Then we went to the annual microbrewing conference in 1986, and Tom met a bunch of businesspeople who convinced him that with the right capitalization, we had a good business idea. We got our money together and signed on it a few days before the stock market crash in October 1987." Great timing!

Hindy and Potter were contracting at Matt's, up in Utica, after having talked a sternly doubtful F. X. Matt into taking a chance on them. "The first time I talked to him," Steve recalled, "he basically called me an idiot, said, 'What makes you think you can sell beer?' I really got nowhere." Then F. X., who'd been an English major in college, found out Hindy was a journalist and decided to give him a serious listen.

It helped that they had Bill Moeller formulating beers for them, a retired brewmaster with decades of experience and two generations of brewmasters' notebooks in his family records. Bill ran up two beers for them: Brooklyn Lager, a hoppy amber lager, and Brooklyn Brown Ale, a shockingly hoppy brown ale.

Beers brewed: All bottled beers brewed at Matt's in Utica under contract and Brooklyn's supervision. Some draft is brewed at Matt's. Brooklyn Brewery won the F. X. Matt Memorial Cup at TAP NY in 2001. Year-round: Brooklyn Lager (GABF Gold, 1992), Pilsner, Brooklyn Pennant Pale Ale '55, East India Pale Ale, Brown Ale (GABF Bronze, 1991, 1992, and 2000), Brooklyner Weisse (GABF Gold, 1997; TAP NY Bronze, 2001). Seasonals: Black Chocolate Stout, Breukelen Abbey Ale ("Breukelen" is the original Dutch spelling of "Brooklyn"), Monster Barleywine, Dry Stout, Blanche de Brooklyn (GABF Bronze, 1997; TAP NY Gold, 2001), Star of Manchester Porter.

After lining up famous designer Milton Glasier to do their logo in exchange for a piece of the company, Hindy and Potter hit the streets to sell beer. That's when they ran headlong into the New York market. It was such a sobering experience that they eventually came to the realization that their plans for a brewery would have to be put on hold until they solved the distribution problem.

It wasn't something they wanted to do. "This is all a necessary evil, the distribution thing," Steve told me in an interview back in 1994. "If there were a good distributor in New York, we wouldn't have needed to do this." But they did, and it turned into the Craft Brewers Guild, a distributor of not only Brooklyn beers, but other great micros and imports as well.

When that part of the puzzle was firmly in place and making money in 1994, it was time to finally start the brewery they'd planned since

1986. That's when Garrett Oliver entered the picture. He'd been brewing at a brewpub, Manhattan Brewing, since 1989. He could see the writing on the wall there, and one day when no one was in, he brewed up a batch of big imperial stout. "I took it over to Brooklyn as my resume," he told me. In one of their smartest moves, Hindy and Potter hired him and sent him up to Utica to brew the stout, which would be labeled as Brooklyn Black Chocolate Stout. I still have one bottle left from that first batch; I drank the other in 2000 and it was marvelous.

Garrett rigged in the big 25-barrel Newlands system and three fermenters and went to work. "All we did at first was Brooklyner Weiss," he told me. "Then came the East India Pale Ale, then the others. We grew slowly, but now we have twelve fermenters that are full all the time." I asked him which beers were brewed at Matt's and which at Brooklyn. "It's complicated," he said. "But all the bottled beer is done at Matt, because I do *not* want a bottling line. A bottling line will make a grown man cry."

Garrett's been a great ambassador for the beer. He's an articulate proponent of beer and food as the equal of wine and food and just wrote a book about it, *The Brewmaster's Table*. That's why Brooklyn makes such a wide range of beers. "Food choice needs something for everyone," he pointed out. "With all those beers, we can cover a wide range of tastes."

It's been a long journey for Brooklyn, but at 38,000 barrels in 2001, they've made it. They even showed growth in 2001, after the disaster of September 11 struck right in the middle of their core market. "The press says the air's gone out of the sales of craft-brewed beer," Garrett said earnestly. "They don't get it: *We won.* Our share is growing, food and drink is a different relationship from what it was, we're part of the community."

Steve Hindy was completely optimistic when I last talked to him. Brooklyn had just doubled its New Jersey business, thanks to a new dis-

The Pick: Brooklyn Lager has been one of my favorite beers from any brewery since long before I started writing about beer. I was lucky enough to find this beer in 1988, shortly after it came out, and drank it often. I was terribly impressed by its hoppy nose, solidly medium body and malt heft, and bitter, clean finish—and I still am. This is one of the best beers out there for serious session drinking, when you've got old friends together or are making new ones and you want to talk forever. Brooklyn Lager's so good you won't want to switch, but not so over-the-top that it distracts you. Best of all, the bottles taste almost exactly like the draft, something that is unfortunately all too rare in beer. I'd also like to make mention of the Star of Manchester porter, a recent one-shot brew that I hope makes a return someday. This beer, brewed from a century-old British recipe, was velvety smooth, rich, and flavorful. It tasted like cask ale when I had it on CO_2 push at Mugs, and when I got it on cask at Sparky's, I just about lost my mind. What a delicious beer, Garrett: Make it again!

Directions to Brooklyn Brewery

tributor, and he and Potter had sold part of their distribution business for a nice profit to a company they trusted. He agreed with Garrett. "There's still high interest in regional breweries," he said. "You just gotta get out there and keep preaching. The old-time religion still works." Preach it, Brother Steve.

Opened: October 1987.
Type: Brewery and contract brewery.
Owners: Stephen Hindy, Tom Potter.
Brewer: Garrett Oliver.
System: 25-barrel Newlands brewhouse, 10,000 barrels annual capacity.
Production: 38,000 barrels in 2001 (in-house production plus con-
    tracted production at Matt's in Utica).

Tours: Saturdays, noon to 5 P.M. Also open Fridays, 6 P.M. to 10 P.M., selling packaged and draft beer; bar snacks are provided. There is live music some Fridays; call for details.

Take-out beer: Six-packs and cases, plus by-the-drink ($3 pints!).

Extras: There is a large area full of tables for Friday nights, plus a dartboard and pool table.

Special considerations: Cigars not allowed. Kids welcome. Handicapped-accessible.

Parking: Plentiful free street parking.

Chelsea Brewing Company

Pier 59 (across from 15th Street)
Chelsea Piers, New York, NY 10011
212-336-6440
www.chelseabrewingco.com

New York started its rise to greatness as a port city. It still is a major port, but some of the trade has been pried away by cities like Baltimore and Philadelphia, leaving unused facilities in New York. One of the more innovative uses of these relics is at Chelsea Piers, where an enormous sports and entertainment complex has been developed, including a studio where interior scenes of *Law and Order* are shot, and a driving range out on one of the piers.

I wasn't there to hit a bucket of balls, though. I was there to watch other people do that while sipping a relaxing glass of porter in the Chelsea Brewing Company lounge, a less strenuous but equally rewarding activity. Considering the heft of the porter Chris Sheehan brews, I'm not so sure it is less strenuous; this is some big beer.

Chris has the pedigree for big black beers. Before brewing at Chelsea, he brewed at the late and much-lamented 20 Tank Brewery in San Francisco, where he helped produce the stunning Heart of Darkness XXX Stout and Kinnikinick Old Scout Stout, which dominated the dark end of the Great American Beer Festival in the mid-1990s. An upstate native, Chris returned from California to take a brewing job at the short-lived Neptune brewery, also in Manhattan. He could see that job wasn't too secure, so one day he had lunch at Chelsea with then-brewer Russell Garret. He was quickly hired as an assistant brewer, and when Garret left to open a microbrewery in Ireland a year later, Chris moved up to the head brewer slot.

That was in 1997, and Chris has settled in pretty well now. He's happy with the brewery, though there are two flies in the soup of his contentment. "I've got a 30-barrel kettle," he explained, "with 60-barrel fermenters and 15-barrel serving tanks." He shrugged, and a wry grin twisted his long face. "That makes it . . . difficult sometimes," referring to the juggling act of double-batching and tank transferring he has to go through at times to keep the beer fresh and flowing.

The other problem is the bottling line. Chelsea used to bottle the Checker Cab Blonde Ale and Sunset Red Ale for sale off-premises. Chris put an end to that. "I had bad experiences with distributors," he recalled. "They'd let the beer sit in the summer heat, and then they'd sell it six months later; we had no control over it. We have no cold storage on-site, so we can't store it ourselves. So I don't bottle anymore." But it's a tough market for used bottling lines, so the bottling line still sits in the middle of the brewery, taking up space that Chris would love to use for things like a new bright beer tank.

Beers brewed: Year-round: Checker Cab Blonde Ale, Sunset Red Ale (GABF Gold, 1997). Seasonals: Chelsea offers some beers by categories. There is always a wheat beer on that changes with the season: Autumn Harvest Amber, Frosty's Winter, April Showers-May Flowers, or Summer Solstice. There is always a stout or porter: Chelsea Cream Stout (GABF Gold, 1997; Bronze, 2001), Chelsea Export Stout, Tsar's Revenge Imperial Stout, Ard Righ Irish Stout, Chelsea Oatmeal Stout, and Porter of Authority (one of my favorite beer names anywhere). The pale or India pale ales rotate through: Pier 59 Pale Ale, Henry Hudson IPA, HopAngel IPA, CBC ESB, and the winter holiday version, Hoppy Holidays Special Ale. There is also always a fruit beer: Raspberry, Cherry, or Blueberry Wheat.

Chelsea does still sell beer off-premises, but it's all draft, which actually helps with the beer juggling problem by emptying the tanks. "It's a significant amount of our business," Chris noted. "In fact, it's over half our monthly business during the winter. We have a number of accounts in Manhattan, a few in Brooklyn, and three bars out at JFK Airport." Chelsea also has a number of house taps, where the beer is sold under a bar's own name, in places like Greenwich Brewing Company (a Village bar, not a brewery) and the landmark bar Chumley's.

I just happen to think you're better off drinking these beers at their home. Not only is there a lot of fun to be had at the Piers, but the bar is long and the staff is personable, the food's good, and the view out over the Hudson River is spectacular at sunset. If the weather's good, you can sit outside on the extensive waterside deck in the breeze and listen to the slap of the waves. If the weather's not so good, stay inside in the padded horseshoe-shaped booths that face the water by the western glass wall.

In any case, stick around till it's dark. In your glass, that is. Because the big black beers are where the real fun is at this place for a beer lover like you.

Opened: March 1996.

Type: Brewpub and brewery.

Owner: Pat Green.

Brewer: Chris Sheehan. Assistant brewer, Mark Szmaida.

System: 30-barrel DME brewhouse, 6,000 barrels potential annual capacity.

Production: 1,748 barrels in 2001.

Brewpub hours: Seven days a week, noon to 1 A.M.

Tours: Monday through Friday, 9 A.M. to 5 P.M. at the brewer's convenience. Large groups, schedule in advance.

Take-out beer: Half-gallon growlers, half kegs (call for availability).

Food: Try the hot beer bread with honey butter to start the meal, or an order of steamed mussels or clams. Salads are popular, ranging from greens to taco salad to fruit salad. Sandwiches include a wide range of burgers, blackened catfish po'boy, and bratwurst hero; vegetarians will enjoy the roasted vegetable wrap. This is New York, so there's pizza (Chris's favorite is the barbecued chicken pie, but you can build your own). You'll find an understandable emphasis on seafood, including a dinner portion of steamed mussels and teriyaki salmon. Pick a pasta—linguini, capellini, spaghetti, with a variety of sauces or scampi. If you're really hungry, you can tie into a full entree, like the pork tenderloin in mustard-stout sauce or a filet mignon. You'll find the fajitas and burritos in the entree section because they're that big. There's something here for almost everyone, including a "chef's whim" dessert menu.

Extras: Chelsea has eight TVs in the bar. There's a room for private parties; call for details. The main draw in good weather is the large area for outdoor seating, with a view of the marina and sunsets over the Hudson River and New Jersey.

Special considerations: Cigars allowed at the bar. Kids welcome. Vegetarian foods available. Handicapped-accessible.

Parking: Available in the Chelsea Piers lots.

The Pick: I have a bit of a problem here, and it's all Chris Sheehan's fault. Porter of Authority was on when I visited Chelsea, and it brought me to my knees (figuratively, that is): almost opaque, rich, and bitter. Anywhere else, this would be a stout, but Chris's stouts, his favorite style, are so damned assertive that this actually represents a step back. Anyway, the problem is, Chris told me he doesn't do the Porter very often. I guess it's your problem now. If you can't get the Porter, there's no shame in settling for one of Chris's stouts.

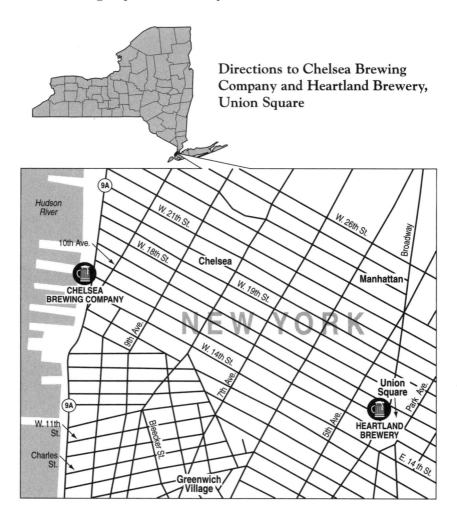

Directions to Chelsea Brewing Company and Heartland Brewery, Union Square

Area attractions: The brewery is located in the **Chelsea Piers Sports Complex** (www.chelseapiers.com), next to the driving range. The Sports Complex is amazingly varied, offering venues and classes for ice and in-line skating, rock climbing, soccer, boxing, swimming, baseball, dance, kayaking, lacrosse, basketball, sailing . . . as well as batting cages, a driving range, bowling lanes, and a huge fitness center. The Sports Complex is right alongside the Hudson River promenade and bike trail, part of the **Hudson River Park,** which is eventually intended to run the whole way to Troy! This part of the park and path is well described at the NYCSK8 website: www.skatecity.com-nyc-where-manhattans.html.

Heartland Brewery, Union Square

35 Union Square West, New York, NY 10003
212-645-3400
www.heartlandbrewery.com

There's a look to older New York City bars, the long-established places in the older buildings. They've got a lived-in look, an easy-on-bleary-eyes atmosphere of dark wood and low lighting, and a lot of times you can see the brick walls of the building. The long bar is a little cluttered, but the surface is shiny and clean from many rounds of club soda and bar towel. If there are tables, they're low, and they may be separated from the bar by ornamented structural pillars.

Heartland Union Square's got that look, and it's not by chance, and they didn't just move into a great old bar. Owner Jon Bloostein knows that look, and he wanted it, strove for it. "I don't like places where it looks like they just waxed the floor and polished everything," he told me. "I like places that look like they're fifty years old. It's a struggle to give it that lived-in feel, that looks like it's been there forever, that makes you want to relax, sit back, and have two or three beers."

That's a planned look, a worked-at look. This may remind you uncomfortably of the Fadò pubs' "add-Irish-and-stir-briskly" phenomenon, but Bloostein's work rings more solidly than those. For one thing, the breweriana up on the walls is all from Jon's own collection. "I love the breweriana," he said, with obvious enthusiasm. "I'm an addict of that stuff. And it lends flavor and history to the places." The collection at Union Square is great, varied and nostalgic.

For another thing, Jon's a real beer guy. I have to admit that I was suspicious of the man when I read the press releases back in 1995 when Heartland Union Square opened. He was a mergers and acquisitions guy. At the time, I was convinced that they and their stockbrokering, investment banking ilk were ruining the small brewing revo-

Beers brewed: All beers brewed on the premises. Year-round ("The Classics"): Cornhusker Lager, Harvest Wheat, Indian River Light, Red Rooster Ale, Indiana Pale Ale, and Farmer Jon's Oatmeal Stout (GABF Gold, 1997; Silver, 1999; and Bronze, 1995). Seasonals: Summertime Apricot Ale, Grateful Red Lager, Smiling Pumpkin Ale, Oktoberfest, Bavarian Black Lager, Old Red Nose Ale, Full Moon Barleywine, Old Faithful Steam Beer, Stumbling Buffalo Brown Ale, Eliminator Doublebock, Maibock, and Not Tonight Honey Porter. Sodas: Black Cherry, Root Beer, Ginger Ale, and Mocha Soda.

lution, spending stupid money to make ho-hum beer in overdone premises because they thought they'd make a bundle.

I still think I was right in general, but I was dead wrong about Jon Bloostein. He was a genuine beer geek with money, and he did things right. Just look at the brewpub scene in Manhattan: Heartland dominates, with three pubs, and a fourth planned for late 2002 at the South Street Seaport. Commonwealth is gone, Highlander is gone, Zip City and its Tap Room successor, Times Square Brewing. . . . Is this town particularly hard on brewpubs? No, but it's hell on restaurants that don't have a solid vision and good business practices to back it up.

The Pick: First of three Picks, and the easiest: Farmer Jon's Oatmeal Stout. Nitro-poured dark chocolate brown beer with a deep tan head yields a nose full of baker's chocolate, coffee, graham, and those sugar wafer cookies, and the first mouthful yields all that the aroma promises, plus some delicious estery-fruity sidenotes. This is great stuff. Kelly Taylor tells me that customers love a mix of the stout and Smiling Pumpkin Ale, and call it a "Stumpkin."

The restaurant business is definitely the hard part for Jon. "Running a brewpub is easy; it's fun," he told me as we looked around Union Square. "Running a restaurant is nuts." He rolled his eyes. "But if I didn't have food, just beer, no one would come in."

Boy, the things you'll put up with for love! Luckily, Jon doesn't take out his occasional exasperation on the food. This is a great bar menu, full of well-prepared savory sandwiches and serious entrees that all get to your table fast. Union Square "is the beer-drinking pub," Heartland's head brewer, Kelly Taylor, told me. "We do twice as much beer here as at the other Heartlands." Maybe so, but don't overlook the menu.

There's more to hear from Bloostein and Taylor, but we've got two more entries to do it in. Meanwhile, relax, sit back, and have two or three beers. That's what Jon would want you to do.

Opened: April 1995.

Type: Brewpub.

Owner: Jon Bloostein.

Brewer: Kelly Taylor. Assistant brewers, Allan Duval and Scott Osborg.

System: 15-barrel DME brewhouse, 2,000 barrels annual capacity.

Production: 1,500 barrels in 2001.

Brewpub hours: Monday through Thursday, noon to 1 A.M.; Friday and Saturday, noon to 3 A.M.; Sunday, noon to midnight.

Tours: On request, or by appointment. Scheduled beer-tasting groups go through the brewery.

Take-out beer: Half-gallon growlers.

Food: Food at Union Square is delicious pub food, and it comes *fast*. I got a smoking hot, perfectly cooked buffalo burger about thirteen minutes after I ordered it. Talk about "in a New York minute." It's not just sandwiches, either; you can tear into Maine crab cakes, hickory-smoked ribs, and filet mignon. There's some real vegetarian meals here, too, like vegetarian chili and wild mushroom ravioli. This may be a beer-drinking pub, but the food's worth your notice.

Extras: High-end sound system that doesn't blow your hair back, but does do a great job of providing crystal-clear background music that runs to classic rock, alternative, and blues.

Special considerations: Cigars allowed. "Though there's not too much of that anymore," Jon noted. Kids welcome, but more geared for adults. Vegetarian foods available. Handicapped-accessible.

Parking: Don't even think about it. Union Square subway station is right across the street.

Heartland Brewery, Midtown

1285 6th Avenue at 51st Street, New York, NY 10019
212-645-3400
www.heartlandbrewery.com

Heartland Midtown is tucked back off the northwest corner of 6th Avenue and 51st Street, but you'll easily find the big red neon sign. Walk in and you'll find yourself in another of Jon Bloostein's creations, a classically styled New York barroom, dark wood and plenty of bar space. I find Midtown to be the most true to Bloostein's midwestern "heartland" imagery; it just seems a bit older and more plain-spun.

What's with all that midwestern imagery, anyway? Who would have thought midwestern theming would have worked in a Manhattan brewpub? Oh, maybe the people who thought a revival of *Oklahoma!* would knock Broadway dead. Like *Oklahoma!* Heartland is a romanticized, eastern view of the Midwest: reassuring, quiet, honest, just what your average Manhattan office worker is looking for after a stressful day of dealing with a couple dozen screaming liars.

One of the things they'll be looking for first is one of Heartland's great beers. I asked Jon Bloostein which of his beers he liked the best, and he did the only dithering I've ever heard from the man. "I like all of them; what can I tell you?" he finally said, laughing. "The Farmer Jon's Oatmeal Stout is a favorite for watching other people drink it. You can read it on their lips how much they like it; they smile, they lick their lips. I like that, that's great."

The Farmer Jon's has won gold, silver, and bronze medals in its category at the Great American Beer Festival. It's an excellent beer, especially on the creamy nitro pour Heartland uses. But the relatively new Indian River Light is, as Jon put it, "something different, an interesting light beer." Kelly Taylor called it "Hoegaarden Light," referring to the classic Belgian *witbier*; both are spiced with coriander and orange, but Indian River is only 4 percent ABV. Light beer for geeks.

Beers brewed: All beers brewed on the premises. Year-round ("The Classics"): Cornhusker Lager, Harvest Wheat, Indian River Light, Red Rooster Ale, Indiana Pale Ale, and Farmer Jon's Oatmeal Stout (GABF Gold, 1997; Silver, 1999; and Bronze, 1995). Seasonals: Summertime Apricot Ale, Grateful Red Lager, Smiling Pumpkin Ale, Oktoberfest, Bavarian Black Lager, Old Red Nose Ale, Full Moon Barleywine, Old Faithful Steam Beer, Stumbling Buffalo Brown Ale, Eliminator Doublebock, Maibock, and Not Tonight Honey Porter. Sodas: Black Cherry, Root Beer, Ginger Ale, and Mocha Soda.

Heartland's seasonals are popular too, particularly the cloudy golden Summertime Apricot Ale and the beloved Smiling Pumpkin Ale. "The Smiling Pumpkin is always a big seller," Bloostein said. "We'll sell a thousand pints of Pumpkin on Halloween. It's our biggest holiday for beer sales."

The prices are higher at Midtown, but that's the price of fame in this zip code. Think of it as an escape from fast-paced, stressful Midtown to the less-frenzied ease of the wide-open prairies.

Opened: March 1998.
Type: Brewpub.
Owner: Jon Bloostein.
Brewer: Kelly Taylor. Assistant brewers, Allan Duval and Scott Osborg.
System: 4-barrel Price-Schönstrom brewhouse, 400 barrels annual capacity.
Production: Pilot system only; no commercial production in 2001.
Brewpub hours: 11:30 A.M. to midnight every day.
Tours: On request or by appointment. Beer-tasting groups go through as well.
Take-out beer: Half-gallon growlers.
Food: See page 61.

Extras: A great sound system that plays mostly blues, classic rock, and R&B. This Heartland is just a little more "down-homey," and you can see it in one thing I was happy to see: bar puzzles, the chains and rings and horseshoe puzzles that are a staple in upstate rural bars.

Special considerations: Same as Heartland Union Square.

Parking: Fuhgeddaboudit. Take the subway to the 49th Street or Rockefeller Center station and walk a couple blocks.

The Pick: Indian River Light, and boy, doesn't that surprise me! This was unexpectedly good, full of the classic *witbier* aromas of orange and coriander spiciness, and so light that it practically evaporates from the glass. No, wait, that's me, drinking this so fast. An exceptionally clean beer for a *wit*.

Directions to Heartland Brewery, Midtown; Heartland Brewery and Chophouse; and Typhoon Brewery

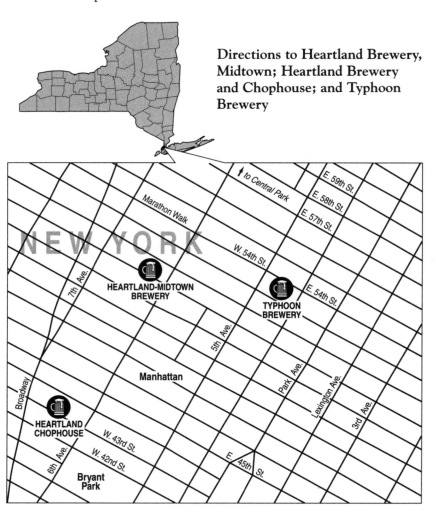

Heartland Brewery and Chophouse

127 West 43rd Street at Times Square,
New York, NY 10036
646-366-0235
www.heartlandbrewery.com

Shifting gears from the other two Heartland brewpubs, the Chophouse is decidedly more sophisticated and upscale. Jazz plays on the crisply precise sound system, brighter lighting rules in frosted glass partitions and mirrored columns, and the bar is smaller and ornate, with hammered copper panels. There are a lot more suits here, grabbing a poached salmon lunch (but scared to death to have a beer midday) and arguing with someone on their cells. This is a business lunch and pretheater dinner place and is usually pretty quiet by 10 at night.

Jon Bloostein is working magic again. The Chophouse's more imposing entrance and jazz background are deliberate. "It's a new place that we're trying to lend a tradition to, infuse some history to it," he explained. "The other places have classic rock, blues, and reggae, more timeless stuff."

I admit to having more egalitarian tastes when it comes to brewpubs, so places like the Chophouse can put me off a bit. That's why it's comforting to this beer geek to see that whatever other design tricks have been used here, the brewery is still right there, with all its gleaming stainless, clearly in view from the main dining room. Like I said, Jon Bloostein is a real beer guy.

He's got himself a real beer guy for a head brewer, too. Kelly Taylor is another guy with a business background. "International business relations, with a specialty in Russian and Eastern European interests," he noted. "But beer is the real international language!" After working at places

Beers brewed: Most of the beer at the Chophouse is brewed at Heartland Midtown, kegged off, and brought here. The beers are the same as at the other two Heartlands, with the substitution of Chophouse Blonde Ale, a light pale ale, for the Cornhusker Lager.

The Pick: As I said, Kelly Taylor is a fan of balance. Sometimes, though, you just feel *un*balanced: that's when you reach for an Indiana Pale Ale. I saved it for last when I did my formal tasting, and wrote in my notes, "So this is where the hops have been hiding!" There's a deft hand here; the hops come through in huge flavor and aroma, as well as bitterness. This is a big, full-bodied IPA with a minutes-long hop finish. Great beer!

like Karl Strauss in San Diego and Whidbey Island Brewing in Washington (and a stint in marketing at Pyramid Brewing), Kelly wound up in Manhattan, back in international commerce.

It didn't last. He missed brewing, and when the Heartland position came open, he interviewed for it and got it. It's worked out well for all involved. Taylor has a surprisingly European approach to brewing for a West Coaster (must be the international commerce background). "It's all about balance," he said, explaining his brewing philosophy. "You have to balance the malt and the hops, not overwhelm with one or the other." That's why hopheads might not be happy with anything but Kelly's Indiana Pale Ale, but then, not everyone's a hophead, which is near the core of the philosophy.

Bloostein and Taylor see eye-to-eye on that balance. That's what Heartland is about: Rarely over the top (though at 9 percent and aged almost a year, the Full Moon Barleywine comes close), always interesting, comfortable, and approachable—all the things designed to get the most people in the door. There's a little compromise here, but no sellout. Bloostein, thankfully, enjoys beer too much for that to happen.

Opened: June 2001.

Type: Brewpub.

Owner: Jon Bloostein.

Brewers: Kelly Taylor. Assistant brewers, Allan Duval and Scott Osborg.

System: 15-barrel DME brewhouse, 2,500 barrels annual capacity.

Production: 600 barrels in the first six months of operation in 2001.

Brewpub hours: Seven days a week, 11:30 A.M. to midnight.

Tours: On request or by appointment. Beer-tasting groups go through as well.

Take-out beer: Half-gallon growlers.

Food: As you might expect, the menu is tonier and pricier here: poached salmon salad, beefsteak tomato salad with Bermuda onions and Maytag blue cheese, mahi mahi fra diavolo. Still, the food comes quickly, well presented, and well prepared.

Special considerations: Same as Heartland Union Square.

Parking: Get serious. Hop the subway to the Times Square station and walk off some of that beer.

Typhoon Brewery

22 East 54th Street, New York, NY 10022
212-754-9006

Typhoon could only happen in Manhattan. Chelsea Brewing could easily be a Legal Seafood with a brewhouse on the docks in Boston. Heartland's brewpubs could have happened in Philadelphia; Dock Street almost pulled it off. But the only place on the East Coast that you'd see a brewpub menu full of dishes like wok-charred squid with chilis and fried garlic, chicken coconut soup, duck pizza, and shrimp skewers with peanut sauce and pickled cucumbers . . . would be Manhattan.

Because Typhoon is a brewpub mated to a Thai restaurant (and isn't it a brilliant name for a Thai restaurant?), it's something of a shotgun wedding, design-wise. Sit at the bar in a conversation with any of the string of friendly bartenders that have been through here, and you'll think you were in a comfortably dark, upscale brewpub bar. But turn around and you'll see a stylish, arty lounge area; head upstairs and you'll find a brightly lit and brashly light restaurant dining room with all the accouterments of high-level Asian dining.

Is Typhoon schizo? Maybe, but so what? Think about a nice fresh IPA with that wok-charred squid and tell me if you really care about the jarring juxtaposition of cultures. I don't, but apparently I'm not most people, because that's been a problem at Typhoon.

Beer geeks don't like the way the brewhouse at Typhoon seems to be an afterthought, grafted onto a Thai restaurant. Thai food lovers, despite the strong beer tradition in Thailand (think of the hoppy Singha and the Singaporean brands Tiger and ABC, both popular in Thailand), apparently couldn't care less about fresh-brewed house beers. On top of that is the famously fickle New York taste for restaurants, which can bury a new restaurant in throngs of people and just as quickly desert a place that is somehow deemed no longer interesting.

Where does that leave Typhoon? On 54th Street, about two-thirds of the way between 5th and Madison Avenues. In short, it's made its bed

Beers brewed: Golden Ale (GABF Gold, 1998; Silver, 1997), Simply Red Ale, Spring Wheat, British Pale Ale, USA IPA. Seasonals: Witbier, Brown Ale.

The Pick: The USA IPA is an easy choice for The Pick. A deep coppery-garnet color, this pint's got punch. It's a solid beer with good hop flavor and aroma, teasing ale-fruit esters, and a bitterness that sets off the spicier Thai dishes. Reach for this one.

and now must lie in it. I find it a particularly interesting situation, because Typhoon is so much more restaurant than brewpub. Restaurant people outside the brewpub part of the industry have been telling us that to be successful, a brewpub must be a restaurant first and a brewery second. I doubt that, myself. Heartland has put their beer just slightly ahead of the restaurant and is doing very well.

Pronouncements about the balance of restaurant and brewery in a brewpub all have a flaw: They're drawing on a database that's barely ten years. I have seen plenty of "beer first" places do just fine, thank you. If the restaurant's good and the beer's good, you've got a shot, but there are a host of other factors.

Till all that gets argued out and the years deliver their verdict, you can make your own decisions about the shotgun wedding on 54th Street. If you like Thai food, go on upstairs and enjoy. If you're a real beer lover, sit at the bar and order up a glass of IPA and some of that squid. Just don't turn around.

Opened: March 1996.
Type: Brewpub.
Owner: Walter Steinmann.
Brewer: Jack Burkett.
System: 15-barrel Liquid Assets, 2,000 barrels annual capacity.
Production: 450 barrels in 2001.
Brewpub hours: Monday through Saturday, noon to closing; closed Sunday. On Saturday, kitchen is open for dinner only.
Tours: By appointment.
Take-out beer: Not available.
Food: The bar menu is good, with all the dishes mentioned in the narrative and then some, many available as a fixed-price lunch special: entree, salad, and a pint of beer for $11, a good deal in Midtown. Upstairs, you can drop serious money on serious Thai food.
Special considerations: Cigars allowed in the bar. Parents, take note: Typhoon is not really set up for kids, by atmosphere or menu. Stash them somewhere safe and do this one by yourself; you deserve it. Vegetarian foods not available. Handicapped-accessible.
Parking: None.

A word about . . .

Brewing Beer

You don't need to know much about beer to enjoy it. After all, I don't understand how the electronic fuel injection on my car works, but I know that when I stomp on the accelerator, the car's gonna go!

Knowing about the brewing process can help you understand how and why beer tastes the way it does. It's like seeing the ingredients used in cooking a dish and realizing where the flavors came from. Once you understand the recipe for beer, other things become more clear.

Beer is made from four basic ingredients: water, hops, yeast, and grain, generally barley malt. Other ingredients may be added, such as sugars, spices, fruits, and vegetables, but they are extras. In fact, the oft-quoted Bavarian Reinheitsgebot (purity law), first promulgated in 1516, limited brewers to using only water, hops, and barley malt; yeast had not yet been discovered.

In the beginning, the malt is cracked in a mill to make a grist. The grist is mixed with water and heated (or "mashed") to convert the starches in the grain to sugars (see *decoction* and *infusion* in the Glossary). Then the hot, sugary water—now called wort—is strained out of the mash. It is boiled in the brewkettle, where hops are added to balance the sweetness with their characteristic bitterness and sprightly aroma. The wort is strained, cooled, and pumped to a fermenter, where yeast is added.

A lager beer ferments slow and cool, whereas an ale ferments warmer and faster. After fermentation, the beer will either be force-carbonated or naturally carbonated and aged. When it is properly mature for its style, the beer is bottled, canned, kegged, or, in a brew-pub, sent to a large serving tank. And then we drink it. Happy ending!

Naturally, it isn't quite that simple. The process varies somewhat from brewery to brewery. That's what makes beers unique. There are also major differences in the ways micro and mainstream brewers brew beer. One well-known distinction has to do with the use of nonbarley grains, specifically corn and rice, in the brewing process. Some micro-brewers have made a big deal of their Reinheitsgebot, proudly displaying slogans like "Barley, hops, water, and yeast—and that's all!" Mainstream brewers like Anheuser-Busch and High Falls all add significant portions of corn or rice or both. Beer geeks howl about how these adjuncts make the beer inferior. Of course, the same geeks often rave about Belgian ales, which have a regular farrago of ingredients forbidden by the Reinheitsgebot.

Mainstream brewers boast about the quality of the corn grits and brewer's rice they use, while microbrewers chide them for using "cheap" adjunct grains and "inferior" six-row barley. Truth is, they're both right . . . and they're both wrong.

Barley, like beer, comes in two main types: two-row and six-row. The names refer to the rows of kernels on the heads of the grain. Six-row grain gives a greater yield per acre but has more husks on smaller kernels, which can give beer an unpleasant astringency. Two-row gives a plumper kernel with less husk but costs significantly more. Each has its place and adherents.

When brewing began in America, farmers and brewers discovered that six-row barley did much better than two-row in our climate and soil types. Two-row barley grown the same way as it had been in Europe produced a distinctly different malt. This became especially troublesome when the craze for pale lagers swept America in the mid-nineteenth century. The hearty ales they replaced had broad flavors from hops and yeast that easily compensated for these differences. But pale lagers are showcases for malt character, and small differences in the malt mean big differences in beer taste.

Brewers adapted and used what they had. They soon found that a small addition of corn or brewer's rice to the mash lightened the beer, smoothed out the husky astringency of the six-row malt, and gave the beer a crispness similar to that of the European pale lagers. Even though using these grains required the purchase, operation, and maintenance of additional equipment (cookers, storage silos, and conveyors), almost every American brewer did it. Some say they overdid it, as the percentages of adjuncts in the beer rose over the years. Is a beer that is 30 percent corn still a pilsner?

Microbrewers say adjunct grains are cheap substitutes for barley malt. In terms of yield, corn and brewer's rice are less expensive than two-row barley, but they are still high-quality grains. Similarly, six-row barley is not inherently inferior to two-row; it is just not as well suited to the brewing of some styles of beer. Mainstream brewers have adapted their brewing processes to six-row barley. The difference is in the beer those processes produce.

Another difference between micro and mainstream brewers is the practice of high-gravity brewing. The alcohol content of a beer is mainly dependent on the ratio of fermentable sugars to water in the wort, which determines the specific gravity of the wort. A higher gravity means more alcohol.

Large commercial brewers, in their constant search for ways to peel pennies off the costs of brewing, discovered that they could save money by brewing beer at a higher alcohol content and carefully diluting it later. To do this, a brewer adds a calculated extra amount of malt, rice, corn—whatever "fuel" is used—to boost the beer to 6.5 percent alcohol by volume (ABV) or higher. When the fermented beer has been filtered, water is added to bring the ABV down to the target level of 4 to 5 percent. You may remember an ad campaign in the early 1990s in which Anheuser-Busch accused Coors of shipping "beer concentrate" across the country in tank cars for packaging at its Virginia facility. The so-called "beer concentrate" was this high-alcohol beer prior to dilution.

How does this method save money? It saves energy and labor costs during the brewing process by effectively squeezing 1,300 barrels of beer into a 1,000-barrel brewkettle. While 1,000 barrels are boiled, 1,300 barrels are eventually bottled. It also saves money by allowing more efficient use of fermentation tank space: 10,000-barrel fermenters produce 13,000 barrels of beer. It sounds great, so why not do that with every beer? Because the high-gravity process can produce some odd flavor and aroma notes during fermentation. That's what brewers aim for in big beers like doppelbocks and barley wines. But these characteristics are out of place in a pilsner. I also feel that beer brewed by this high-gravity method suffers from a dulling phenomenon similar to "clipping" in audio reproduction: The highs and lows are clipped off, leaving only the middle.

With a studied nonchalance, big brewers keep this part of their brewing process away from the public eye. To tell the truth, of all beer styles, American mainstream lager is probably the style least affected by this process. It is mostly a practice that just seems vaguely wrong, and you won't see any microbrewers doing it.

So now you know how beer is made and a few of the differences in how the big boys and the little guys do it. It's probably time for you to do a little field research. Have fun!

FDR Territory
The Hudson Valley

First, let's get one thing straight: The Hudson is not a river. At least, it isn't till you get to Troy. Check the elevations and you'll find that Troy Pub & Brewery is only a few feet above sea level. The Hudson is tidal up to the dam north of Troy; it's an estuary. Given the steep banks along most of its length through this area—the Palisades, the Hudson Highlands, Storm King Mountain—you could even call it a fjord.

This may seem to be a trivial point, but it had a great effect on the history of the Hudson River Valley. Navigation was a snap with no current and no waterfalls, leaving Henry Hudson an easy road to explore, even though it wasn't the Northwest Passage he'd been hired to find. That ease of navigation was what made the Hudson an important battleground in the Revolutionary War. The Americans stretched barriers across the Hudson to deny the British easy access to the interior. This was where Benedict Arnold, embittered by frustrated ambition, made his traitorous plot to deliver West Point to the British. At war's end, Washington declared victory from his headquarters in Newburgh (Washington's Headquarters State Historical Site, 84 Liberty Street, 914-562-1195).

As the area was settled, sailboats regularly plied the wide waters all the way to Albany. Towns grew up all along the Hudson, leading to rich trade up- and downriver with fruit, produce, furs, and meat. In later years, the wealth would come from the factories that lined the Hudson and dumped their waste into the estuary, creating problems for generations not yet born. Starting in the 1970s, a cleanup of the Hudson began, first with an end to dumping, and culminating in the massive PCB dredging project now going on.

This is the land where my wife and her brothers grew up, and they've shown me a lot of it. We've boated in the summer and picnicked on the sandy shores of Little Stony Point (where I dozed on a sandbar and learned firsthand about how tidal the Hudson is). We've rambled in the fall, visiting the apple orchards and cider presses along the shores. We've hiked the woods in the winter and shared a bottle of strong beer in a snowfall. And one memorable spring, I flew a light plane over the Hudson and saw the whole Newburgh-Beacon area spread out below me, the dark mystery of the Catskills in the distance.

To me, the Hudson's bucolic charms have been foremost. I love the glorious foliage in fall, when the leaves on the slopes seem to hold the light at sunset and the whole valley glows. The greening of the slopes in spring is a foretaste of the lush cover of summer. There are several gorgeous drives along the Hudson, but one has become a favorite of mine.

Seven Lakes Drive runs northeast from Sloatsburg, not far from Suffern and Ramapo Valley Brewery, through Harriman State Park (845-786-2701) and into Bear Mountain State Park (same number), linking seven of the lakes and giving access to the swimming beaches. Harriman is more wild than Bear Mountain, which can get absolutely jammed with people on summer weekends. If you come during the week, a drive up Perkins Memorial Drive to the summit of Bear Mountain offers breathtaking views of the Hudson and the forested slopes of the Ramapo Mountains. When you come down, drive across the Bear Mountain Bridge, a beautifully compact silver-painted suspension bridge, one of the prettiest bridges I know of for construction and setting.

There are charms of civilization on the Hudson as well. Some would find it ironic that I would apply that to the U.S. Military Academy at West Point, but I know John Eccles at Hyde Park Brewing would agree. West Point is a fascinating look at America's oldest military academy. There is a visitors center at the Thayer Gate, off Route 218 (845-938-2638), and the West Point Museum houses a deep variety of the paraphernalia of war. You can get a guided tour of the academy, beginning at the visitors center, or you can tour on your own.

On up north, over on the east shore about a mile north of Garrison, is the Boscobel Restoration (845-265-3638), a restored mansion from the early 1800s. The house is filled with period furniture, china, silverware, and fancy wallpaper, but the gardens, when at their peak, outshine the man-made gauds inside.

Drive on up past Poughkeepsie, and you'll see Hyde Park Brewing. Tear your eyes away and look on the other side of Route 9, and you'll see Franklin Delano Roosevelt's home, Springwood. You can tour the home and see how the great man lived. The Roosevelt Library and Museum (511 Albany Post Road, 800-FDR-VISIT) is next door, with exhibits on FDR and Eleanor's lives together and apart. Eleanor built herself a house to escape the constant political bustle at Springwood: Val-Kill. Simple in comparison to Springwood, Val-Kill (on an unpaved access road off Route 9G, 845-229-9115) is a more intimate look at the life of Eleanor Roosevelt and her own important political activities.

The Old Rhinebeck Aerodrome (42 Stone Church Road, 845-758-8610) stages World War I–era dogfights and aerial demonstrations—in World War I–era aircraft. Excited airplane enthusiasts watch the dragonfly-weight aircraft turn and loop, thrill to the clattering roar of rotary engines, and breathe deep the burnt castor oil lubricant—okay maybe they don't breathe *that* deep, but it's all part of the show, folks! This is a rare opportunity to see these historic aircraft fly. Airshows are on Saturdays, June through October; the museum is open daily during that period.

That's a start on the attractions in the Hudson Valley. Come on up and enjoy the fjord. You'll find natural and man-made beauty to thrill you, some of the most impressive scenery in the state.

Ramapo Valley Brewery

122 Orange Avenue, Suffern, NY 10901
845-369-7827
www.ramapovalleybrewery.com

Ramapo Valley Brewery is in Suffern, just barely inside New York. If you walk across the street to the Suffern train station and look left as you do, you can see New Jersey down the road. You've seen it? Okay, now just walk back across the street and into the brewpub. Your beer's getting warm, and someone took your pool table.

Ramapo Valley is a joint, a rocking good time. It's also got a history that goes back to the roots of microbrewing in this area. Ramapo Valley was Mountain Valley Brewing; same building, same brewer. Mountain Valley was a link in a chain of brewers and apprentices that went back to Jay Misson, at the brewery in the water park in Vernon

Beers brewed: All beers brewed on the premises. Year-round: Horny Blonde Lager, Stud Copper, Trailquencher IPA, Suffern Station Porter. Seasonals: Habañero Pilsner, Skullcrusher Scotch Ale, Blarney Stout, Walking Home Wit.

Valley, a brewery that Michael Jackson praised as "outstandingly traditional" and "a great contribution to American brewing." It was also, as John Eccles at Hyde Park Brewing (who also trained under Misson) says, "a brewery ahead of its time." A water park wasn't the right place to educate people about unfiltered lagers, and the Vernon Valley Brewery petered out.

Mountain Valley picked up the torch and made it work well for a while, putting out bottled beers under the Ruffian line, beers that won some well-deserved GABF medals. But they lost sight of the brewpub in the drive to put beer on store shelves. It didn't help that Mountain Valley bartenders had a wide reputation as some of the most surly, beer-ignorant people behind a microbrewed tap. Finally, as Ramapo Valley partner Danny Scott put it, "They just didn't make it."

Danny and his two partners had been to Mountain Valley. "Two of us were regular patrons," he said. After some consideration, they decided they could make a go of it there. Danny had no experience in the field of brewing or restaurant management. "I was a glazier by trade," he said with a chuckle in his voice. Why a brewpub? "We figured we wanted to do something different." But buying a brewpub that had already failed? "No, that didn't worry us in the slightest."

And that's the way they run the place. Don't worry. Come in, have a good time, drink some beer, shoot some stick, listen to some music. (Try not to notice the cavelike decor, a leftover from the Mountain Valley days.) It helped a lot that they managed to get former Mountain Valley brewer Neill Acer back. I asked Danny what it took to get Neill to come back. "We just asked him!" Danny said, laughing. "We were happy with his beermaking at the old place."

I'm pretty happy with his beermaking at the new place. He's a funny guy, too. When we were sampling the Stud Copper Ale, a malty, biscuity ale with similarities to Fuller's ales, he started saying, "You taste toffee, and pears, and—those are dogwhistle flavors." Eh? "You can't taste them unless you're a brewer," he explained with a grin, "or unless the brewer tells you they're in there. Once I tell them, they taste them, and go, yeah, yeah, I taste them!"

The Pick: Neill really cut loose on the Trailquencher IPA. It's brewed with a big load of floor-malted Maris Otter barley for a base, then hopped with Magnum, Fuggles, Cascades, Challenger, and East Kent Goldings. Though the beer is bitter (more on that shortly), it attains a beautiful blend of hop and malt character. But "balanced" it's not: It's bitter right up front, hoppy and bitter in the mouth, and there's a long bitter finish of hops. That's IPA, buddy. And for those of you who miss Mountain Valley, stop. The Suffern Station Porter is the same porter that's been made in this building since 1994, when it won GABF Gold. It's smooth and a little sweet, with a hint of bitterness—a great mouthful of beer.

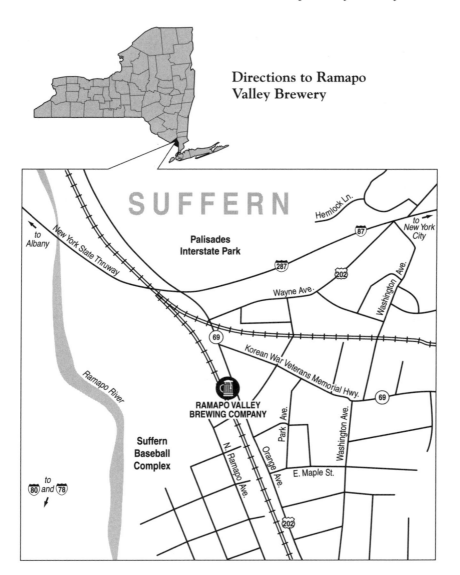

Directions to Ramapo Valley Brewery

He also told me about a habañero pilsner he made once, spiced with the little yellow-orange death peppers. "It didn't smell spicy," he recalled. "It didn't even taste spicy, but when you swallowed, the back of your throat came off. And it made people drool. It didn't sell too well, but there was a dental hygienist, a regular, who really liked it." Must have been the drool.

Ramapo Valley has an extensive schedule of live music, a great pub grub menu ("It's a basic pub menu," Danny said, "but it's good food, and you're not going to spend too much"), and lots of things to do, *bar* things. There's a pool hall with four big tables, a rank of video games, and dartboards. There's a dance floor—in a brewpub! Best of all, the bartenders at the big copper-covered bar now have a clue about beer, and they're friendly.

"It's simple," Danny said. "You supply good beer, good food, and good entertainment." Sounds like a formula for success to me.

Opened: June 2001.
Type: Brewpub.
Owners: Private partnership.
Brewer: Neill Acer.
System: 14-barrel Pub Brewing System brewhouse, 1,400 barrels annual capacity.
Production: 1,000 barrels in 2001.
Brewpub hours: Seven days a week, noon to 4 A.M.
Tours: At brewer's convenience.
Take-out beer: Half-gallon growlers, and you get a free glass of beer when you get a growler refill; nice deal.
Food: This is an unabashedly pub grub menu, with 15¢ wings, curly fries with cheese and chili, hot dogs, burgers, and fish and chips, but they've also got ribs (which are delicious) and steaks, and two veggie sandwiches. There's also a complimentary happy hour buffet, Monday through Friday, 3 P.M. to 7 P.M.
Extras: There's lots of music at Ramapo Valley, and there's room to dance. Tuesday is an open music jam, and there's live entertainment Thursday, Friday, and Saturday (call or check the website for schedules). There are TVs hanging all over the bar for sports fans. A pool room has been added, with four pool tables and video games to play while you're waiting for a table, and there's a darts room for tossers.
Special considerations: Cigars allowed. Kids welcome. Vegetarian foods available. Handicapped-accessible (Ramapo Valley is all about smooth ramps).
Parking: Off-street lot.
Lodging in the area: Holiday Inn Suffern, 3 Executive Boulevard, 914-357-4800; Wellesley Inn, 17 North Airmont Road, 914-368-1900; The Castle at Tarrytown, 400 Benedict Avenue, 914-631-1980.
Area attractions: Nearby Tarrytown is the setting for Washington Irving's *Legend of Sleepy Hollow*, and the **Washington Irving Memorial** stands at the corner of Sunnyside Lane and Broadway, by Irving's home, **Sunnyside** (914-631-8200). The home is restored, complete

with the indoor plumbing that was advanced for its day, and can be toured with the help of guides in period dress. Irving is buried in the *Sleepy Hollow Cemetery* (along Route 9 in Sleepy Hollow, 914-631-0081), as is Andrew Carnegie.

Other area beer sites: There's Guinness aplenty at **Ireland's 32** (ironically at 6 Orange Street, Suffern, 914-357-9863), a no-nonsense Irish-owned bar with good pub food.

Brotherhood Winery

100 Brotherhood Plaza Drive, Washingtonville, NY 10992
845-496-3661
www.brotherhoodnywines.com

Yes, you're still in the right book. Brotherhood Winery is the business, and it's a real winery: America's oldest winery—in fact, established in 1839. But now they've got Nat Collins brewing for them, and I just hope for pride's sake that their wine is up to the challenge, or they're going to wind up changing their name to Brotherhood Brewery.

Those of you who've been following the New York brewery scene for as long as I have will recognize Nat's name and know just what I mean. Nat Collins was the man behind Woodstock Brewing, of Kingston. My first experience with Nat's beers was at River Station in Poughkeepsie, where I enjoyed a smooth, fresh glass of Hudson Lager in 1990. Nice beer, but it left me totally unprepared for my next Woodstock beer, the Big Indian Porter.

Woodstock Big Indian Porter was only a porter because Nat decided to call it that. It was big, almost as big as the mutant Baltic porters, and wonderfully rich without being heavy. Then came Ichabod Crane Pumpkin Lager, a richly spiced whopper made with gobs of sugar pumpkin, and Braveheart Scottish Ale, a malty sledgehammer. "I believe there's a definite niche for strong beers," Nat understated to me once, familiar grin on his face, as he poured Bravehearts for an appreciative crowd at a beer festival.

Beers brewed: All beers brewed on the premises. Year-round: Pilsner, Lager, Porter, Scotch Ale. Seasonal: Holiday Ale. Woodstock Brewing (same brewer, same equipment); winner, *Matthew Vassar Cup, 2000.*

Nat's beers were great, and I couldn't get enough of them. But I ran into problems with the bottles, some sour, some really awful. I stopped drinking the beer except on draft, and then I couldn't even find that. When I caught up with Nat at Brotherhood, I asked him what had happened.

"I brought in a partner in 1998," he told me. "I left the brewery in his hands in May of 2000. He sold it to Black Bear Brewing, and they ran it into the ground. They left things hanging, left a lot of people in the lurch." Bad news, and I mourned the loss of the beer.

But Nat's back, and working on the new brewery at Brotherhood. Well, the old brewery, actually. Nat's got the old brewhouse from Woodstock, his baby, and that's what is going in at Brotherhood. I'll admit it: As I write this, the brewery's not open, and Nat hasn't brewed a drop of beer there yet. Relax. Nat's unleashed, he's eager, and believe me, people—he's good.

He's also excited. "We already have a full lab here at the winery," he said, "with a full-time, in-house microbiologist. And we'll be aging beer in the wine cellars. I've got access to those big French oak barrels! I'll be able to do a bunch of great things, because the infrastructure's all in place already: sales, lab support, distribution, even tour guides. I'll be able to do so many things now."

Brotherhood is putting in a combined wine-brewpub, and Nat will be brewing a pilsner and a more mainstreamish lager for that. But for the more adventurous, and for off-premises sales, "we'll stick to the specialty beers," Nat promised, "a porter, Scotch ale, and some kind of holiday beer." That sounds wonderfully familiar to this old Woodstock fan. Nat Collins, unleashed. Man, that gives me beer goosebumps.

The Pick: Hey, I haven't tasted any of these beers. They hadn't been brewed when I wrote this. But I know Nat, and I know this system, and I *know* that my Pick is going to be the porter. Woodstock's Big Indian Porter was one of my favorite beers anywhere—big, rich, a little winey, even—and I doubt that Mr. Nat "there's a definite niche for strong beers" Collins is going to back off from it at all. Try it and see if I'm not right.

Opened: Winery established 1839 (America's oldest), brewery scheduled for September 2002.

Type: Brewpub and brewery.

Owners: Cesare Baeze, managing partner, and two other partners.

Brewer: Nat Collins.

System: 20-barrel DME brewhouse, 10,000 barrels annual capacity.

Production: None in 2001.

Tours: Seven days a week, 11 A.M. to 5 P.M., except Christmas and New Year's Day. Tours are available of the winery, brewery, and cellars.

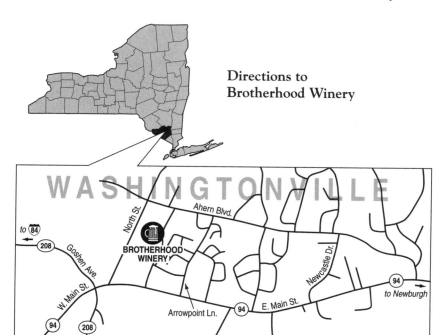

Directions to
Brotherhood Winery

Take-out beer: 12-ounce bottles, occasional releases of 750-milliter bottles, half and quarter kegs. The Brotherhood wines are also for sale.

Food: The pub building was still being renovated from a fire when I visited (as was much of the winery, though operations never stopped). Plans are for a bistro type of menu, with a big outdoor barbecue pit behind the pub.

Extras: Live music every weekend in the summer, and some weekends in the winter. Two-hundred-seat catering center on premises (the winery hosts a number of weddings through the year).

Special considerations: Cigars not allowed. Kids welcome. Vegetarian foods will be available. The cellars are not handicapped-accessible.

Parking: On-site lot.

Lodging in the area: Holiday Inn West Point, 90 Route 17K, Newburgh, 914-564-9020; Comfort Inn, 5 Lakeside Road, 914-567-0567; Windsor Motel, 2976 Route 9W, New Windsor, 914-562-7777.

Area attractions: George Washington's last headquarters in the Revolutionary War, the building from which he declared victory, has been restored as the ***Washington's Headquarters State Historical Site*** (Liberty and Washington Streets, 845-562-1195). The site includes the house, a museum on the Continental Army, and the Tower of Victory monument. A more interactive experience is available at the **New Windsor Cantonment State Historical Site** (Temple Hill Road, one mile south of I-84, 845-561-1765) where the Continental Army made its last winter encampment. There are demonstrations of military drill and military-related crafts such as blacksmithing.

Other area beer sites: *The Raccoon Saloon,* in Marlboro (1330 Main Street, 914-236-7872), is one of the first bars I ever wrote about as a pro. It's a fun place, with a little raccoon door by the bar, delicious burgers, and a great selection of bottled beer. See also the beer sites on page 87 and page 90.

Gentleman Jim's

522 Dutchess Turnpike, Poughkeepsie, NY 12603
845-485-5467

"I had been interested in putting in a brewpub for a number of years," Jim Fahey told me as we sat in the little greenhouse room at his Gentleman Jim's restaurant. Fahey is an older man, soft-spoken and genial, and what he doesn't know about running a restaurant in Dutchess County isn't worth knowing. He's owned Gentleman Jim's for almost thirty years. The name's a reference to the father of modern boxing, "Gentleman" Jim Corbett; the restaurant was previously known as John L's, after the hard-hitting bare-knuckle fighter John L. Sullivan.

"But the equipment was too expensive," Jim continued, "and too large for what I wanted and the space I had. Then I heard about this three-barrel brewing equipment that DME made. I took a look at it, and went ahead with it. I had figured that as the only brewpub in the area, it would give me an edge." He paused, then gave a wry smile and shook his head. "We ran into some slowdowns with the state, with the paperwork, and by the time we got cleared and started brewing, Hyde Park Brewing opened one day later."

Beers brewed: All beers brewed on the premises. Year-round: Sweet Sheila's Wheat, Galway Gold, Renegade Red, Poughkeepsie Porter, Butternut Brown, Blarneystone Bitter, Without a Doubt Stout. Seasonals: Aran Islands Irish Ale, Bridal Ale, Belgian Strong Golden, Scotch Ale, Pilsner, Old Ale.

He paused, as if to once again go over in his mind something he'd weighed many times. "I have no regrets," he said, finally, "but I'm not sure I'd do it again. Retrofitting it into the bar was not the best way to do it. We hadn't developed around beer. It's a wash on costs compared to regular beers, but it's a unique product, and the beer John makes is excellent."

He's talking about his brewer, John Calen. John's very happy doing the brewing at Gentleman Jim's. He's in his first professional brewing job. He was a serious homebrewer—a past president of the Hudson Valley Homebrewers and a certified home-brew judge with a national ranking. He was also an IBM employee, and like many of his colleagues in the Hudson Valley, he got laid off.

The Pick: John's Poughkeep-sie Porter is based on an 1850s recipe he researched. It has a very crafty way of delivering gobs of flavor on a light-bodied frame with some nice chocolate notes, gulpable as a classic porter should be. I was also very impressed by a one-shot Bridal Ale John brewed for his wedding: an ale brewed with honey and brown sugar. He ought to stretch like this more often; this beer was real good and very different.

IBM had a generous severance package, which included a retrain-ing allowance. John took his retraining money to the University of Sunderland in England and used it to take their Brewlab course. He came home, and his current, part-time job with Fahey at Gentleman Jim's became part of his livelihood. He's living a dream.

"We do mostly ales," John said, "in British and American styles. It's a small system, but it's full mash, and I use all malt, except for a few interesting adjuncts. Given free rein, I tend toward the eclectic."

Eclectic? I didn't think John knew what the word meant while I was sipping my way through an enjoyable lineup of bitter, brown, porter, stout, Irish red . . . but then I got to the Bridal Ale he brewed for his recent wed-ding. This was brewed with honey and brown sugar and came out with a ton of estery fruitiness. "I think I got some wild yeast from the honey," John commented. Better tame that one; it's a keeper. Eclectic indeed.

Is Gentleman Jim's a "real" brewpub? Frankly, this is what the restaurant consultants condescendingly speak of when they imagine a brewpub: a restaurant with a brewery attached. The brewery at Gentle-man Jim's was an afterthought. Before I visited every brewery in New York, I thought such a thing was bound to deliver second-rate beer and be a black eye for brewpubs. Then I had the beer here, and at Bootleg-gers, and at Eddie's . . . and realized I was wrong. Good beer is where you find it, and you can definitely find it at Gentleman Jim's.

And yes, the food's pretty good, too. Jim Fahey wouldn't have it any other way.

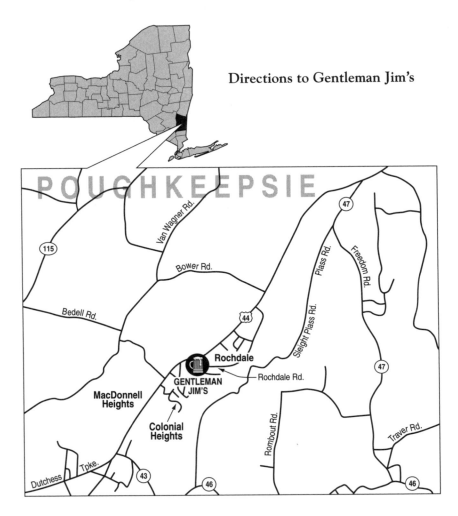

Directions to Gentleman Jim's

Opened: Restaurant opened in 1973, brewery opened April 1996.
Type: Brewpub.
Owner: Jim Fahey.
Brewer: John Calen.
System: 3-barrel DME brewhouse, 300 barrels annual capacity.
Production: 150 barrels in 2001.
Brewpub hours: Tuesday through Saturday, the bar opens at 4 P.M., the dining room at 5 P.M.; Sunday, the bar opens at 1 P.M., the dining room at 2 P.M. The kitchen closes at 9 P.M. Tuesday through Thursday and Sunday, and at 10 P.M. Friday and Saturday. Closed Monday.
Tours: By appointment or at brewer's convenience.

Take-out beer: Not available.

Food: Jim Fahey has been in the restaurant business in New York a long time, and it shows. The menu centers on classics: steaks (Jim really delivers great steaks and has no qualms about cooking them as rare as you want them), seafood, pasta, and ribs that brewer John Calen pronounced "awesome" as he drooled all over the table. Appetizers are similarly classic and just as well prepared: wings, beer-battered onion rings (these are more than classic, they're divine), and small orders of the ribs.

Special considerations: Cigars not allowed. No children's menu. Vegetarian foods available, plus a large and exceptional salad bar, Handicapped-accessible.

Parking: Large on-site lot.

Lodging in the area, area attractions, and other area beer sites: See pages 86–87.

Hyde Park Brewing Company

4076 Albany Post Road, Hyde Park, NY 12538
845-229-TAPS (8277)
www.hydeparkbrewing.com

"I feel like I'm off, every day." John Eccles told me that while we were sitting out on the patio at Hyde Park Brewing, watching the preparations for Memorial Day across Route 9 at the FDR Home. He was trying to explain to me just how much he loved brewing. I'd gotten his point about five minutes before, to be honest, but I know better than to interrupt a man when he's signifying, and he was doing it so well.

John gets a little Zen sometimes; he lives in the moment, and right then he was savoring the rightness of a universe that put him in a brewery where the owners, he said, "are two really bright guys, restaurant guys, who know how to lead, and how to let others lead." He took a long drink of ice water and sighed expansively. "I wouldn't leave here for twice the money somewhere else."

Lots of brewers would think of future negotiating points and not say such a thing. But it's true, so Eccles says it. He came out with another one when we were talking about his love for lager brewing, and why he moved Hyde Park's beers to the cold side of the beer family: "Ales!" He snorted. "I could train a chimp to make ales. You have to know what you're doing to make lagers."

John learned lagers from one of the first lager microbrewers in America, Jay Misson, who brewed at Mountain Valley (now Ramapo Valley), and at Vernon Valley before that. Vernon Valley was a pioneering micro at Action Park, a big water park in northern New Jersey. "Jay was using all wooden fermenters, a cascade wort chiller, all the traditional Czech lager brewing equipment," John said with reverence. "It was a hazy, lightly filtered beer, way ahead of its time." I was lucky enough to get some beer at Vernon Valley, and even though it was served a whisper above freezing in a plastic cup, he was right: That was great beer.

What kind of beer does John like to make? "Good beer," he replies quickly and seriously. "And what's a good beer? A beer that sells. You have to remember, 99 percent of your customers are not aficionados or homebrewers. I'm market-driven when it comes to deciding what to brew. I always keep in mind that beer is just one pillar of the business."

Hyde Park is popular because everyone understands that. Everything works together to keep the customers happy. It's a real "can-do" staff. The menu is designed to appeal to a broad audience without being a boring reiteration of sports-bar grease-fodder. The space is a little odd, with the long, narrow bar (check out the Howard Johnson's logo on the floor; this was one of the original HoJo's) and the high-ceilinged dining room (with a big *Quiet Man* poster), but it's been made friendly.

That wasn't easy. "We got hit with an $80,000 septic surprise just before opening," John said, recalling an unforeseen plumbing expense. "We got it taken care of, but it ate our decoration budget. We looked like a high school cafeteria when we opened, but we had great food, great beer, and a great staff. It didn't matter what we looked like. We're entrenched now."

Beers brewed: All beers brewed on the premises. Year-round: Winkle Lager (TAP NY Bronze, 2002), Big Easy Blonde, Rough Rider Red Ale, S.O.B. ("Special Old Bitter," GABF Silver, 2000), Mary P's Porter, Chaos Dry Stout. Seasonals: "Barrel 9 Brewer's Choice," which is John's way of saying he made something just for fun. Seasonals vary widely at Hyde Park; just ask the bartender. Oktoberfest, Dark Bock, Maibock, and Hefeweizen are the four main ones.

The Pick: I like John's insistence on brewing lagers, but I'm afraid I like his S.O.B. best. With a rich copper color and beautifully entwined aroma of malt and hops, this beer holds great flavor under a tenacious cap of creamy foam. There's good hop flavor as well as bitterness here, and the malt's big enough to stand up to it. Great beer, John, and I'll bet no chimp could brew this!

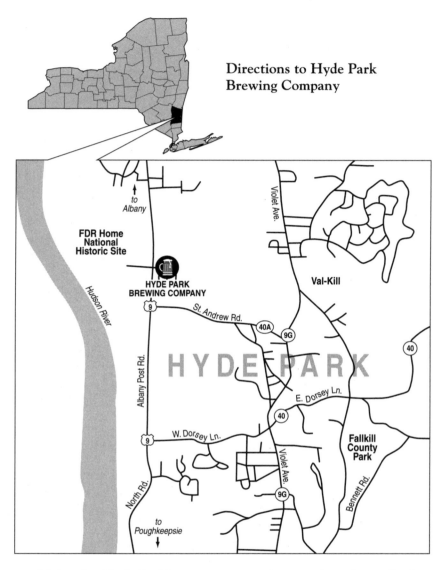

Directions to Hyde Park Brewing Company

He's right. Hyde Park's not going anywhere, and neither is Eccles. He's bought a house here, and he's settling down. That's good news for those of us who enjoy a well-made lager.

Opened: April 1996.
Type: Brewpub.
Owners: Mel Diciccio, Joseph LoBianco.
Brewer: John Eccles.
System: 7-barrel Pub Brewing System, 1,200 barrels annual capacity.

Production: 760 barrels in 2001.

Brewpub hours: Monday through Saturday, 11 A.M. to 2 A.M.; Sunday, noon to midnight.

Tours: On request; groups can make appointments.

Take-out beer: Half-gallon and 2-liter growlers.

Food: Hyde Park is right down the road from the Culinary Institute of America, and you can see the influence of CIA-trained chefs on preparation and presentation. It is a fairly standard-looking brew-pub menu, but the secret is in the preparation: This is great food, not stamped-out nutrition. Be sure to save room for dessert, something I don't usually bother with in brewpubs.

Extras: Full schedule of live music. Tuesday nights are an open jazz jam: Bring your . . . whatever and sit in with the Joe Carozzo Trio. Wednesday is blues night, with the Upstart Blues Allstars. There's a band every Friday and Saturday night, playing blues, jazz, folk, bluegrass, or whatever (call for schedule). Dartboard, video games.

Special considerations: Cigars allowed on terrace; in the bar after dinner is over. Kids welcome. Vegetarian foods available. Handicapped-accessible.

Parking: Large on-site lot.

Lodging in the area: The Golden Manor is right next door, and it's where John Eccles stays after a late night brewing (522 Albany Post Road, 845-229-2157); Beekman Arms (billed as America's oldest inn), 6387 Mill Street, Rhinebeck, 845-876-7077; Holiday Inn Express, 2750 South Road, Poughkeepsie, 845-473-1151.

Area attractions: In addition to the attractions mentioned in the Hudson Valley intro (see p. 71), there is a fine art museum on the campus of Vassar College, the *Frances Lehman Loeb Art Center* (124 Raymond Avenue, 845-437-5632), with pieces by European masters and American artists as diverse as Georgia O'Keeffe and Jackson Pollock; there is also a strong collection of Hudson Valley landscapes. If you still feel like mansion-hopping after you visit the FDR homes, the *Vanderbilt Mansion National Historic Site* (2 miles north of FDR site on Route 9, 845-229-9115) is as much a monument to excess as the Roosevelt estates are to restraint—even though this was the smallest of Vanderbilt's estates. Note: You can get a combination ticket to tour all three homes. You can also visit the CIA; the *Culinary Institute of America* (433 Albany Post Road, 845-452-9600) gives tours on Mondays, by reservation only. The four restaurants on campus are also open to the public but are reserved far in advance; plan accordingly.

Other area beer sites: *Park Discount Beverage,* about a mile south on Route 9 in Hyde Park, isn't a bar, but it does have an outstanding selection of craft beer and out-of-the ordinary imports (3969 Albany Post Road, 845-229-9000). *River Station* (1 Water Street, Pough-keepsie, 845-452-9207) has been a favorite of mine for years for the food, the beer, and the view of the Hudson from its deck. My kids like the train around the ceiling, even when it's not running. *The Beekman Inn's* 1766 Tavern (6387 Mill Street, Rhinebeck, 845-876-7077) is authentically old and should be experienced, just for bragging rights.

Gilded Otter Brewing Company

Corner of Main and Huguenot Streets, New Paltz, NY 12561
845-256-1700
www.gildedotter.com

Ah, New Paltz, funky little New Paltz, with its winding Main Street, distinctly Bohemian air, and uplifting view of the Shawangunk Mountains. The 'Gunks, as they're called here and in the rock-climbing world, are a major draw for this area—some of the finest rock climbing on the East Coast and one of the places where American climbing lost its technical purity and took on its ragged energy and edginess.

The Gilded Otter is on the 'Gunks-ward side of town, right on the western edge by the Walkill River, and the view out its big plate windows at sunset is like something out of a Frederic Edwin Church landscape. The glass is framed with big logs with a hand-hewn look, and climbing gear hangs from hooks on the logs. You're lucky your waitress doesn't rappel down from the second floor to serve your jambalaya and pale ale.

No, I'm just kidding. I wouldn't want to give you the wrong idea. There aren't any gimmicks here, except for maybe the otters painted on the brewery tanks. This is an honest place, with solid food and good beer, and loyal locals. And the brewer, Darren Currier, fits right in, an honest, open guy without an ounce of guile in him.

He's a local, like the managing partner, Rick Rauch. Darren grew up in nearby Wappingers Falls and studied geology right here in town at SUNY–New Paltz. "I started homebrewing in my first year of college," he told me. After college, it was postgraduate work, but not in geology. Darren took the brewing course at the Siebel Institute and got broken in at Mountain Valley in Suffern (now Ramapo Valley) before hiring on at the Otter in 2000.

I remember the first time I had Darren's beer. It was a hot afternoon in the late summer of 2000, and the kids and I had escaped the punishing heat by driving over to New Paltz to see *Star Wars Episode I*. We got to the theater half an hour early, so I tempted them with promises of root beer and tooled down the hill to the brewpub.

Drinks in hand, the kids looked out at the sun-scorched landscape with dread while I tore into my hefeweizen. Totally refreshing, that beer, and full of all the classic hefe details: clove, banana, plum, a hint of smoke, and sublime quaffability. I decided right then that we would be back for dinner after the movie. It was delicious, too, a grilled meatloaf sandwich with a big glass of Grizzly Brown Porter.

The pub's name, the Gilded Otter, comes from one of the ships that brought New Paltz's original Huguenot settlers to America, fleeing religious persecution in France; the brewpub is located on Huguenot Street, a National Historic Landmark. New Paltz's Huguenot heritage is one more thing that makes this an interesting spot, along with the 'Gunks and the Minnewaska State Park Preserve at their summit, the cool little shops and restaurants in town, and, naturally, the Otter. It's a little oasis of hipness in rural New York.

Beers brewed: All beers brewed on the premises. Year-round: Huguenot Street American Lager, New Paltz Crimson Lager, 3 Pines IPA, Rail Trail Pale Ale. Seasonals: Winter Wassail, Walkill River Wheat, Düsseldorf Altbier (GABF Bronze, 2001), Grizzly Brown Porter, Double Bogie Bitter, Die Pfalz Schwarzbier (TAP NY Silver, 2001), Highland Pilsner, Belgian Spring Wit, Mohonk Muncher, Wallkill River Wheat, Chapter II in the Red Ale, Dortmunder Gold, Sundown Rye, Indian Summer, Hefeweizen, Dunkleweizen, Buck Burch Summer Lager, Kristall Weizen, Bavarian Dopplebock, Nut Brown Ale, Awosting Amber, Apple Brown Ale, Otter Trotter Red Ale, Clove Pumpkin Ale, Octoberfest Ale, Stone House Imperial Stout (GABF Gold, 2000). *Winner, 2001 Matthew Vassar Cup.*

Opened: November 1998.
Type: Brewpub.
Owners: Catskill Mountain Brewing Co., Inc., a private corporation. Rick Rauch is the general manager.
Brewer: Darren Currier.
System: 7-barrel Pub Brewing Systems brewhouse, 1,500 barrels annual capacity.
Production: 860 barrels in 2001.

Brewpub hours: Monday through Thursday, 4 P.M. to 1 A.M.; Friday and Saturday, 11:30 A.M. to 2:00 A.M.; Sunday, noon to midnight.

Tours: On request, during regular business hours.

Take-out beer: Growlers; kegs by special order.

Food: Pretty pub-grubby—pizza, good soups, salads, and sandwiches—but there are also some pasta and jambalaya dishes, and some interesting appetizers, like the escarole with sausage and white beans, and Prince Edward Island mussels steamed in lemon juice.

Extras: There is a small game room upstairs with a pool table and video games. The Gilded Otter does have live music; call for schedules.

Special considerations: Cigars allowed. Kids welcome (kids eat free on Wednesdays). Vegetarian foods available. Handicapped-accessible.

Parking: Large on-site lot.

The Pick: I like confounding the beer geeks, and the 3 Pines IPA might just do that. Chock full of British hops but still plenty bitter, this is the kind of IPA that doesn't taste "right" to American geeks, brought up on the piney grapefruit tang of Cascade hops. But it's real, and it's bitter, and it's different, and it's my pick: a hops education in a glass. If the Stone House is on tap, though . . . don't miss it. It's a stone killer.

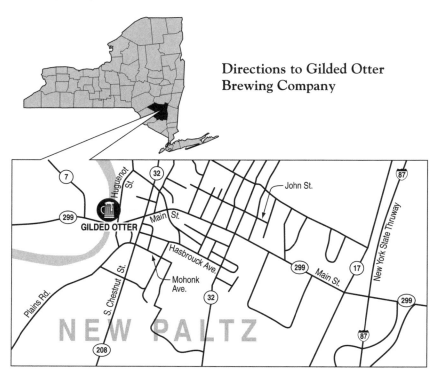

Directions to Gilded Otter Brewing Company

Lodging in the area: Minnewaska Lodge, intersection of Routes 299 and 44/55, Gardiner, 845-255-1110; Super 8, 7 Terwilliger Lane (right off the thruway exit), 845-255-8865; Swiss Country Inn, Route 44/55, Gardiner (just around the corner from the Mountain Brauhaus and has its own good German-Swiss restaurant), 845-255-9772.

Area attractions: It is claimed that New Paltz's **Huguenot Street,** where the brewpub is located, is the oldest continuously inhabited street in America. It is a National Historic Landmark and features several original homes that are open to tours. Call the Huguenot Historical Society at 845-255-1660, or visit the excellent website at www.hvnet.com-museums-huguenotst-index.htm for more information and tour instructions. Shopping is an intercultural experience in New Paltz. There's a strong independent streak to the town, seemingly inherited from the Huguenots, and you can find shops selling all kinds of "neat stuff," as my daughter says. Take some time and stroll around town. Don't forget that you're in the midst of apple country. There are many orchards around New Paltz, many with fresh-pressed cider in season, fresh produce, home-baked pies, and other goodies.

The only way to legally climb in the 'Gunks anymore is to get a permit. Go to the Peter's Kill entrance to the park, on Route 44/55, go to the ranger station off the parking lot, get your permit, and start climbing. You might want to get a copy of *The Gunks Select*, by Dick Williams, one of the original Vulgarians, the gang of wild-men who revolutionized climbing in the Shawangunks. Williams was the man who first climbed the 'Gunks naked: Now that's a revolution. For the less aerially inclined, the **Minnewaska State Park Preserve** (845-255-0752) has trails, paved roads, waterfalls, and the breathtaking views from the 'Gunks, all without hanging from a knob of quartz by one hand. The strikingly blue Lake Minnewaska is naturally fish-free; it has always had a high acid content because of the rock it lies in. Swimming is allowed when lifeguards are present, but beware: It's *cold* in there.

The Wallkill Valley Rail Trail is a pleasure for bikers (hybrids or mountain bikes recommended), hikers, and cross-country skiers, as it runs for miles along the Shawangunks. It also runs right alongside the brewpub. Check the website, www.gorailtrail.org, for history and parking area directions and a nice printable map.

Other area beer sites: "We're going over to New Paltz" used to be the favorite refrain of brother-in-law Chris and me: This is a fun area for bar-hopping. If you're on foot, just head up Main Street from the Otter. The first cross street is Chestnut; turn right and try out **Bacchus** (4 South Chestnut Street, 845-255-8636). Don't let the name fool you; although there is a good wine selection, with thirteen good taps and 250-plus bottles, Bacchus is the best place for beer variety in town. It's comfy and worn, too. On up Main Street is **McGillicuddy's,** an Irish-themed sports bar. They've got the obligatory Guinness and Saranac, but try their draft Anchor Steam. It's popular in the bar and turns over quickly—one of the freshest Anchor Steam drafts I've ever had in the East (84 Main Street, 845-256-9289). Two more excellent places are west of town. Drive out of town on Main Street and keep going past the Otter, as if you were going up to the 'Gunks. About halfway up the mountain is the **Mountain Brauhaus** (intersection of Routes 299 and 44/55, Gardiner, 845-255-9766—if you haven't figured it out by now, the intersection of Routes 299 and 44/55 is a happening place!). This is a great German bar and restaurant, with draft Spaten and weissbier. Try the Gunksburger, a unique cheeseburger served with fried onions on pumpernickel raisin toast. Farther west, in Krumsville, is a real gem of the Catskills, **Larry Erenberg's Country Inn** (1380 NY Route 2, Krumsville, 845-657-8956). Somehow, way out in the woods, Erenberg has kept a largely unknown beer mecca going for over twenty-five years. It's well worth the trek for his carefully chosen twelve taps and over four hundred bottles. Don't worry about freshness: Even though you didn't know about this place, lots of people do. Larry claims to have regulars from as far away as Long Island.

A word about . . .

Ales and Lagers

If you're going to go to the breweries in this book, you'll have to know how to talk shop with the bartenders and tour guides and not embarrass yourself on the tour. First off, beer is any fermented beverage made from malted barley, usually with an addition of hops. The two main types of beer are ales and lagers.

What's the difference between the two? It's quite simple: two different yeasts. These have a number of small differences, the most important of which is that the optimum temperature for fermentation and aging is higher for ale yeasts (in the 60s°F) than for lager yeasts (in the 40s°F). That's more than just a thermostat setting. The warmer operating temperature of ale yeast encourages a faster, more vigorous fermentation that creates aromatic compounds known as phenols and esters. These can give ale-fermented beers aromas such as melon, banana, raisin, clove, and vanilla. (I call these aromas "alefruit.")

On the other hand, the cooler lager fermentation produces a very clean aroma and flavor palette. Lagers generally have purer malt and hop characteristics. A lager brewer will tell you that there's nowhere to hide when you make lager beer; the unadorned nature of the beer makes flaws stand out immediately.

I like to think of the two yeasts in terms of jungles and pine forests. Warm ale fermentations are like lush jungles—exotic arrays of flavors, splendid in their diversity. By comparison, cold lager fermentations are more like northern pine forests—intense, focused, and pure.

Among small brewers in America, ale brewers outnumber lager brewers by more than ten to one. Given that lagers are by far the most popular beers in the world, how did this come to be? Tom Pastorius of Penn Brewing once explained it to me somewhat bluntly: "More ale is being made because it's cheaper, easier, and more flexible." Hard words, perhaps, but the facts bear them out.

After lagers are fermented, they undergo an extended aging period of at least three weeks at low temperatures. The cooling and the tank time required add energy costs and decrease turnover. In the same amount of time, it would be possible to put twice as much ale through those tanks. Add the energy and labor costs of the more complicated decoction brewing process used for lagers, and you wind up with a product that costs substantially more to brew than ales but has to be priced the same. No wonder there are more ale brewers!

When it comes to lager, New York is blessed to have one large and two midsize brewers of deliciously varied lagers in Matt's, Brooklyn, and Mendocino. Add in the medal-winning lagers from Black Forest and from brewpubs like Hyde Park, and you've got some great lager beer being brewed here. How did we get so lucky?

In a word, ethnicity. It's no coincidence that the areas of the United States where old brewers survived and new lager brewers sprang up are those that welcomed vast numbers of German, Scandinavian, and Eastern European immigrants. Where those lager lovers settled—New York, Pennsylvania, Wisconsin, and Minnesota—is where lager brewing thrives today.

Whatever your tastes—ale jungles or lager forests—you'll find something to your liking in the Empire State.

Dutch Country Albany and the Capital District

Albany, miles up the Hudson River from New York, is a year older than the coastal metropolis. Dutch fur traders founded a settlement here at the head of navigation on the river in 1624, underscoring the importance of this broad and placid water route to the interior.

The Dutch had a strong influence on the area, an influence that remained strong into the 1800s and can be seen in the place names today: Watervliet, Schenectady, Rotterdam, Rensselaer, and the numerous "kills," the Dutch word for "stream." But their power was slowly eclipsed by the political power stemming from the rest of the state when Albany became the capital of New York in 1797, a waning that increased rapidly when the Erie Canal opened in 1825.

The Erie Canal was both engineering marvel and social leveler. Trade flowed through Albany in a great river, and plenty of the money and people associated with it stayed in the city. The railroads followed the canal, and soon the Capital District was not just trading, it was taking in raw materials and manufacturing heavy machinery and a host of consumer goods.

Albany was more of a counterweight to New York City in those days, an upstate financial center and the center of a statewide power that held its own against the clout of the Big Apple. Teddy Roosevelt and Franklin Roosevelt both vaulted into the presidency from the governor's mansion; Al Smith unsuccessfully tried the same thing.

The underworld moved freely between Albany and the city as well, the best-known example being Jack "Legs" Diamond, who was finally killed in Albany in 1931. William Kennedy's Albany cycle of novels, which includes the Pulitzer Prize winner *Ironweed*, explores this side of Albany, along with its connections to the above-world of politics. These books show a dirty, human side of Albany that most cities are lucky enough never to have exposed, but it sure makes good reading.

As it has a way of doing, the area's success contained the sources of its downfall. The great factories along the Mohawk and the Hudson polluted the rivers, the railroads and the highways that came later made it easy for people to move out of the cities into growing suburbs, and the success of industry and labor led to higher wages that priced their products out of the market. Albany, Schenectady, Troy, all of them proud, successful cities, fell hard in the 1950s and 1960s as industries closed or moved.

Albany now lives largely on government. In 1962, then-governor Nelson Rockefeller decided to turn the city into a showplace for the state, a capital the state could be proud of. Although New York wasn't prepared for the billion dollars it would eventually cost, it is hard to argue that Rocky's plan didn't save the city. The Empire State Plaza is a stunning expanse of almost 100 acres of marble, with scattered modern sculpture and a long reflecting pool. It can get a bit windy, but it is breathtaking.

The state capitol building is at the north end of the plaza, a breathtaking sight in its own right. The capitol is a bit of a jumble, architecturally speaking, looking more like a castle than a capitol. The free tours are a fascinating ramble through this lavish building (518-474-2418); pay particular attention to the Million Dollar Staircase, and try to find the seventy-seven famous faces among the three hundred carved into it.

At the other end of the plaza is the New York State Museum (518-474-5877). The major exhibits concentrate on New York City as metropolis, the wilderness and logging exploitation of the Adirondacks, and the life of the state's Indian peoples, an exhibit that includes a full-size Iroquois longhouse replica.

There are two other little places in Albany I'd like to tell you about. First, the Big Dog. You're all familiar with the RCA dog, Nipper, who was originally the mascot of the Victor company till RCA bought Victor and took Nipper as its own. Nipper was usually pictured with his head cocked toward the horn of a Victrola gramophone, and in old representations the picture was titled *His Master's Voice*. You can see Nipper, larger than life (if that's accurate for a dog that was only an illustration), at 991 Broadway, a 25-foot-tall Nipper on the roof of a former RCA distributor. The company's gone, but Nipper remains, and all of Albany uses him as a landmark: "The Big Dog."

Just down the road from The Big Dog is the Miss Albany Diner, at 893 Broadway, the only place I go for breakfast in Albany. They only do breakfast and lunch (when they will do your french fries to order, lightly cooked to "brittle"), and their breakfasts are fun and eclectic and delicious. Listen to a few: Georgian eggs are eggs any style on a bed of sweet potatoes and onions, topped with peanut sauce; MAD eggs, two eggs served on a split English muffin topped with sliced scallions and a light curry sauce; and MAD Irish toast, thick slices of Texas toast dipped in French toast batter, filled with pecans and cream cheese, and "drowned in a butterscotch Irish whiskey sauce." If that doesn't get you going in the morning, you're just not trying.

I've included the two breweries in Saratoga Springs in the Capital District; via the Northway, they're not far off at all. Mendocino Brewing Company strongly considers the Capital District to be the market for its new beer, Old Saratoga Lager, and the Original Saratoga Springs Pub and Brewery's brewers both come up from Albany to make the beer, so it's not too much of a stretch.

Poke around in this area and there's no telling what you might find. Go and explore. I found things to love about all these towns, and now it's your turn.

Note: With the tight concentration of brewpubs in the Capital District, I have decided to consolidate the **Lodging in the area, Area attractions,** and **Other area beer sites** here to avoid repetition. Listings for Saratoga Springs are found on pages 115 and 116.

Lodging in the area: Mansion Hill Inn, 115 Philip Street, Albany, 518-465-2038; Microtel Inn, 7 Rensselaer Avenue, Latham, 518-782-9161; Albany Fairfield Inn, 1383 Washington Avenue, 518-435-1800; Super 8, 1 4th Street, Troy, 518-274-8800.

Area attractions: *The Albany Pump Station* brewpub is located in the same building as the *Albany Urban Cultural Park Visitor Center,* a fun, hands-on museum of Albany history, which also includes the *Henry Hudson Planetarium,* with regular shows, 25 Quackenbush Square, Broadway and Clinton, 518-434-0405. The high-end venue for performance in Albany is the *Empire State Performing Arts Center,* "The Egg." That's the strikingly odd building just off the plaza, clearly visible from I-787, that looks like half an egg on four legs. It's a carefully designed concert space, and the acoustics are incredible (518-473-1845 for schedules). For big shows, it's the

Pepsi Arena: music, sports, spectacle, you name it (Pearl and Market Streets, 518-476-1000, www.pepsiarena.com). More music of a different sort takes place at the **Old Songs Festival of Traditional Music and Dance,** an annual event in late June at the Altamont Fairgrounds (west on Route 20/Western Avenue to Route 146, 5 miles west to Altamont, 518-765-2815, www.altamontfair.com). The fairgrounds also host the **Altamont Fair,** a classic country fair with lots of farm exhibits (518-861-6671).

The **USS Slater,** a World War II destroyer escort, is tied up in the Hudson at the foot of Madison Avenue (518-431-1943). An interesting tour emphasizes the cramped quarters that served as an extended home for over two hundred men. While we're talking ordnance, the **Watervliet Arsenal Museum** (on Broadway, 1.25 miles west of the 23rd Street Exit of I-787, Watervliet, 518-266-5805) is the home of the Big Guns. Watervliet Arsenal opened in 1813 and has been making artillery for America ever since, from cannons to mortars to the big 16-inch naval rifles on battleships like the USS *New Jersey*. The museum goes back further than that, to sixteenth-century European cannons, and traces artillery development up to the nuclear shell.

Other area beer sites: Touring the bars of the Capital District was almost as grueling as my pubcrawl in Buffalo; there are a *lot* of good bars around here!

Albany

The first bar to mention in Albany has to be **Mahar's** (1110 Madison Avenue, 518-459-7868). Mahar's has twenty-six taps and hundreds of bottled beers, so many that they have a constantly updated, computer-generated list—and Mahar's will keep track of what you've already had. There's no music, and the lights are on all night so you can actually see who you're talking to. Jim Mahar gets beers no one else in Albany gets, because he knows he can sell them. Just behave yourself in here. Mahar has been known to throw people out for beer pretension. Really, he has. If Mahar's is the most famous beer bar in Albany, **Valentine's** (17 New Scotland Avenue, 518-432-6572) might be Albany's unknown beer bar. Most people know Valentine's as a music venue (and it is an excellent one; call for schedule), but they also have some great taps and a good bottle selection.

Albany goes to bed early, generally, but Lark Street keeps on rocking. You can start at the **Lark Tavern,** just around the corner at 435 Madison Street (518-463-9779), an older hangout with plenty of good, if not great, taps and a big spirits selection. There are pool tables in the back. The food's good, the onion rings are exceptional. Walk around the corner to **Justin's** (301 Lark Street, 518-436-7008). It's down below street level but easy to find. Justin's is pleasantly sophisticated for a place with a beer selection this good; there are well-dressed professionals here, drinking from the small but excellent spirits selection and from taps like Fuller's London Porter and Brooklyn Pilsner. Across the street and down a bit is **Lionheart** (258 Lark Street, 518-436-9530), a polar opposite. Lionheart is about bluesy funk and come-as-you-are. The small, cozy bar next to the performance space is well stocked with some astonishing bottles (Aventinus, Coniston's Bluebird, Sinebrychoff Porter, and Stegmaier Porter) and good taps. Very enjoyable bar.

Beff's (15 Watervliet Avenue, 518-482-2333) is an acronym: Big Ed Fat Fields, the owner's dad's nickname. I like a man who would be proud of a nickname like that! Beff's has a lot of good taps, particularly for a sports bar. It also has great food, winning Albany Metro's Best Burger and Best Pub Food in 2001. Maybe the chicken toes did it; they're bigger than chicken fingers, and they're beer-battered. Take the time to read the menu; it's a howl. Not far away is Albany's oldest bar, **Pauly's Hotel** (337 Central Avenue, 518-426-0828); a sign outside says "since 1862," while the mirror inside says "established 1889." Whatever. I'm not actually recommending Pauly's, just noting it. When a place advertises over twenty taps and five of them are Miller High Life. . . . But they do have Guinness. They also have holes in their floor from the rowdy college crowd. This is a stop of largely historical interest.

There are two bars within easy walk of Big House and the Pump Station. **Victory Cafe** (10 Sheridan Avenue, 518-463-9113) is a neighborhood bar with good food (the Greek pizza is excellent), good service, friendly patrons, and a small but good tap and bottled selection. Up the street is **McGeary's** (4 Clinton Square, 518-463-1455), an Irish pub that also caters to Parrotheads (Jimmy Buffett fans). McGeary's has a surprising thirty-six taps, representing a good spread of beers. Their selection of Irish, bourbon, and Scotch whiskies is even more surprising, and gratifying.

Schenectady

I found Schenectady very confusing to drive in because of the fan-shaped street grid; keep your wits about you. **Van Dyck's** (237 Union Street, at Broadway, 518-381-1111) was a brewpub until recently, and may be again in the future, but for now the house beers are brewed at an Albany brewpub. I promised I wouldn't say where, but if you think about it, you can probably figure it out pretty easily. You can see the brewery across the small courtyard in the back of the building. Van Dyck's is mainly about serious jazz acts; they get them in, and judging from the performers' comments, they love to play there. Call for a schedule, and be prepared to be amazed at the airy, open, and intimate performance space. You can easily walk from Van Dyck's to **Pinhead Susan's** (38 North Broadway, Schenectady, 518-346-6431). The bizarre name comes from a long-lived graffito on the adjacent railroad bridge: "Susan is a pinhead!" Everyone in Schenectady knew immediately where the place was. Susan's is an Irish pub, but it's nicer, more varied in beer selection, and quirkier than most; the last comes as no surprise, I'm sure. Try the house beer, and lean back against the bar to people-watch through the windows along Broadway.

Troy

Holmes and Watson, Ltd. (450 Broadway, 518-273-8526), is a famously good beer bar that has been a favorite of the geekerie for years, and rightly so. With twenty-one excellent taps and a good selection of single malts, you're well outfitted for drinking, and the comfortably worn bar, tall windows, attentive bartenders, and great food make it a very pleasing experience. Add in the subtly understated Holmesian references, and you've got a real winner. **The Man of Kent** tavern (518-686-9917) is not in Troy at all, but 20 miles out Route 7, near Hoosick Falls. Proprietor John Stoate, who is a man of Kent, England, is as much a beer fanatic as anyone reading this book. I never saw draft Coniston Bluebird Bitter before I saw it at the Man of Kent, and that's just one of fifteen excellent taps. The atmosphere is completely, classically English pub, and the patrons are a mix from every social class, brought together by the beer. Man of Kent shows up frequently on lists of the best bars in America; Wendy Littlefield suggested it as a stop for visitors to Brewery Ommegang. It's not easy to find—it's on the south side of the road; look for the wooden sign with the smiling huntsman—but few hunts are more rewarding.

Big House Brewing Company

90 North Pearl Street, Albany, NY 12207
518-445-2739
www.bighouseonline.com

Drew Schmidt, the long, tall head brewer at Big House, and I have a good friend in common. Drew brewed for three years at Oxford Class in Linthicum, Maryland, under the strict tutelage of Tom Cizauskas. I met Tom at Oxford in late 1994, while Drew was there, so chances are we were both sitting around the same table in the brewery that cold December morning when I was making my first "official" brewery research trip as a beer writer. I know everyone pitched in when a shipment of raspberry puree arrived, so Drew and I have worked together.

I'd like to say we remember meeting, but we don't. It doesn't really matter, because between Drew and his beers, there's plenty of charisma to fire up a fast friendship. This is a guy with a quick smile and a good line of brews, and the Big House is doing just fine with them.

Drew's been in since the beginning, back when Big House was just an empty building being used for storage, "a business dumping ground," as he put it. That was back in 1995. Big House's principal partner, attorney Steven Waite, owned the building next door. He was just sick of having this empty eyesore next to his building, so he made an offer on it. The owner came back with a counteroffer, saying there were other people bidding on it.

Steven thought, "Who are these guys?" He made some inquiries, and found out his competition, Eric Schilling and Mike Galonka, wanted to open a brewpub in the building. That sounded good to him, so they formed a partnership and let the final bid stand. After a massive cleanup, the brewery went in, and it opened in July 1996.

It was hard sailing the first few years. "There was nothing open in downtown after five o'clock," Drew recalled. As usual, a brewpub changes that, for the better. Now there are about fifteen places. Big House holds up its end as a cornerstone of that business by offering dining, barroom relaxation, and

Beers brewed: Year-round: Ma Barker Light, Al Capone Amber, Legs Diamond Pale Ale, Bootlegger Berry Wheat, Prohibition Porter, Bonnie & Clyde IPA. Seasonals: Bad Boy Brown, Irish Red, Vice Weizen (TAP NY Gold, 2002), Whiskey Dick's Porter, Barleywine, Pilsner, Oktoberfest, Spiced Ale, Dortmund, English Pale, Scotch Ale, Vienna, Bock, Kölsch. *Winner, Matthew Vassar Cup, 1999.*

a frenzied DJ dance hall on the third floor—a little something for everyone.

Why "Big House?" Well, originally it seemed that there was plenty of theming fun to be had with a prison atmosphere. That faded, and not much is made of it past the names of the beers these days. To be honest, I always like it when a place outgrows theming on the merits of food, service, and beer.

With an upcoming third Big House scheduled for a November 2002 opening in Clifton Park, the vagaries of New York brewing law are leading to a probable move of brewing operations off-site to a bigger, stand-alone facility. That's going to change how things work at Big House, but it won't change the beer. Drew's going to be watching over that. Hey, I trust him. We've known each other for years. Kind of.

The Pick: The elbow bender here is the Irish Red, a Bass-like beer with a real British nose of malt and a hint of cookie sweetness, with a smooth, buttery note sneaking in to confirm the Irish style. "Bass-like," forsooth—Bass wishes it tasted like this. But the beer that laid me out was Whiskey Dick's Porter, a batch of Prohibition Porter that Drew aged in a Jack Daniels barrel. The beer was "good night" in a glass: a huge vanilla nose, very thick body and rich texture, and enough malt to stand tall in the whiskey. Beer-booze candy.

Directions to Big House Brewing Company and C. H. Evans Brewing Company

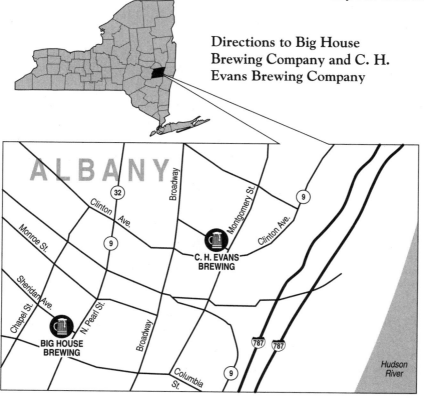

Opened: July 1996.

Type: Brewpub.

Owners: Stephen Waite, Mike Galonka, Eric Schilling.

Brewer: Drew Schmidt. Assistant brewer, Mike Breunig.

System: 20-barrel Specific Mechanical brewhouse, 3,000 barrels annual capacity.

Production: 1,200 barrels in 2001.

Brewpub hours: Sunday, Tuesday, and Wednesday, 4 P.M. to 11 P.M.; Thursday, 4 P.M. to 1 A.M.; Friday and Saturday, 4 P.M. to 3 A.M. Closed Monday.

Tours: None.

Take-out beer: Half-gallon growlers, quarter and half kegs; call for availability.

Food: Big House was going to be a white-linen, fine-dining establishment, but . . . "We had a hard time supporting it," said Drew. So they changed to a pub menu—pizza, burgers, sandwiches, and some wicked garlic fries—and everyone was happy. Except maybe the chef.

Extras: Dance hall on third floor, pool tables on second floor. Dance floor is open 11 P.M. to 3 A.M. Friday and Saturday only. Thursdays often have live music, sometimes Fridays; call for schedules.

Special considerations: Cigars allowed. Kids welcome. Vegetarian foods available. Handicapped-accessible; elevator to all floors.

Parking: Street parking; large pay lot across street.

Big House Grill

112 Wolf Road, Albany, NY 12205
518-458-7300
www.bighouseonline.com

A few years ago, there was an operating, successful restaurant and sports bar on Wolf Road. When the owner decided he wanted to sell, the partners at Big House decided they wanted to buy. They stuck a small (3.5-barrel) brewery in the front corner and called it the Big House Grill.

There the brewery sits, gleaming copper and stainless steel, looking very nice and very much like a brewery. But that's probably not where your beer is coming from. Big House head brewer Drew Schmidt was pretty open about that. "We don't brew there often," he told me. Once a month? "Maybe once a month." Almost all the beer served at the Grill is brewed on the big system downtown.

New York law requires a brewing system to have the brewpub license, so they put one in the Grill. It's kind of an odd law: If you have one brewery, the amount you can sell off-premises is essentially unlimited. Once you own another, the amount allowed as off-premises sales goes down, and goes down more when you own more. The upshot is that Big House may be moving all their brewing operations out to another site; Troy Pub and Brewery is considering the same thing.

So the story on the Grill's beer is pretty much the same as the downtown, original Big House. But here the emphasis is on the restaurant, a dark, quiet place with a full menu. There are

Beers brewed: Ma Barker Light, Al Capone Amber, Legs Diamond Pale Ale, Bootlegger Berry Wheat, Prohibition Porter, Bonnie & Clyde IPA. Seasonals: Bad Boy Brown, Irish Red, Vice Weizen, Whiskey Dick's Porter, Barleywine, Pilsner, Oktoberfest, Spiced Ale, Dortmunder, English Pale, Scotch Ale, Vienna, Bock, Kölsch.

The Pick: Prohibition Porter gets the nod. It's good, it's roasty (but not too much so), it's bitter (but not too hoppy), and has a great medium body, just heavy enough to be soothing rather than quenching.

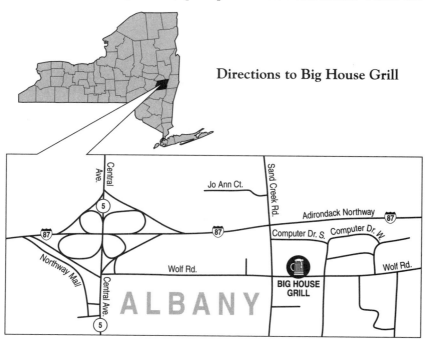

Directions to Big House Grill

still TVs showing sports in the bar, though, so you can hang here all day, sent up to the Big House.

Opened: September 1999.
Type: Brewpub.
Owners: Stephen Waite, Mike Galonka, Eric Schilling.
Brewer: Drew Schmidt. Assistant brewer, Mike Breunig.
System: 3.5-barrel Specific Mechanical brewhouse, 250 barrels annual capacity.
Production: 50 barrels in 2001.
Brewpub hours: Seven days a week, 11:30 A.M. to 11 P.M.
Tours: On request.
Take-out beer: Half-gallon growlers, quarter and half kegs; call for availability.
Food: Pretty standard pub stuff, with some good classics; the meatloaf was outstanding.
Extras: Plenty of sports-dialed TVs in the bar area.
Special considerations: Cigars not allowed. Kids welcome. Vegetarian foods availables. Handicapped-accessible.
Parking: On-site lot.

C. H. Evans Brewing Company at the Albany Pump Station

19 Quackenbush Square, Albany, NY 12207
518-447-9000
www.evansale.com

"We make anything," was one of the first things Pump Station brewer George Depiro told me. "Almost anything." I was willing to believe him; while I was waiting to talk to him, I'd sampled a triple he'd made that had been second fermented with hefeweizen yeast. It was bright and bubbly, explosively tinged with spicy cinnamon and birch notes, sweet and lively, but good Lord, where does an idea like that come from?

From a self-confessed wacky homebrewer like George Depiro. "I was a homebrewer for five years," the former chemist said. "I got in deep and quick, right into full mash brewing after three extract brews. I was wacky about it," he added, without a trace of embarrassment. "My basement was a lagering cellar, rigged out with an air conditioner and a homemade walk-in refrigerator." He was good, too, winning several national awards. If he hadn't gotten into professional brewing, some independent filmmaker might have done a black-and-white documentary on him.

The whole Evans Brewing Company story might be worthy of a documentary as well. The Evans name is an old one in brewing, dating back to 1786, when Cornelius H. Evans opened his little brewery down the river in Hudson, New York. The brewery grew and exported beer to England and France, as well as all over the northeastern United States. The family called it quits when Prohibition came along, as did many brewers. But the family retained the memory of its legacy, and descendant Neil Evans started things again in July 1999.

Why July 1999? "That's when the money ran out," George explained. "Brewpubs open when you run out of money and need to make some." He also pointed out that there was a bit of a design flaw—the dining room and the kitchen were at opposite ends of this huge building. "I'm good at pointing out flaws," he said matter-of-factly. "I'm a cynical person."

Let's talk about the huge building, because it is a great setting for a brewpub. It was originally built as the pumping station for the city's water supply, housing massive pumps that forced water from the Hudson up to the Bleecker Reservoir, now Bleecker Stadium. To repair the pumps, two 20-ton overhead cranes were built into the overhead. They're still very much functional and were used to hoist the serving tanks onto their perch high over the main bar.

You can look a long way up to the ceiling, 40 feet away. Check out the climbing guy on the big stone wall in the dining room (let me know if he made it to the ceiling yet). I love these old industrial spaces, places like the Foundry Ale Works in Pittsburgh and Empire in Rochester. They're so solid, and so overengineered, they seem to be the work of giants.

Beers brewed: All beers brewed on the premises. Year-round: Quackenbush Blonde, Scottish Light, Kick-ass Brown Ale (GABF Gold, 2000), Pump Station Pale Ale, Hefeweizen, Evans Amber. Seasonals: Triple, Doppelbock, Barleywine, Wit, Porter. Additional beers at George's whim; check the well-updated (by George, not some marketing weenie) website.

The Pick: Yes, the Hefeweizen's as good as billed by everyone I talked to, but I can't ignore the Kick-ass Brown Ale. Typed as an American brown ale by George Depiro, this is nothing less than a dark IPA. There are some chocolate notes in a solid malt body, but this baby's all about hops, smack in your face from bold beginning to a minutes-long hop finish. Rock on.

It's in the hands of humans now, and one of them has some very definite opinions about how to sell beer in a brewpub. "We don't sell anyone else's beer," George stated. "Why? If you're selling Budweiser; you've given up, if you're selling Sierra Nevada Pale Ale . . . well, again, why? I can make beer like that. Actually," he added with a quick grin, "I think I could sell almost anything labeled Pale Ale. They really like the Pale Ale."

It's good to know your audience. Judging from the business (beer sales were up 25 percent in the first half of 2002) and the raves on beer websites like Pubcrawler, he's right: They really like the Pale Ale, and the Hefeweizen as well. As long as he keeps pumping them out and throwing in the occasional wacky homebrewer idea, things should be humming along at the Pump Station.

Opened: July 1999.

Type: Brewpub.

Owner: Neil Evans.

Brewer: George Depiro. Assistant brewer, Tim Matias.

System: 10-barrel New World Systems brewhouse, 900 barrels annual capacity.

Production: 650 barrels in 2001.

Brewpub hours: Monday through Thursday, 11:30 A.M. to 11 P.M.; Friday and Saturday, 11:30 A.M. to midnight; Sunday, 11:30 A.M. to 8 P.M.

Tours: By appointment.

Take-out beer: 2-liter and 1-liter growlers, half, quarter, and sixth kegs; call for availability.

Food: Yes, you can get pub grub here, but why not break out of the habit? The Pump Station has more adventurous dishes than you'll see in most brewpubs. For a starter, try the Thai peanut wings or a portabello mushroom stuffed with a mixture of three mushrooms, aged cheddar, and sun-dried tomatoes. Then it's raspberry grilled duck salad, followed by French Quarter gumbo or seafood pot pie. Vegetarians: This is one of the better brewpub menus for you, with a house-made veggie burger, eggplant lasagna, grilled vegetable primavera, and the vegetarian Thunder and Lightning, a dish of soba noodles with chickpeas, garlic, fresh sage, and pecans.

Extras: Very occasional live music. Occasional weekend cask ales.

Special considerations: Cigars allowed. Kids welcome. Vegetarian foods available (see above). Both floors handicapped-accessible.

Parking: On-site lot plus street parking and nearby pay lots.

Malt River Brewing Company

800 New London Road (in Latham Circle Mall), Latham, NY 12110
518-786-6258
www.maltriver.com

MALT RIVER
BREWING COMPANY

Goose Gosselin's come home to Latham, and at the time, it seemed like I was the only person in the Capital District who knew it.

Gary "Goose" Gosselin had been the original brewer at Malt River. He'd come to Malt River by a strange path, as a philosophy major and rugby player, construction painter and heavy equipment rigger, and finally into the brewhouse at Boston Beer Works. "It was fast beer in those days," he recalled. "They were selling beer like crazy, and it was brew it, filter it, screw it: on tap in six days. That's a problem. If you drop a popular beer, people will just shift to another beer. If you start serving six-day beers, they might leave."

He left for Union Station brewpub in Providence, but it was the same thing. When John Harvard's took over Union Station, they liked Goose's experience with setting up breweries and wanted him to be the setup guy for the then-expanding chain. He didn't want to move around that much and was starting to feel pressured, when Mark Weiss contacted him about starting things up at Malt River.

"I'd been hosed by these things before," Goose said. "So I took a good look at this. Mark's dad owns the mall, and there's a lot of money in the place, and a lot of mahogany, so it doesn't look that mall-ish. I liked what I saw, and when Mark started talking about a Bohemian system, I signed up and went to Budapest to overlook the construction."

Hungary was evidently still pretty Soviet-influenced at the time. "There were armed guards at the brewery fabrication plant!" Goose told me, laughing. But aside from a rumble with some Romany and a run-in with some less than optimum steak tartare, things went well, and soon

Beers brewed: All beers brewed on the premises. Year-round: Malt River Red, Old Albany Pale Ale, Goose's Golden Ale. Seasonal: Razz-Ma-Tazz, Maple Porter, Pat's Porter, Blonde Ale, IPA, Oatmeal Stout.

The Pick: Let's see, have I picked too many hoppy beers already? No? Great, make it the IPA! Goose shoveled in the citric hops on this one, and it's clean and piney, dry-hopped with Chinooks. Get a big glass of this and pretend you're in Oregon, drinking the hop-juice they call beer out there. Punishing but rewarding at the same time. You should also try whatever's on cask, because Goose does it right.

Goose and the system were headed back across the Atlantic to Latham and Malt River.

"We opened on time, and I was happy," he recalled. But life had another nasty surprise in store for him. Still footloose, Goose couldn't leave well enough alone. He left Malt River, lured away to brew on a big 50-barrel system at a New England brewery. "It enticed me," he said. But things didn't work out the way they were supposed to, and Goose was left hanging, laid off, with a wife who was eight months pregnant. "I got a sales job," he said, "and I mowed greens on a golf course. I actually liked that, mowing greens."

Then Mark got in touch with him again. His brewer had left; would Goose be interested in coming back? As it turned out, he was, and in January 2002, he returned to the Bohemian system he'd shepherded to Latham from Budapest.

And things are good. Honestly, I was told by a number of people to skip Malt River when they found out I was visiting breweries in the Albany area. After trying Goose's beers twice, I cannot imagine that these folks have been there since he took over the helm again, because these are good beers. Maybe it's the fact that Malt River is in a mall, but come on, people—the place is clean, it's got plenty of room, the beer's good, and the staff was friendly and competent. Maybe it's the contentious nature and sharply divided geekerie I noticed in the Capital District, with fierce preferences and "love it or hate it" evaluations of these breweries.

All I know for sure is that the Goose has landed on the River again, and the sooner people learn what that means, the better.

Opened: June 1996.

Owner: Mark Weiss.

Brewer: Gary "Goose" Gosselin.

System: 15-barrel Bohemian brewhouse, 3,000 barrels annual capacity.

Production: 800 barrels in 2001.

Brewpub hours: Opens at 11:30 A.M. and stops serving food at 10 P.M. seven days a week (except in summer: closed Sunday, open at 4:30 P.M. on Monday). Closing time varies widely after 10 P.M., depending on the crowd.

Tours: Upon request.

Take-out beer: Half-gallon growlers, half kegs.

Food: Malt River's Thai peanut wings are hot stuff, not your run-of-the-mill wings. You can cool off with a helping of "aled pub cheese," made with house beer; real good eating. Tuck into the big Rio

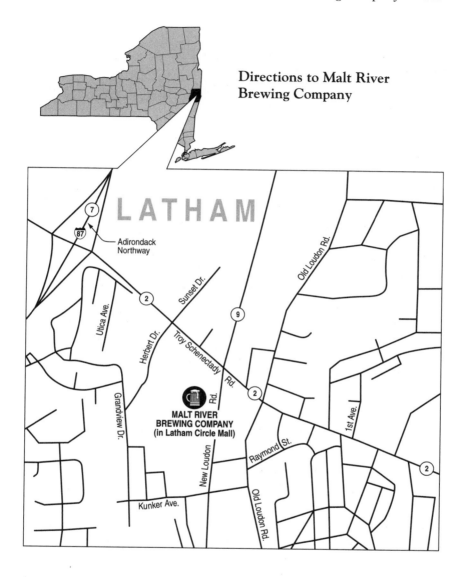

Directions to Malt River Brewing Company

Grande burrito, a Cuban marinated pork tenderloin, or buffalo meatloaf to tamp down any hunger you may have.

Extras: Darts, billiards, big-screen TV, live music on Thursdays. Beer on sale at Valley Cats stadium in Troy.

Special considerations: Cigars allowed. Kids welcome. Vegetarian foods available. Handicapped-accessible.

Parking: Mall lot.

Troy Pub and Brewery

417–419 River Street, Troy, NY 12180
518-273-2337
www.troypub.com

When I was in college, I worked two summers at a lumberyard. We did a lot of fabrication work in the mill shop: stairways, prehung doors, double windows. With all those tools and materials, whenever we needed something—a tool cart, a stool—we just made it. One morning the place was infested with flies, so I grabbed a strip of trim, nail-gunned it to a flap of thin sheet steel, and put some serious swatting on them.

That's the vibe at Troy Pub and Brewery. The place is, to quote brewer Peter Martin, "in a state of continuous renovation. We do all the work ourselves." The old building on River Street was originally a grocery warehouse, then a printshop. After a fire, there were plans to renovate the place for office space, but Troy had hit hard times, and new office space was the last thing the market needed. The plan was shelved.

That's when Gary Brown came along, a man with a plan and some welding and construction experience. He took on the building and started ripping and redoing. Peter came along in 1994 with a background in equipment design. Things clicked, and Peter's been doing the brewing ever since.

Take a look at the brewery from the big window at the end of the bar. This is a wide-open brewhouse with clearance through three stories, and Peter uses all the height. It's a gravity brewhouse; the malt gets lifted once, to the second floor, where it drops into the mill and then drops into the mash tun, and then the wort drops into the kettle. It's all chains, pulleys, hooks, and hoists, much of it muscle-powered, and lots of manual cleaning. Peter may look slight, but don't offer to arm-wrestle him. Years of brewing here have made him wiry and surprisingly strong.

"I like whole hops in some of my beers," he told me, "but the brewhouse didn't come with a whirlpool. So we built a hop filter." Built a hop filter? That's right. Brown has a 50-acre mill prop-

Beers brewed: All beers brewed on the premises. Year-round: Trojan Pale Ale, Cherry-Raspberry Ale, Sid's Brown Ale, Harwood's Porter, Uncle Rodney's Oatmeal Stout, Bridgekeeper's Lager, Lighthouse Wheat Beer, Uncle Sam Amber, Black Collar Stout. Seasonal: Pumpkin Ale, St. Brendan's Red Ale, Rauchbier, Altbier, Rye Beer, Barley Wine. *Winner, Matthew Vassar Cup, 1998.*

erty out near Bennington, where he has a steel fabrication company and a crane company. When they need something at the brewpub, they just build it, bring it to town, and rig it in, big or small, no matter: a little hop filter or the big steel-support deck beside the Hudson River.

Brown and Martin have plans for building a bigger packaging brewery on that property. "We've got to jump out there at some point," said Peter. "We can sell the beer, and we have a distributor's license, that's no problem. It sells well. But we're getting close to capacity, and that's scary."

Don't be too scared, though, because they don't have any plans to do away with the pub. In fact, they're building a major music venue next door with seats for around four hundred people. Meantime, enjoy the pub, one of my favorite for just hanging around. Check out Kevin Clark's murals (I love the big outdoor ones) and look for the baseball in the wheatfield upstairs. Get an order of "famous" spiedies; this is one of the few places you'll find these grilled skewers of meat outside of Binghamton.

Most of all, settle in and have some of Peter's beers. There are usually twelve on tap, they range from good to excellent (don't miss the Rauchbier if it's on), and you can be sure . . . he built them himself.

The Pick: I'm not a big fan of most "amber" beers. That's all too often an excuse to put a little color in a light beer and pawn it off on people. But the Uncle Sam Amber is what an amber should be, as it's been established out on the West Coast. It's got an aroma of ale-fruit spiked with hoppy spiciness, and a solidly medium body with a clean, delicious taste that delivers on every promise the aroma makes.

Opened: Opened October 1993, as Brown and Moran Brewing; name and ownership changed in 1994.

Type: Brewpub.

Owner: Garrett "Gary" Brown.

Brewer: Peter Martin.

System: 15-barrel Stainless Steel Specialists brewhouse, 2,000 barrels annual capacity.

Production: 1,200 barrels in 2001.

Brewpub hours: Monday through Saturday, 11:30 A.M. to 2 A.M.; Sunday, noon to 11 P.M.

Tours: Anytime during restaurant hours.

Take-out beer: Growlers, quarter and half kegs.

Food: Classic pub fare, including a range of pizzas, wings, burgers, shepherd's pie (the stout version is fantastic), and fish and chips, with a few signature differences. This is one of the few places outside of Binghamton where you can find spiedies, a delicious grilled skewer of marinated meat, and maybe the only place you can get

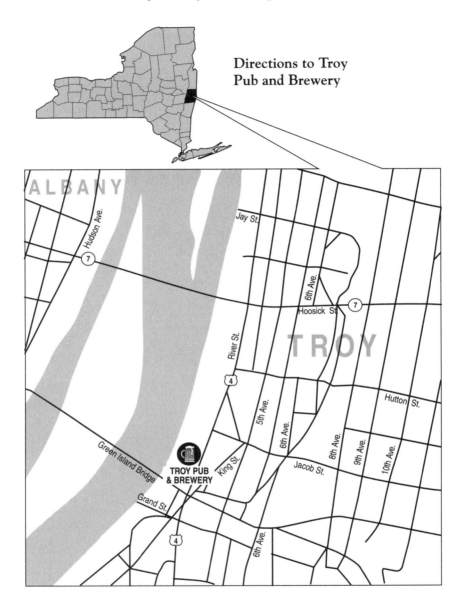

Directions to Troy Pub and Brewery

an eggplant parmesan sandwich. There are also more substantial meals, like steaks, seafood, and a variety of pasta dishes.

Extras: Darts are available. The pub has a large outside deck overlooking the Hudson River; the deck, as with almost every serving area in the pub, has murals, but the size and scope outside are particularly catching. They're visible from the Route 7 bridge. There is live music, and work is progressing on a larger venue in the adjoining building.

Special considerations: Cigars allowed. Kids welcome. Vegetarian foods available. Handicapped-accessible.

Parking: Free street parking. Large rear lot available after 5 P.M. on weekdays, all day on weekends.

Mendocino Brewing Company

131 Excelsior Avenue, Saratoga Springs, NY 12866
518-581-0492
www.mendobrew.com

Mendocino? In upstate New York? Isn't Mendocino a California name? Yes it is, and thereby hangs a tale—a twisted, involved tale that explains how this artifact of brewing hubris washed up in Saratoga Springs. There's a hero, foreign intrigue, rags-to-riches glory, and riches-to-rags despair. Oh yeah, it's all here. Buckle up, let's go for a ride.

First stop, Oregon, where Jim Bernau started the Nor'Wester brewery. It shot to the top of the Portland beer market with a raspberry beer, one of the first. Bernau decided to go national with a network of small, aggressive breweries. The Aviator and Mile High breweries were the first two, and things looked great.

They looked especially great to Glens Falls resident Bob Craven when he got laid off. He gathered a bunch of information, called Bernau, and the next thing you know, Saratoga was one of thirty-five towns vying for the big Nor'Wester brewery. Bob went for it, pushed hard, handed out Nor'Wester at festivals (I talked to him at one in Kingston in 1994), and then flew out to Oregon. In two weeks, he nailed down the deal. "Jim told me, 'Go build a brewery,'" Craven recalled. The North Country brewery was under way.

Then things got weird. Instead of a 50-barrel facility in Saratoga Springs, Bernau changed the plans to a 100-barrel brewhouse. Okay, Bob refigured the plans and got back to work putting up the brewery. While he was building, Bernau was

Beers brewed: All beers brewed on the premises. Year-round: Red Tail Ale, Blue Heron Pale Ale, Eye of the Hawk Strong Ale, Black Hawk Stout, Kingfisher Premium Lager, Old Saratoga Lager.

raising money but didn't keep a good grip on where it was going, and ran out. He cut a deal with Indian brewing magnate Vijay Mallya, the owner of India's UB brewing group, for a loan to get Nor'Wester to full production. North Country was the collateral.

Can you see it? The shakeout hit, Bernau had no margin for error, and defaulted. Mallya shut everything down and foreclosed on the North Country brewery. Around the same time, he took control of the landmark Mendocino Brewery in Hopland, California. He sent a management team to Saratoga Springs, and the big brewery starts turning out Mendocino for the East Coast. The brewery tried its own ten Springs brands, which were good but never caught on.

The Pick: I'd love to give Old Saratoga Lager the nod; it's a good beer, a solid beer, a quaffer. But I'd be lying if I didn't say that Eye of the Hawk is the drop-dead killer in this lineup. It's full-bodied, richly malty, and packing some serious esters, and the best thing about Eye of the Hawk is that it's no longer a seasonal: You can get it all year long now. Rejoice.

Bob finally left, stressed out. Getting out didn't help. "I worked in manufacturing for a year," he said, "and I hated it. I wanted to get back into beer." Things happened to intersect, and Bob got hired back running the brewery again, which UB had renamed Mendocino, just like the one on the West Coast. He got production of UB's flagship Kingfisher brand going, they've got contract brews in from the Sackets Harbor brewpub and others, and now he and brewmaster Paul McErlean are working on a local brand, something to sell on draft in the Capital District.

That's Old Saratoga, a vienna-style lager, "the ultimate crossover beer," as Bob calls it. "We're at the birth level with Old Saratoga," he said, "pounding the pavement—all grassroots sales you have to hustle for. I feel some of the old North Country fire again." He grinned and leaned forward. "It's great to work at something you love!"

At 100 barrels, this plant is some big iron. But with automation, it's an almost intimate process of a few guys here, a couple guys there. The brewhouse is cavernous, with enormously high ceilings, and the fermentation hall is roomy, with all the space for expansion. Bob sighs to see the empty floors, poured to accept tanks to take the brewery to higher capacities. "If this had been a 50-barrel brewery," he says, "things would have been very different. Nor'Wester may not have gone under."

Oh, what might have been. I felt a little guilty because I knew enough of the story to prompt Bob into remembering details and running over old ground again. He's much happier thinking about what might *be*, these days. The Mendocino brand is catching on, Kingfisher Premium Lager is an easy sell to Indian restaurants, and the contract business is slowly increasing. Old Saratoga keeps it fun.

It's a long story, but I think Bob's really happy that it isn't over. I know how he feels about beer; once you've worked with this stuff, with these people, it's hard to go back. Drop in at Mendocino's fine tasting room some evening and get a taste of it yourself.

Opened: September 1997.
Type: Brewery.
Owner: United Breweries of America, Mendocino, California. Brewery manager, Bob Craven.
Brewers: Paul McErlean, Sanford Fogg.
System: 100-barrel Santa Rosa Stainless brewhouse, 100,000 barrels annual capacity.
Production: 12,000 barrels in 2001.
Tours: Tours are generally by appointment only. The tasting room is open Monday through Friday, 5 P.M. to 8 P.M.; Saturday, noon to 7 P.M.
Take-out beer: Single bottles, six-packs, cases, half kegs.
Extras: The tasting room has a dartboard, two TVs, and an assortment of board games for the kids.
Special considerations: Kids welcome. Handicapped-accessible.
Parking: Small lot in front, large lot in back.
Lodging in the area: Saratoga Motel, 440 Church Street, 518-584-0920; Saratoga Bed & Breakfast, 434 Church Street, 518-584-0920; The Inn at Saratoga, 231 Broadway, 518-583-1890. Note that all room rates skyrocket during the racing season, between mid-July and early September, and reservations must be made far in advance for those weeks.
Area attractions: Well, it's all about the season, isn't it? If you're a horse-racing fan, chances are you already know about this. If you don't, you can get all the details from the official website, www.nyra.com/saratoga, or by calling 518-584-6200. There is harness racing from February to November at the **Equine Sports Center,** and polo matches in the summer (Crescent Avenue, 518-584-2110). The **National Museum of Racing and Hall of Fame** (Union Avenue and Ludlow Street, 518-584-0400) is all about Thoroughbred racing in America, with a hall of fame for horses, jockeys, and trainers; illustrative videotapes explain how a race is run from the jockey's viewpoint. Broadway, in the center of town, has pricy but interesting specialty shops.

If you want to "take the waters," the springs that made Saratoga Springs famous originally are still available. **Saratoga Spa State**

Park (entrance off South Broadway, 518-584-2000) has bathhouses that are pretty bare-bones stuff, but you're not here for fluff, you're here for the cure! You can take a twenty-minute bath in the mineral springs (and they are mineral-laden) for a $12 fee. There are also pools, two golf courses, and walking trails.

Other area beer sites: *The Parting Glass* (40 Lake Avenue, 518-583-1916) is a rambling Irish bar and restaurant, with a lot of taps and a great whiskey selection. It also has regular live Irish and American folk music; call for schedule. If you get out of town to Saratoga Springs' old competition for the medicinal waters trade, Ballston

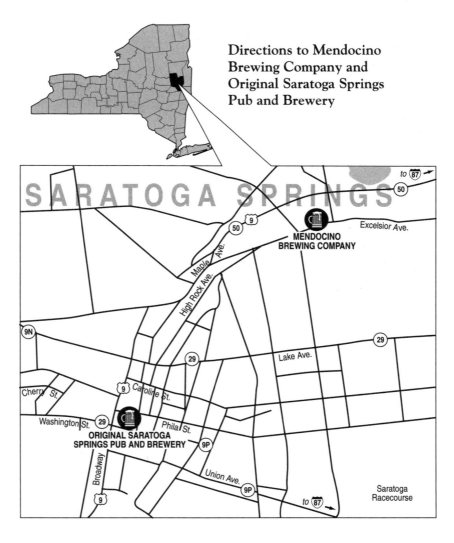

Directions to Mendocino Brewing Company and Original Saratoga Springs Pub and Brewery

Spa, there's the **Spa Brauhaus** (200 East High Street, 518-885-4311), a German bar and restaurant. Don't be put off by the exterior; like a number of German restaurants, the Brauhaus is kind of run-down on the outside but immaculate on the inside. Have a fresh Spaten Pils, listen to the accordion music, and maybe stay for sauerbraten. You can also head up to Glens Falls, another 15 miles up the Northway (see page 126).

Original Saratoga Springs Pub and Brewery

14 Phila Street, Saratoga Springs, NY 12866
518-583-3209
www.restaurant.com/brewpub

Like almost every sport these days, the essence of horse racing has been diluted by spectacle and celebrity. We all watch the Kentucky Derby (and in my house we do it with roses pinned and juleps chilled), we may watch the Preakness and the Belmont Stakes . . . and that's about it. We go to baseball games for the fireworks and the semi-illicit joy of open-air beer drinking, we go to football games for the tailgating and to blow those long plastic horns.

But every sport has its true fans, the ones who keep the box scores, the ones who are there when it's 20 below in Buffalo. This is life and breath, food and drink for them. Fans come to Saratoga for the intense six-week horse-racing season like migrating birds, drawn irresistibly to watch the races and handicap the horses, see and be seen, and then party all night. It's what they do, an equine religion of sorts, and this is one of the holy cities.

Well, good for them. As for the rest of us, we'll see you at the Original Saratoga Springs Pub and Brewery. Food and drink is our food and drink.

This is a good place to enjoy them. The Pub has one of my favorite bars, a long hollow rectan-

Beers brewed: All beers brewed on the premises. Year-round: American Pilsner, Saratoga Pale Ale, Big Red Ale, Mile and a Quarter Porter, Raspberry Wheat. Seasonals: Golden Bock, Dunkel, Doc's Machinegun Stout, Oktoberfest. A mixed-pour "black and tan" is also popular.

gle of dark wood fitting neatly in the two-story well created by the balconies of the second-floor dining area. Pull up a stool, order a beer, and check the big-screen TV at the end of the bar for the latest news and sports. If you've got friends with you, grab one of the booths there on the first floor, or climb up to the somewhat quieter second floor.

You pass the brewery on your way in, a 10-barrel JV NorthWest system, a real high-end setup. The brewer's in there, working away. Wait a minute— that guy looks familiar. He should, because it's either Drew Schmidt or Mike Breunig from Big House in Albany.

The Pick: Call me difficult, but I really like that hand-mixed black and tan. It tasted like all afternoon drinking to me, playing cards, talking, watching a football game, whatever. The hops in the pale ale shred up the roastiness of the porter a little, and the darker malts in the porter smooth out the brightness of the pale ale. Try one, and try other beer mixes, too; they can be a lot of fun.

What's up with that? Drew and Mike independently contract out their time and expertise to the Pub. There's not a lot of competition between the two brewpubs; with three other brewpubs and bars like Mahar's and Holmes and Watson in Albany, not many people are going to drive half an hour up the Northway for a beer. The beers are good, and they're not the same beers as they do at Big House; I've got no problem with a couple guys making a little money.

Besides, it gives Mike a chance to stretch his wings a bit. He does most of the brewing up here, and he's doing a good job on it. I got some of his Golden Bock: What a big, juicy gumball of a beer, with plenty of the overnotes of fruit you get from massive malty lagers, and this is a massive mouthful of beer. "Come back and try the Oktoberfest," Mike urged me. "It's really good." After tasting the bock, I'm more than willing; just call me when it's tapped.

So if you're in town for the beautiful scenery, historic homes, and great restaurants, or if you're here for the horse racing, figure on stopping in for a pint at the Original. Especially if you're a true fan of beer.

Opened: November 1995.
Type: Brewpub.
Owners: Jerry Bender, Dave Tarrella.
Brewers: Contracted services of Drew Schmidt and Mike Breunig.
System: 10-barrel JV NorthWest brewhouse, 1,000 barrels annual capacity.
Production: Approximately 300 barrels in 2001.
Brewpub hours: Seven days a week, 11:30 A.M. to 4 A.M. (the brewpub will close earlier if no one's in, but Saturday nights almost always go till 4 A.M.).

Tours: Upon request.

Take-out beer: Half-gallon growlers.

Food: There are two menus: for the dining room and for the bar. The bar is, as you'd suspect, pub grub, but with some twists, like "Irish" nachos, which are nacho fixings put on waffle fries instead of chips. The dinner menu tends more toward big steaks and chicken, with an Italian influence; there's a great eggplant parmesan.

Extras: Big-screen TV. Open mike and $1 pints Thursday, live music Friday, and karaoke Saturday. Bands during the Hats Off weekends at the beginning and end of the racing season. Hats Off is a big deal in Saratoga Springs.

Special considerations: Cigars allowed, and are sold at the bar. Kids welcome. Vegetarian foods available. Handicapped-accessible.

Parking: On-street parking and town lots.

Lodging in the area, area attractions, and other area bar sites: see page 113.

Bars

Sometimes the pint is not the point. I've been collecting great bars for over twenty years, and that's one thing I've learned. There are more bars all the time that have a good selection of beer. But not all of them are great bars, because it takes more than beer to make a bar, a tavern, a saloon, a joint. Beer is a social drink, and you've got to have that socializing for a great bar.

I don't like nightclubs and big chain bars. The Nazis had a slogan, *Kraft durch Freude*, "strength through joy," that referred to the night-clubs where soldiers and sailors were sent with orders to have a good time. All too often I get that same feeling of enforced enjoyment at nightclubs. It's all about buying the next beer and shoving you off the stool to make room for the next big tipper.

The Switzerland Inn is a good example of a "bar bar," the kind of place I'd send you to for a good time without caring about the beer. The Switz is a rambling place that kind of tumbles down the hill to the east shore of Keuka Lake, north of Hammondsport. The beer's okay: You can get Saranac and draft cans of Guinness, but most of the beer sold here is bottles of Labatt Blue and Coors Light. When we're at Keuka, we can go to the Village Tavern in Hammondsport and have a great time doing a tap dance that includes lambics, IPAs, stouts, and doublebock. We often do, but other nights we wind up at the Switz, drinking Blue and talking trash with the locals. It's got a great view, especially from down on the dock, the people are friendly, and the staff always treats you like a regular.

Not that great beer and lots of taps means you won't have fun. The MacGregor's on Gregory Street in Rochester is my favorite of that excellent chain of multitaps. They've got a ton of taps and bartenders who actually know what they're pouring. Beer-ignorant bartenders are a red flag for me; if they don't know about it, why are they here? But you can get great beer on Gregory Street in a completely natural atmosphere laced with pure fun. I had so much pure fun there one afternoon during a $5 pitcher special on Spaten Optimator that my wife had to come and drive me home.

The Sterling Place, in Buffalo, doesn't have a lot of atmosphere, to be honest, but I liked it right away. What it has is a ton of personality.

The people here know each other, they know their neighborhood, and you can become part of it almost immediately. They care about the beer, too, and you'll find some of the most knowledgeable beer geeks in Buffalo here, because they know they can get well-cared-for beer served by a bartender who sees them as more than just another tip.

You can certainly find great bars in New York City. Mug's Alehouse in Brooklyn was a new experience for me while doing this book, and I liked it so much I went twice in one day. They have a fantastic selection of taps, including incredibly fresh Brooklyn beers from the brewery just around the corner, and a big bottle array with beers from all over. And it's cool, it's relaxed, it's friendly.

Another place, right in Midtown, is St. Andrew's, which isn't even known for its beer selection: When you've got over 140 single malts, even thirty taps tend to get overlooked. The place is well lit, so you can see the people you're talking to; there are no stools, so you can't just lock your face to the backbar; and there are enough partitions to keep the noise down to a manageable level. Within five minutes of getting my beer, I was deeply engaged in a conversation with two strangers about management styles.

Awful Al's Whiskey and Cigar Bar in Syracuse is a surprisingly long warren of a bar, with a long bar, a front lounge, and an extensive "snug" area in the back full of overstuffed couches and armchairs. People here love to talk whisky and beer, or whatever else is on their minds. Al's is one of three outstandingly great idiosyncratic bars in Syracuse, the other two being the Blue Tusk and Clark's Ale House, both within a five-minute walk.

Then there are weird little places like Fadely's Deli & Pub, in Patchogue. A couple of booths, a small stage with a few basic bar stools, and three chairs are in a room with an 8-foot stand-up bar. The decor is mostly plywood with Grateful Dead concert posters, and plaques for a beer club that ceased operations years ago. They have no food except a jar of pickles that everyone warned me not to eat. They also have eight taps of great, fresh beer at a reasonable price and a beautiful "hey, it's okay" attitude. I've been to bars that are more physically comfortable, but I'd happily go back to Fadely's tomorrow.

So what makes a great bar? It's hard to say. Good beer is part of it, and I don't mean this IPA or that helles, I mean fresh beer served through clean lines into a clean glass (and not a frosted one, *please!*). But it's also about bartenders that see you, not through you, and who keep things moving without losing their personality. It's about a look that didn't come out of a box that someone else will open in another town six months later. There's enough light to see the person you're talking to, and not so much volume on the sound system that you can't hear the conversation. The regulars are good people, and you can feel like a regular quickly. The beer and the food (and there doesn't even have to be food) are reasonably priced and well presented. And even when it's full, everything still feels right.

It's not that tough to do it. As I wrote that last paragraph, I was smiling to myself, thinking, yeah, like d.b.a. and the Ginger Man, like the Country Inn, like Papa Jake's, like Holmes and Watson, like. . . . There are plenty of great bars in New York.

And sometimes it's all about memories and experiences. The day before my brother-in-law Chris got married, his dad took him and his two brothers and me to River Station in Poughkeepsie. It was a gray day in November, but as we sat at the bar and drank smoky-bitter pints of Guinness with salty-sweet oysters on the half shell, it felt like a sunny day in May. The bartender caught our vibe and kept the drafts coming with a smile, and the whole place responded. I felt like the fourth brother that day, and River Station will always be a great bar for me, till the day they tear it down.

Sometimes it's about great beer. But it always tastes better in a great bar.

Forever Wild
The Adirondacks

My introduction to the Adirondacks came with a road trip I took with my dad and my father-in-law back in the 1980s. We drove up from Dutchess County to Lake George and into the Park. About 20 miles northwest of Lake George, it began to snow lightly, and by the time we got to Blue Mountain Lake, there was enough for a snowball fight in the parking lot at the Adirondack Museum.

We drove on to Tupper Lake, to Saranac Lake, and then down through Lake Placid. It was still snowing, but it only ever put down enough to make things softly white, not dangerous. We stopped in Keene Valley at the Noon Mark Diner (Route 73, 518-576-4499) for a piece of their excellent pie, then reluctantly got on the Northway and went home. I was enthralled by the beauty of the mountains, the deep forests, and the lakes like frozen jewels set in the pine surroundings.

The popular theory is that "Adirondack" is an Iroquois word meaning "barkeater," a derogatory term the Iroquois tagged on the Algonquin Indians of the mountain area, implying that they were such poor hunters that they had to eat bark off the trees. I'm not satisfied with that, but neither am I about to suggest we change the name of this magnificent wilderness area.

The Adirondack Park is an astounding achievement. It is amazing that it all came about from greedy self-interest and started with the search for the source of the Hudson River.

Surveyor Verplanck Colvin went into the Adirondacks in 1872, when the mountains were still largely unexplored and unsettled. He and his survey team traced the Hudson's sources, seeking the highest. They found it on the west slope of Mount Marcy, the highest peak in the Adirondacks.

123

"Far above the chilly waters of Lake Avalanche," Colvin's report read, "at an elevation of 4,293 feet lies summit water, a minute, unpretending, tear of the clouds—as it were—a lovely pool shivering in the breezes of the mountains and sending its limpid surplus through Feldspar Brook to the Opalescent River, the well-spring of the Hudson." This was Lake Tear of the Clouds, a poetic name, and for once one not stolen from Indian legend.

With the credibility gained by this discovery, Colvin continued to survey the Adirondack region and sent reports to Albany urging that this last wilderness be preserved. He might have been ignored, as so many similar pleas in that era were, had it not been for the silt in New York Harbor. Clear-cut logging in the Adirondacks sent cubic miles of runoff dirt downstream, and the water grew foul with rotten bark. Business interests in the city and in towns along the Hudson saw that their best interests lay in plugging this fountain of filth.

Unbelievably, this strange alliance of conservationists and developers persuaded the state legislature to create an initial 680,000-acre Adirondack Forest Preserve. Somewhere, the words "forever wild" crept into law, probably in a flourish of nineteenth-century rhetoric, a phrasing that would cause years of argument between conservationists and Adirondack residents.

The state made additional purchases, bringing the Forest Preserve within the park to almost 3 million acres. But the park is often quoted as 6 million acres. Why the discrepancy? Six million acres are "inside the blue line," within the boundaries of the park. But that line includes towns like Lake George, Saranac Lake, Lake George, Tupper Lake, and Speculator, it includes the right of way of I-87, it includes railroad lines and even the big prison at Dannemora—land, in other words, that is anything but a forest preserve or wilderness. Add to that all the privately owned land that checkers the park, and you see where the missing 3-plus million acres is hiding.

That's why "forever wild" is such a controversial wording. There are limits on development—in some parts of the park. There are poor people who are caught between a need for work and a love for their homes, who are caught by a lack of jobs in an environment of strictly controlled development. There are the fragile Adirondack ecosystems that are being damaged even by the limited use allowed. Where's the balance?

I don't know; no one does. All I can tell you is to try to use the Adirondack wilderness in a wise way, a careful way. Ask the experts at the Adirondack Mountain Club (www.adk.org) about the best ways to camp, follow the posted regulations, be a good citizen. And when you're in the towns, spend freely to support the local economy!

What to do? Just a few suggestions. First, go hiking and really see the mountains and the meadows. You can get guidance from the Adirondack Mountain Club by writing to 814 Goggins Road, Lake George, NY 12845, visiting the visitors center at that address, or purchasing guidebooks online at the website. Read the guidebooks, be prepared.

The other way to see the Adirondacks is by canoe or guide boat, the lightweight, beautiful wooden boat that is an Adirondack icon. Again, the Adirondack Mountain Club has you covered for guides.

Get a sense of the history of the area at the Adirondack Museum in Blue Mountain Lake (Route 30, 518-352-7311). There are a variety of exhibits on life in the Adirondacks: logging, fishing, mining, and so on. It's a wooded setting, a nice place for a museum.

Do yourself a favor: Don't just go where the brewpubs are. Get out to the other towns in the Adirondacks, get off the road. Go to Tupper Lake, Cranberry Lake, Ausable Forks, and see the place. And as they say, take only pictures, leave only footprints.

A final note about my geography. The two brewpubs in Glens Falls are not "inside the blue line," but Glens Falls is much closer to the Adirondacks than it is to Albany, in distance and in spirit. But why is Red Lion here and Sackets Harbor Brewing, 12 miles away, in the Lake Effect section? It's because of Fort Drum. Watertown is the post town for Fort Drum, home of the Tenth Mountain Division. There was no way I was going to put Tenth Mountain anywhere but in the Adirondacks.

Cooper's Cave Ale Company, Ltd.

Sagamore Street and Dix Avenue, Glens Falls, NY 12801
518-792-0007
www.cooperscaveale.com

Cooper's Cave Ale Company is named for the real cave in Glens Falls featured in the opening of James Fenimore Cooper's *The Last of the Mohicans*. It is the smallest non-brewpub brewery in New York. At 700 barrels, its annual capacity is less than 1/10,000 of the capacity of the Anheuser-Busch brewery in Baldwinsville. Hometown owners Patty and Ed Bethel aren't fazed a bit by the comparison. "In this business," Patty told me, "you either get big or go home. I'm not going home!"

The Bethel family (their son Adrian works in the brewery also) may not have the biggest brewery, but they've got plenty of energy and ideas. You could easily be forgiven for thinking you'd walked into a general store or an old-time drugstore soda fountain when you walk in the front door. In a room about the size of a kitchen, you're presented with books, racks of jerky, postcards, fish-identifying guides, gift baskets, a rainbow of T-shirts and hats, candy, and taps of beer and soda. Things hang from the ceiling, they're displayed in the window, clever shelving holds stuff everywhere, and there's cheese, sausages, horseradish, and pickles in the walk-in cooler behind the taps.

There are usually about eight beers on tap (and a few sodas), but don't figure on trying them all. First off, Patty won't sell you any. The brewery has no license for on-premises beer sales, so it's all free samples of about 4 ounces each. Second, there's an iron-clad three-sample limit. "They call me the beer Nazi," Patty said, "but I don't want a pub. We're kid-friendly, women-friendly, and nonsmoking, and that's how I like it."

"I don't want a pub," she says, and it's not, but . . . at the same time, this is a very social place. Neighbors drop in for a couple growlers ("We've filled over thirty thousand growlers with beer and soda," Patty told me, an average of twenty-eight a day), chat with Patty and Ed and each other, and wind up staying about twenty minutes, having a

Beers brewed: Year-round: Tavern Ale, Bumppo's Brown Ale, Radeau Red, Cooper's Cave Pale Ale, Pathfinder's Porter, Sagamore Stout. Seasonals: Fenimore Froth Holiday Ale, Blind Rock Maibock, Altbier, Raspberry Wheat. Sodas: root beer, birch beer, cream soda, orange cream, wild cherry cream, spicy ginger beer, sugar-free root beer, sugar-free orange cream.

sample or three. Brewpub, brewery—I'm not sure what it is, but it's one of the most successfully integrated community brewing businesses I've ever seen.

Then there's the ice cream business. In May 2000, the Warren County Bikeway, a rails-to-trails project, was extended right along the brewery's back wall. Families would stop, and the parents would stick their heads in to see what was going on, and maybe have a sample. Potential was recognized, and soon Cooper's Cave was doing a good business in soda and soft ice cream. A hard ice cream machine was added late in 2001, and sodas, cones, and ice cream floats are selling like mad.

With all that stuff, it was inevitable that someone would want to do their Christmas shopping at Cooper's Cave, and that's how the gift baskets got started. Patty whips them up to order (and there are a few ready to go if you're in a hurry), anywhere from a couple 22-ounce bombers, a glass, and a jar of cheese spread for about $17, to a big washbasket full of stuff for $200. "We did three hundred last Christmas," Patty told me. Who knows, maybe you got this book in one!

The Pick: I couldn't make up my mind on this. I tried a lot of the Bethels' beers and took more samples home and tried them again. I still couldn't pick one, I liked almost all of them (okay, I'll admit: I'm not big on spiced beers). Then I had to make a trip past Glens Falls and ducked off the Northway to get more of Whalen's horseradish pickles and two bottles of—Pathfinder's Porter. Hmmm, guess I made a Pick after all! This is just incredible beer. It's dark, almost black, and foams a dark brown head, and it is rich and chocolatey and just a little bitter. "Wow. Wow. Wow." is what I have written in my notes.

But enough stuff; what about the beers? They are extremely drinkable and approachable, but also very rewarding for the discerning drinker. The only one I had that was truly big and approaching overwhelming was the Pathfinder's Porter; most are subtle and delightful. English ale drinkers would find a lot in them that was familiar.

Kind of funny: I've run out of room on the state's smallest brewery. There's a lot more to talk about, but don't worry: You can get it all from Patty and Ed over a couple of samples. Might as well get a growler, too. I know you'll want to come back for a refill.

Opened: St. Patrick's Day 1999.
Type: Brewery (and ice cream maker).
Owners: Edward J. Bethel, Patricia A. Bethel.
Brewers: Edward J. Bethel, Adrian P. Bethel.
System: 2.5-barrel self-designed brewhouse, 700 barrels annual capacity.
Production: 600 barrels in 2001.
Hours: Monday through Saturday, 10 A.M. to 9 P.M.; Sunday, noon to 5 P.M. Closed Christmas Day, New Year's Day, and Easter.

Tours: By request, though it may be a "look-through-the-door" proposition.

Take-out beer: 22-ounce bottles: singles, cases, any quantity. Half-gallon growlers, sixth, quarter, and half kegs.

Food: When the weather's warm, both soft-serve and Cooper's Cave's own-make hard ice cream is available at the bike trail service window. You can also get the ice creams in a float with Cooper's Cave soda, or you can buy the sodas separately, by the glass or in half-gallon soda growlers. Patty also sells a variety of excellent Whalen's horseradish products (the pickles are great, and the hot dog relish mustard is worth a trip), local cheeses, and smoked meats in the gift shop, and she'd be happy to make you one of her attractive gift baskets with a selection of 22-ounce bottles, foods, clothing, books, or whatever other doodads she's got that you like.

Special considerations: Cigars not allowed. Kids welcome. Handicapped access is planned.

Parking: Good on-street parking, and plenty of space to park your bike.

Lodging in the area: Days Inn of Lake George, 1454 Route 9, Queensbury, 518-793-3196; Glens Falls Inn B&B, 25 Sherman Avenue, Glens Falls, 518-743-9365; Merrill Magee House, 2 Hudson Street, Warrensburg, 518-623-2449; Lake George RV Park (on the bike trail), 74 State Route 149, Lake George, 518-792-3775, www.lakegeorgervpark.com.

Area attractions: The brewery is located right on the **Warren County Bikeway,** a "rails-to-trails" conversion for bicyclists, in-line skaters, and pedestrians. The Bikeway connects to other bike-multiuse trails: the **Feeder Canal Park Heritage Trail** and the **Old Champlain Canal Towpath,** which runs down to Fort Edward and the Rogers Island Visitor Center (see below). Call 518-623-2877 or 518-623-5576 for information and a free map for the Bikeway, or download a map at www.agftc.org; 518-792-5363 is the number for the Feeder Canal Trail. The brewery's namesake cave, which figures prominently in the beginning of *The Last of the Mohicans*, is located between Glens Falls and South Glens Falls under the Hudson River bridge. If you want to ride that river, bring your canoe or kayak; there are plenty of places to put in.

Glens Falls has a surprising treasure in the **Hyde Collection** (161 Warren Street, 518-792-1761), a small but exceptional art museum with works by Monet, Degas, Rembrandt, and others. **The Rogers Island Visitor Center** at Fort Edward (518-747-3693) is a reconstruction of a French and Indian War fortification, the area and era where Robert Rogers of Rogers Rangers made his mark. If you're feeling like a little spectacle, you could catch an Adirondack Lumberjacks baseball game at **East Field Stadium** (175 Dix Avenue, 518-743-9618). Thanks to the Northway, the world-famous **Saratoga Race Course** is only fifteen minutes away and offers top-notch Thoroughbred racing. Get all the information

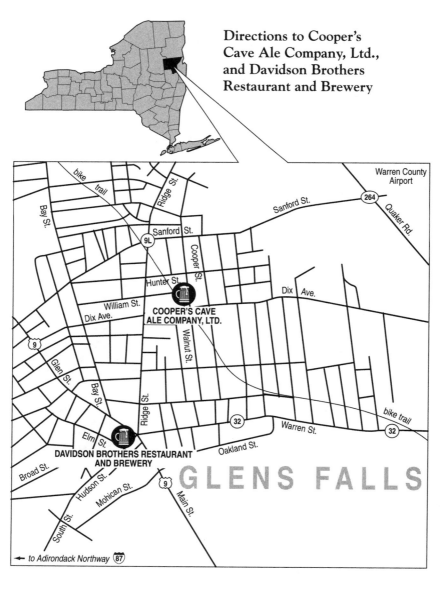

Directions to Cooper's Cave Ale Company, Ltd., and Davidson Brothers Restaurant and Brewery

at www.saratogaracetrack.com. You're also about fifteen minutes from **Lake George** (see the Lake George attractions on page 133, or check www.visitlakegeorge.com).

Other area beer sites: *Dango's,* just two blocks down Dix Avenue on the corner of Maple Street (518-792-9861), is a high-ceilinged sports bar with some of the best wings I came across in eastern New York. They also have seven Cooper's Cave ales on draft, big TVs behind the bar, and exceptionally friendly bartenders. ***Jake's Round-up,*** in South Glens Falls (23 Main Street, Glen Street becomes Main Street as you cross the river), 518-761-0015, is a comfortably kitschy Tex-Mex place that won't blow the roof off your mouth (you can ask for hot if you want it), with a good selection of tequilas and some good taps. Here's a weird one: the ***Sunnyside Par 3 Golf Course.*** It's up the road a piece, west of Oneida Corners (168 Sunnyside Road, Queensbury, 518-792-0148), and it's a pretty nondescript-looking place. But when you get into the bar, your eyes will pop at over twenty-five *good* taps and about two hundred bottled beers. I don't know how they do it, I'm just glad they do. It's a public golf course, too.

Davidson Brothers Restaurant and Brewery

184 Glen Street, Glens Falls, NY 12801
518-743-9026
www.davidsonbrothers.com

This is one of my favorite bars or brewpubs anywhere for hanging out, just because of the space. I love old, worn bars that look authentic (even if they aren't) and are in context with their surroundings, not ones that look like they were blown out of a spray can. Davidson Brothers has that feel, that vibe, and I groove on it.

What's so great about it? The age of the 1865 brick building, the exposed ceiling, the lack of any white walls, the wooden floor. . . . I find it hard to pin down. But I could sit here all day, drinking Ezra Musselman's good beer, and never regret a minute. It wouldn't hurt to have Rick Davidson at the table to tell stories, because he's got a bunch of them.

Most of his brewing stories center on Alan Pugsley, of Shipyard Brewing in Portland, Maine, who sold Rick and his brother John the brewhouse. Reluctantly, to hear Rick tell it. "We went up to see him and told him we wanted to open a brewpub," said Rick. "We've never homebrewed, never ran a restaurant, never even worked in one. He told us we were crazy. After we did our homework and went back again, he took us on and said, 'I really suggest you do some homebrewing.'"

When they were set up in Glens Falls, Pugsley came down to get them started. Rick and Alan did the first four brews together. "It was like a spelling bee in front of the class," Rick recalls. "He'd stand there waiting for me to do the next thing, and if I was wrong, he'd just start whistling! It went on for a week, and it was hell, but I had a great time."

Rick got to meet the man who taught Pugsley brewing: Peter Austin. "He's fantastic," said Rick. "He's got four rules, and they're brilliant. 1. Keep the brewery clean. 2. Buy the best ingredients, even if you can't afford them. 3. Boil the copper. 4. Pray to God. Do all that, and the beer will be great."

But Rick doesn't even brew anymore. Ezra Musselman came in and wanted to learn. Rick took him on, and he learned the trade. "Then one day he locked me out of the brewery!" Rick laughs. "He's great, he was born to brew." Ezra keeps about a dozen beers on tap at all times, from summer dust-cutters right up to massive head-thumpers.

The brewery is helped by its huge commitment to Quality Control. That's the name of what would be called a "mug club" anywhere else. The 22-ounce glasses, kept at the brewpub, are clearly marked "Quality Control use only!" They get 22-ounce beers for a pint price, they get a hat and a T-shirt, they get a newsletter, and they get an annual party, for a $50 fee. It's very popular.

Beers brewed: Bottled IPA and American Bright done at Shipyard, Portland, Maine. Year-round: Brown, Smoked Porter, Scotch Ale, Oatmeal Stout, Irish Red, Golden, Amber, IPA, American Light. Seasonals: Spring Ale, Imperial Stout, Fall Brew, Chocolate Porter, Strong Ale (one batch a year, one barrel served a year after Thanksgiving, rest stored). No fruit beers; Rick won't allow it.

The Pick: I screwed up. I liked the Cohan's Porter a lot, very drinkable beer, kind of like a medium-bodied stout with all the roasty bitterness. But evidently no one else liked it, and it didn't sell, so Ezra has stopped brewing it. Okay, fine. My second choice is an easy one, too: Scotch Ale. This big, fat beer just hangs out all over, juicy with alefruit.

Why do I like it here so much? It's a gestalt thing. I like the food—stopping at Cooper's Cave for Whalen's horseradish pickles makes a good excuse to stop in at Davidson Brothers for a bowl of stout and cheddar soup, and the turkey-apple melt is so darned upstate it makes you drool. I like the beer—from the whip-bitter IPA to the malt-fat Scotch Ale. But mostly, I just like this place—period.

Opened: October 1996.
Type: Brewpub and contract brewery.
Owners: Rick and John Davidson.
Brewer: Ezra Musselman.
System: 7-barrel Peter Austin brewhouse, 1,400 barrels annual capacity.
Production: 950 barrels in 2001.
Brewpub hours: Monday through Thursday, 11:30 A.M. to midnight; Friday, 11:30 A.M. to 1 A.M.; Saturday, noon to 1 A.M.; Sunday, noon to 10 P.M.
Tours: On request.
Take-out beer: 2-liter growlers, 12-ounce bottles of IPA and American Bright, half, quarter, and sixth kegs (call for availability). Davidson Brothers also has a limited number of gas tapping systems available for short-term rent with a keg purchase; call for details.
Food: Largely a pub-style menu of appetizers, salads, soups, and sandwiches, with a small number of more substantial entrees (fish and chips, bluefish medallions, ribs, a roasted vegetable ragout, and chicken Fairfield). The soup to get is the stout and cheddar: bliss for the stout drinker. The turkey-apple melt grilled sandwich is delicious. Davidson Brothers proves its kid-friendliness with a "more than the usual" kids menu that comes with an automatic ice cream.
Extras: The Quality Control "club" is a big option and a lot of fun. There is live music every Thursday, Friday, and Saturday; call for schedule. There's also a big happy hour and DJ before the live music on Fridays. For games, there's lots of stuff on the second floor: a pool table, dartboard, pinball machine, flash bowling game (my favorite of all bar games), and some classic arcade games. There's also a TV that's usually set to cartoons for the kids (or the adults).
Special considerations: Cigars not allowed. Kids welcome. Vegetarian foods available. Handicapped-accessible first floor.
Parking: On-street and city lot.

Adirondack Pub and Brewery

33 Canada Street, Lake George, NY 12845
518-668-0002
www.restaurant.com/adkbrewpub

My contract for this book with Stackpole required me to visit every brewery in New York or to revisit them, in the case of those I'd visited in years past. So I toured almost every brewery in six months.

All but one: John Carr's Adirondack Pub and Brewery. It wasn't for lack of trying, either. I got to Lake George more times in six months than I did in the last six years, not that I found that to be a hardship. Lake George is a beautiful spot, one of the most beautiful in the state. The long silver lake, flanked by steep wooded hills, is particularly beautiful at sunset, when the sun pierces the western valleys and throws theatrical shafts of vermilion light across the lake.

I was beginning to think that the brewpub had closed, but I just wasn't hitting things right. Bowing to the seasonal nature of Lake George tourism, the pub is closed in January and March, right when I was hammering on the door. I finally got inside about three weeks before my deadline and collapsed at the bar in relieved disbelief. After a quick restorative glass of incredibly hoppy IPA, I went back through the kitchen to John's office.

Carr is a bright, mercurial guy, tall and energetic, with a lot of drive and a passion for beer. He'd been homebrewing for twelve years before he opened the brewpub. "I love beer," he explained. "Lake George is a great place to be, one of the most beautiful lakes in the world. It didn't have a brewpub. I figured, why not?"

And it's really just that simple. John flings himself into these things and thrives on them. The brewpub was a 1960s-era grocery store, a squat stucco building that Carr rebuilt into an Adiron-

Beers brewed: All beers brewed on the premises. Year-round: Bear Naked Ale, Inman Pond Blonde, Snow Trout Stout, IPA, Steam. Seasonals: Hefe-weizen, Munich Dunkel, Scottish Ale, Marzen, Oktoberfest.

The Pick: I Pick An IPA. John's IPA is a light gold, almost Coors Light color. Don't let that fool you. Under that tenacious white head is a whole lotta hops, enough to drop your jaw and open your eyes. This beer will whoosh right through your mouth, grab your uvula, and hang there, shaking its fist and screaming, "I am HOPPY!!!" Quite an enjoyable rush, really, like eating jalapeños.

dack lodge, complete with log- and branch-framed booths and bar, and a big roofed-over deck that's the favored spot for dining. It's cozy inside, with rustic elegance and camp knickknacks, and a bar that's just longing to be bellied up to.

Speaking of bellies, fear not: This is a hunger-slaying menu. Ribs, steaks, salmon, pork tenderloin, and rainbow trout, burgers, wings, nachos, and overstuffed wraps; as the menu says, "Are YOU hungry?" Not for long, friend!

Don't worry about thirst, either. John's handling the brewing. He had a brewer, but the guy just wasn't up to his standards. The only way to be sure is to do it yourself, so he dove into that as well. I thought the place was a bit overbreweried at first; it's just not that big a pub for a 15-barrel brewhouse. Then John told me about the kind of business they do in July and August, and it all made sense. He's got to have that big iron to handle the rush.

Does the brewing take too much time out of running the place? "It's the only fun I have!" John said laughing. "Beer's *fun!* You got to have fun." He has so much fun with it that he even serves guest beers from New York breweries like Ommegang and Cooper's Cave. "You have to support each other," John preached. "Brewers and distributors just don't get that, and it's frustrating."

I know all about frustrating, Mister Closed-in-March! Next time I'll call ahead and reserve a seat on the deck under the hop vines with a big quaffing glass of Bear Naked Ale.

Opened: October 1999.

Type: Brewpub.

Owner: John Carr.

Brewer: John Carr.

System: 15-barrel Bohemian Brewing system, 3,000 barrels annual capacity.

Production: 400 barrels in 2001.

Brewpub hours: Seven days a week, Memorial Day through September, 11:30 A.M. to 11 P.M.; October through April, Friday and Saturday only. Closed in March and "a few weeks" in January. Best to call ahead between New Year's and April 1.

Tours: Tuesday and Saturday at noon, or by appointment.

Take-out beer: Half-gallon and 2-liter growlers, half, quarter, and sixth kegs (call for availability).

Food: Trout, burgers, salmon, meatloaf, steak, wings, ribs . . . this is "I've been hiking in the mountains and I'm *starved*" food! There

Directions to Adirondack Pub and Brewery

Lake George

Courtland St.

Dieskau St.

W. Brook Rd.

ADIRONDACK PUB
AND BREWERY

Sewell St.

Canada St.

LAKE GEORGE

Fort George Rd.

9

Adirondack Northway

9

to
Saratoga Springs

are wraps and stir-fry dishes on the menu as well, but no one will mistake this for a menu from a health food store.

Extras: John Carr is very proud of the live music on Friday and Saturday nights during the summer: "They are rising national acts, people who are going to be famous in a few years." Call for schedule. If the weather's good, the music is out on the deck, a large area done in Adirondack style, with undressed logs and branches and surrounded with hop vines.

Special considerations: Cigars not allowed. Kids welcome. Vegetarian foods available. Handicapped-accessible.

Parking: Lot in back, plus street parking. Don't use the liquor store lot across Seneca Street.

Lodging in the area: Quality Inn, 57 Canada Street, 518-668-3525; Fort William Henry Resort Hotel, 48 Canada Street, 518-668-3081. John suggests that the thing to do is come in the off-season and rent one of the lakeside cabins. ("Come for the foliage in fall," he says. "They're the same trees as they have in Vermont, and no one's here!") You can try an online agency like CyberRentals (www.cyberrentals.com-NY-NYLG.html).

Area attractions: *Lake George Village* is a grab bag of beach-boardwalk-type attractions, some more attractive than others, largely of interest to kids and party-hearty singles. I leave that to you. There is *Fort William Henry,* the fort from *The Last of the Mohicans,* with a museum and exhibits that include musket and cannon demonstrations and musket ball molding (Canada Street, 518-668-5471). Otherwise, drive up Lake Shore Drive along the western shore at sunset for a view of this handsome lake, or drive up Prospect Mountain Veterans Memorial Highway to the overlook for a tremendous view of southern Lake George. There is also some great shopping to be had at the outlets south of town on Route 9.

Other area beer sites: *King Neptune's* (2 Kurosaka Lane, 518-668-4644) is one place to try in Lake George, with a good beer selection in a largely mainstream beer town. You can also run up to Bolton Landing and settle in at the *Tavern on the Pond* (Main Street, 518-644-5520), which was the universal response when I asked John and the kitchen staff at Adirondack Pub where I could go for a good beer. It's a nice place, with a quiet patio area beside a little pond out back. And of course, Glens Falls is just over the hill (see p. 126).

Lake Placid Pub and Brewery

**14 Mirror Lake Drive, P.O. Box 948,
Lake Placid, NY 12946
518-523-3813
www.ubuale.com and www.lakeplacidpubandbrewery.com**

Chris Ericson is my kind of guy. When I came by Lake Placid Pub and Brewery on my scheduled visit for this book, Chris greeted me, took my wife by the arm, led us to a table overlooking Mirror Lake, and got us beer samplers right away. Interviewing could wait; this man wanted me to hear from his beer first.

That's how this brewpub runs. In recent years since the shakeout of microbreweries, it passes for business wisdom to say things like "a brewpub is really just a restaurant that happens to brew beer." Run a great restaurant and brew "beer," it seemed, and you'd do fine.

Hogwash. That's like saying a duck is really just a fish that happens to fly. I like the way Chris Ericson runs his brewpub: It's a brewery that happens to serve food. Good food, but the food is secondary. "I'm an eater," Chris said with a laugh, "and we serve good food. But it's the beer first."

He's got a good reason for that perspective. "We tried not to overdo ourselves in Lake Placid," he explained. "There are a lot of really good restaurants in this town, and you pay for a really good meal. So we focus on an alternative, really good pub food, and we don't gouge people for it. We try to get their loyalty as soon as they walk in the door."

It works both ways. I heard about the brewpub for years before I ever walked through the door. A beer geek friend of mine, Joe Meloney, builds his vacations around the two brewpubs in Lake Placid. He was always talking about Chris's Ubu Ale, the beer that's spread through the Adirondacks with its big white bone taphandle. I mentioned to Chris that I knew a guy in Philly who loves his beer.

Beers brewed: Year-round: Ubu Ale, 46'er IPA, Moose Island Ale, Barkeater Amber Ale. Seasonals: Fresh Powder Stout, Frostbite Pale Ale, High Peaks Hefeweizen, Big Bear Bock, Norm's Dubbel Bogie Belgian Ale, STrEAM Beer, Bruce's Brown Bag, Dr. Fogg's Oatmeal Stout, 3-Putt Porter, Ectoberfest, Matt's Maibock, Leaping Cow ESB, Logan's Lager, Daystar Dunkelweizen, McCalvin's Mild Ale, Hopscotch Pale Ale, Cascade Pale Ale, Monsoon Pilsner.

"Oh, Joe!" he said. "Yeah, I know Joe." That's the kind of personal attention that makes regulars, and Ericson's got them.

Joe's not the only fan of Ubu, either. Hillary Clinton was campaigning for the Senate in Lake Placid over her husband's birthday. Bill's staffers were in the brewpub all night long, and when they left, they got him a T-shirt and a growler of Ubu for his birthday. "Three days later, the White House called," Chris said, grinning. "They were having a state dinner, and the president really liked that beer. Could they get some? I Fed Ex'd three cases of growlers to them." Not bad for a little place in the mountains.

The Pick: The Fresh Powder Stout is a milk stout, a type of beer you don't see too often. Its rich, sweet aroma tells you exactly what you're going to get in your mouth: a creamy, sweet, and solid beer that manages to finish up roasty and just bitter enough to clean things up for the next big swallow. Very nicely done version, and one worth watching for.

There are two different places here. Downstairs is the pub this place started as twenty years ago, P. J. O'Neill's. It's very much a bar, and locals hang there in the afternoons. It's loud, friendly, and smoky, and it serves a lot of Bud and Blue until the tourists show up after 6:00. Upstairs it's light and open and almost all house beers, and it's nonsmoking.

"Nonsmoking was tough," admits Chris, "but it was the smartest move we made. We get people who'd stopped going out because of smoke, we get athletes, we get families. And we've only had two complaints about it in six years."

The bulk of the beer is the mighty Ubu, a 7 percent strong ale that sells amazingly well, and the 46'er IPA, Brit-hopped and a beautiful dark gold in color. (A "46'er" is someone who's climbed all forty-six "high peaks" of the Adirondacks.) But the seasonals raise a lot of interest with regulars and visitors alike, too, like the Frostbite Pale Ale, which is hoppier than the 46'er. "I want to make hoppier beers," Chris explained, "but there's only one IPA."

Whatever, Chris. As long as the beer comes first, it's okay by me.

Opened: September 1996.
Type: Brewpub and brewery.
Owner: Christopher Ericson.
Brewers: Christopher Ericson, Kevin Litchfield, Matt Ray.
System: 7-barrel McCann Fabrication brewhouse, 1,800 barrels annual capacity.
Production: 1,300 barrels in 2001.
Brewpub hours: Monday through Saturday, 11:30 A.M. to 3 A.M.; Sunday, noon to 3 A.M. Kitchen is open till 10 P.M., 11 P.M. on Friday and Saturday. Note: Off-season hours vary unpredictably, so

the brewpub advises calling ahead in November, April, May, and early June.

Tours: By appointment.

Take-out beer: Half-gallon growlers, 5-gallon and half kegs, six-packs and cases.

Food: A "pub-grub" menu, ranging from nachos to chicken parmesan. Favorites include fish and chips, homemade meatloaf, steak sandwiches, ribs, and chicken caesar salad sandwiches.

Special considerations: Cigars allowed downstairs; upstairs is all non-smoking. Kids welcome. Vegetarian foods available. Downstairs is handicapped-accessible.

Lodging in the area: Mirror Lake Inn Resort, 5 Mirror Lake Drive, 518-523-2544; Northway Motel, 5 Wilmington Road, 518-523-3500; The Adirondack Loj, Adirondack Loj Road off Route 73 south of town, 518-523-3441. The Hotel Saranac (101 Main Street, Saranac Lake, 518-891-2200) is a refurbished grand hotel, part of the National Trust for Historic Preservation's Historic Hotels list, has very reasonable rates, and you can get Ubu Ale there.

Area attractions: *The Olympic Center* (218 Main Street, 518-523-1655) hosts hockey, speed skating, figure skating, ice shows, and curling on its four indoor rinks. You can get on a bobsled run at the *Mount Van Hoevenberg* complex (7 miles south on Route 73, 800-462-6236), or go cross-country skiing—when winter conditions allow. Another fun winter thing is the *Lake Placid Toboggan Chute* (518-523-2591, www.neparkdistrict.com/toboggan.shtml). Once Mirror Lake freezes over, the chute is set up to send toboggans roaring down and out onto the lake, sliding as far as 1,000 feet. John Brown, *the* John Brown, came up with the idea to establish freed slaves on a farm near Lake Placid. It was a dismal failure. It is now the *John Brown Farm State Historic Site* (John Brown Road, Lake Placid, 518-523-3900). John Brown is buried there, and the farmhouse is restored, with a self-guided tour. Lake Placid has plenty of opportunities for summer fun as well: fishing, biking, hiking, canoeing, all the stuff you can do in the Adirondacks, but here you're close to two brewpubs!

Other area beer sites: *Handlebars Hideaway* (1 Station Street, 518-523-9963) is a locals' joint. It's smoky, and the only "better" beer it has is Saranac, but there's a potbelly stove, friendly locals, a pool table, and shelves full of books you're welcome to sit and read. *90 Main* (90 Main Street, 518-523-4430) is a deli and upscale coffeeshop (would there be any other kind in Lake Placid?), but there's a stand-up marble-top bar serving Guinness and Saranac Pale Ale. **The Cabin** (in the Northwoods Inn, 122 Main Street, 518-523-1818) is *very* Adirondacky, with branches and logs all over the place. They also have a fireplace and two taps of Chris Ericson's beers, plus a delicious tap of Spaten Pils. Downstairs from The Cabin is the **Northern Exposure** restaurant (518-523-7258), where you'll find a more casual bar with a wider selection of beers (including taps from both Lake Placid brewpubs). The Adirondack-style bar stools are surprisingly comfortable. **Zig-Zag's Pub** (130 Main Street, 518-523-8221), named for the infamous turn on the Olympic bobsled run, has five good taps that often include

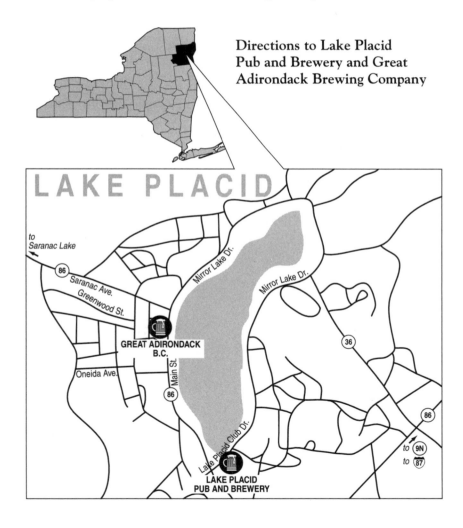

Directions to Lake Placid Pub and Brewery and Great Adirondack Brewing Company

Rob Davis's beer from Great Adirondack. The long bar is a great place to hang out on a snowy afternoon, shooting pool and looking at the money stapled to the wall. **The Brown Dog Deli and Wine Bar** (3 Main Street, 518-523-3036) is indeed mainly a wine bar, but there is a good selection of bottled beers as well, and the atmosphere and food is great. **The Cottage** (5 Mirror Shore Drive, 518-523-9845) is a hopping, popular hangout with some good taps. It's also a great place for dinner before things get nuts. **Water Hole #3,** over in Saranac Lake (43 Main Street, 518-891-9502), is a local legend. It's nothing fancy, some good beers, but it's a great music venue and just a rocking good time.

Great Adirondack Brewing Company

34 Main Street, Lake Placid, NY 12946
518-523-1969
www.adirondackbrewing.com

Lake Placid is an upscale kind of place. I remember thinking the first time I visited, back in the 1980s, that it looked like they'd uprooted part of White Plains and moved it to the North Country. Delis, boutiques, and high-end restaurants and hotels crowd Main Street right down to the Olympic Complex.

In its own rustic way, the Great Adirondack Steak and Seafood Company fits right in. It has a dark wood, Adirondack-style decor, lots of natural branches and logs with the bark still on carefully attentive service, and a kitchen that provides superbly prepared beef, fish, and shellfish in big portions. The dishes are basic—grilled steaks, broiled seafood, with minimal sauces and no "crusting" or "emulsions"—but the execution is flawless.

The Kane family owns the restaurant, and they decided that fresh-brewed beer would be a

Beers brewed: All beers brewed on the premises. Year-round: Haystack Blonde, Ausable Wulff Red (TAP NY Bronze, 2001), John Brown Pale Ale (TAP NY Silver, 2001 and 2002), Adirondack Smoked Porter, Adirondack Abbey. Seasonals: Wee Heavy 80/, Adirondack German Hefeweizen, ESB. Home-make root beer. *Winner, Matthew Vassar Cup, 2002.*

good addition. So in 1996, they built a brewery out back, up against the hill. The brewers get pretty free rein so long as they keep producing great beer, and they've done a great job on that. Rob Davis has been the head brewer since 2000, and he's nuts about the job.

"I love beer. I get my inspiration from Fritz Maytag," he told me, naming microbrewing's patron saint, the George Washington of the movement. Maytag started the whole revolution by purchasing an old regional brewery, Anchor Brewing, and turning it to the path of brewing all-malt beer in a variety of types. Quality and variety have always been Maytag's watchwords, and that's what does it for Rob, too.

Rob's also not afraid to push something he knows should work, even in the face of resistance. I'm talking about his Smoked Porter. Smoked beers are made with malt that has been smoked, usually over hardwoods like beech or alder. They smell and taste like smoked salmon or smoked meat, a hearty smell that some love and some can't stand. American brewpubs that have them on tap year-round could be counted on the fingers of one hand.

The Pick: A beer with this much heart-strong work put into it that comes out so good has to be my pick: Adirondack Smoked Porter. Rob hand-smokes his own malts in a little smoker (you can see pictures at the entrance; maybe you'll even happen by when he's doing it) over fruit-woods and nutwoods. He mixes them up, too; the batch I sampled had been done over pecan, wild cherry, and maple woods. The porter has a great smoky aroma, like standing downwind from a good wood-stove fire. But the beer itself is relatively light in smoke, and Rob attributes that to the wood. "I find it almost impossible to oversmoke with fruit-wood," he told me. What a wonderful beer this is with the big, juicy chunks of meat served here—what a match.

Count Great Adirondack. Not only is the Smoked Porter on year-round, it's popular. Part of that is because smoked beers are natural complements to grilled meat. But part of it is Rob's touch: He smokes the malt himself, on a backyard smoker, over fruitwoods, like cherry and apple, and aromatic woods like pecan and maple. The Smoked Porter smells great, like the smell of a good wood-stove in the fall, but the flavor is mild and deliciously understated.

As city-sophisticated as Lake Placid looks on first glance, there's plenty of Adirondack under the patina: solid, confident, and plain-spoken to the point of bluntness. You'll find plenty of that at Great Adirondack in the solid value, the confident brewing, and their plain-spoken way of presenting their beer and food.

Opened: April 1996.
Type: Brewpub.
Owners: The Kane family.
Brewers: Rob Davis, Kyle Dipatreo, Tonny Munn, Jasmine Hayes, Herron Heffe.

System: 7-barrel JV NorthWest brewhouse, 700 barrels annual capacity.
Production: 500 barrels in 2001.
Brewpub hours: Seven days a week, 11:30 A.M. to 10 P.M.
Tours: Saturday and Sunday, noon to 3 P.M.
Take-out beer: 2-liter and half-gallon growlers, sixth, quarter, and half kegs.
Food: Refreshingly basic steak and seafood dishes, simple and very well prepared. Not a lot of nouvelle cuisine, just really good beef and fish. Note the beer suggestions on menu items.
Extras: Outdoor patio for dining, with a huge flower arrangement during good weather, and the big tasting tent for the brewery.
Special considerations: Cigars not allowed. Kids welcome. There is pasta primavera on the menu for vegetarians, but to be honest, the serious carnivore nature of the place might put vegans off. Handicapped-accessible.
Parking: Street parking can be difficult; there is a small public lot nearby (with clean public restrooms, believe it or not). There is a lot of turnover on street parking, so parking is not always as hard as it looks at first glance.

Bootleggers

411 Cornelia Street (in the Comfort Inn),
Plattsburgh, NY 12901
518-561-6222
members.aol.com/clubgatsby/bootleggers.htm

There was a small controversy in the 1990s over the "Greatness" of Lake Champlain. Late one night, a bill slipped through Congress that made Champlain one of the Great Lakes, a crass move to grab funds earmarked for the Great Lakes. This was mostly met with giggles outside the small circle of people who were affected. Lake Champlain just doesn't support the kind of navigation the Great Lakes do. These days, the biggest traffic on the lake is the ferries that run between New York and Vermont.

But Champlain was important in the days when small boats were crucial. It was a vital highway for sloops and barges carrying redcoats and American militia, a battleground for hastily built squadrons of vest-pocket wooden warships, and . . . a backdoor for a mosquito fleet of speed-boats bootlegging booze across the Canadian border to a thirsty America during Prohibition.

That's the inspiration for Bootleggers, the period-decorated brewpub built into the Comfort Inn by the Northway in Plattsburgh. Motel owner Jim Murray recalls that his parents "never went thirsty" during Prohibition, thanks to the sizable smuggling traffic along the lake. Murray himself never seems dry of ideas. The brewpub is only part of his lodging complex; there is also a sprawling arcade with the latest video games, batting cages, and bowling lanes, an extensive fitness center, a miniature golf course, conference facilities, and an off-site you-pick orchard with hayrides in season.

All this was driven by Plattsburgh's loss of the Canadian traffic in 1992, when the Canadian dollar dropped dramatically against the American dollar. Faced with the loss of tourism, Murray decided to take his location—midway between Montreal, the heart of the Adirondacks, and Vermont ski country—and give his motel guests so much to do that people wouldn't even want to leave. "A hotel should be more than just a place to sleep," Jim says.

Beers brewed: All beers brewed on the premises. Year-round: Easy Blonde, Cardinal Red, Canada Goose Pale Ale, Black Horsemen Stout, Prohibition Porter, 3 Nut Brown, Adirondack Blueberry Ale, Adirondack Raspberry Ale. Infrequent seasonals.

The Pick: Jim told me he's got a bowling team that comes in often, and the whole team drinks nothing but Black Horsemen Stout. I can understand why. This nitro oatmeal stout is roasty but smooth, creamy, and satisfying. The name comes from a Prohibition-era mounted border patrol. As Bootleggers' website proclaims, "This much fun used to be illegal."

It's worked, and the brewpub has played its part. "I originally had an upscale restaurant," Jim told me. "It was working, but not well. Then I thought about brewpubs. Food and beer seemed like a better fit for my clientele." After coursework at the Siebel Institute and an apprenticeship at Bluegrass Brewing in Louisville under brewer David Pierce, Jim was ready.

Almost ready. "We realized the importance of theming to a restaurant," Jim explained. A friend of his, a local artist, went antiquing and found the myriad things decorating the pub's walls. Take a look at the car chase over the main entranceway. The front half of the cop car chasing the back half of the bootlegger's car are actually two halves of the same car, found in a field near Altoona, Pennsylvania. And that pay phone in the booth by the dining room? It's an original antique phone, but drop in a quarter and it really works.

Bootleggers is a fun place to be. The food's good, the beer's good (the Black Horsemen Stout is real good), and you'll have a blast just looking around at all the stuff. You'll know Jim's plan is working when you find that you don't really want to leave.

Opened: December 1995.
Type: Brewpub.
Owner: James Murray.
Brewer: James Murray. Assistant brewer, Dan Minor.
System: 7-barrel DME brewhouse, 900 barrels annual capacity.
Production: 550 barrels in 2001.
Brewpub hours: Monday through Thursday, 3 P.M. to 1 A.M.; Friday, 3 P.M. to 2 A.M.; Saturday, noon to 2 A.M.; Sunday, noon to 1 A.M.
Tours: Available upon request when brewer is present.
Take-out beer: Half-gallon growlers.
Food: Bootleggers has a full menu, with steaks, seafood, and pasta (I had the lasagna and it was classic, with beefy sauce and fluffy ricotta). They also have meats smoked on the premises, including Montreal-style smoked corned beef, which is excellent with a side of *poutine*, the Canadian soul food of fries in gravy with cheese curds.
Extras: Bootleggers has darts, billiards, and a number of TVs tuned to various channels in the bar. Downstairs is one of the largest video arcades I've ever seen: over fifty games, from classics like Pac-Man to the latest big-screen, full-motion madness like HydroThunder. There's also a Laser Tag zone, and a "Soft Zone" padded play area with a giant ball pit for the little ones. Great place to stash the kids! Outside, weather permitting, you can play on the eighteen-hole miniature golf course, use the batting cages, and ride in the bumper boats. And if the brewpub just gets you warmed up, you can shake your bootie at the hotel's Club Gatsby, a full-scale nightclub with light displays, fog machines, and thumping big sound system. If you stay at the hotel, you can work off the night's excesses at the Court Club, a fitness center with a pool (with a 70-foot slide), steam room, sauna, a full line of fitness equipment, basketball and racquetball courts, and more.
Special considerations: Cigars allowed. Kids welcome. Vegetarian foods available. Handicapped-accessible.
Parking: Large on-site lot.
Lodging in the area: Jim's Comfort Inn is wrapped right around the brewpub, 518-561-6222. Pont Auroche Lodge and B&B, 463 Point Au Roche Road, 518-563-8714.
Area attractions: If you ask the natives in Plattsburgh what there is to do, it's amazing how many of them will respond that Montreal,

Lake Placid, and Burlington are all only an hour away. They are, of course, but Plattsburgh's not bad itself. The lakeside views from the streets and parks are beautiful, both in winter and summer. You can get out on the lake on the *Juniper,* a cruise boat that makes a two-hour trip that takes you past **Valcour Island,** where Benedict Arnold fought a naval engagement in the Revolutionary War (May through September, Dock Street, 518-561-8970). You can also take one of the Champlain ferries (802-864-9804, www.fer-ries.com). The Plattsburgh ferry runs twenty-four hours and offers a quick way to Burlington, Vermont, via Grand Isle (though it can be a very exciting fourteen minutes, as I found out one windy day). The Essex–Charlotte ferry crosses in twenty minutes. The Port Kent–Burlington ferry is more of an excursion ferry, taking an hour to make a scenic crossing. Keep an eye out for Champ, the lake's version of the Loch Ness Monster, first sighted by Samuel de Champlain in 1609 . . . maybe.

If you do get over to Burlington, be sure to visit the breweries. **Magic Hat** (5 Bartlett Bay Road, South Burlington, 802-658-BREW) is a whimsical outfit that offers a great tour of their large packaging microbrewery and has a fun taproom. **Three Needs** (207 College Street, 802-658-0889) is a decidedly funky brewpub that is a great contrast to upscale ventures. **Vermont Pub and Brewery** (144 College Street, 802-865-0500) is one of those upscale ventures; try the smoked porter.

Other area beer sites: It might seem odd to start the list of beer places with a wine bar, but **Irises** (20–22 City Hall Place, 518-566-7000) is just too good to overlook. It sports five good taps (including the local Ubu Ale and Magic Hat Fat Angel) and offers a great selection of wines. Urbane sophistication in Plattsburgh, a very nice place. Two other good places are within an easy walk. **The Monopole** is at 7 Protection Street, a small alley off Margaret Street (what City Hall Place turns into one block south). Best known for a thriving alternative music scene, the Monopole hosts bands on the weekends (518-563-2222 for schedule), the more "out there," the better. But it's also a real comfortable bar, dating from the 1880s, with about thirty taps, including Sierra Nevada Porter, Ubu, and three Saranacs, a surprisingly deep spirits selection, and billiards and foosball in the back. Walk down the hill to a work in progress at 9 Bridge Street, the **Teal Lizard** (518-566-8126), which used to be the infamous "fight-a-night" Long Branch Saloon, and may have been renamed McDonough's Inn by now (in honor of the

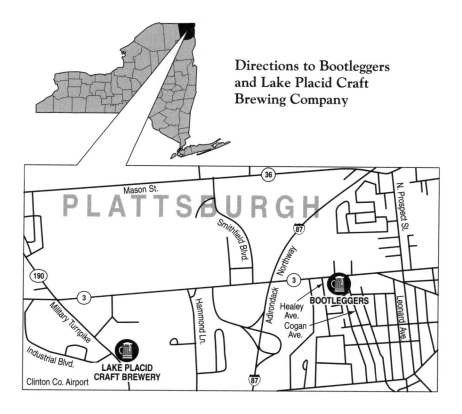

Directions to Bootleggers
and Lake Placid Craft
Brewing Company

American commander at the Battle of Plattsburgh, a War of 1812 naval battle on Lake Champlain). That was new owner Matt Brown's intent, anyway. Brown's got six good taps and plans to add more as soon as he can. Drop anchor at the bar and hoist one with him. I was also fortunate enough to catch the season's opening night at the **Naked Turtle Holding Company** (just off Dock Street, in the Plattsburgh Boat Basin, 518-566-6200), the talk of the town that day in Plattsburgh. It's not all about micros, but even beer geeks have to cut loose occasionally. The Naked Turtle is "naked" (open) from late April to October. It's a ton of fun, the French-Canadian waitresses are gorgeous, and you can get Guinness and Saranac. Relax!

Lake Placid Craft Brewing Company

1472 Military Turnpike, Plattsburgh, NY 12901
518-563-3340, 1-866-4-UBUALE
www.ubuale.com and www.lakeplacidpubandbrewery.com

Ever heard the story about the guy who sees an ad in the paper: "1956 Corvette for sale, $300"? He figures it must be junk at that price but goes and checks it out. The ad was placed by a woman whose son was killed and who just wants to get rid of his car. She takes the guy out to the barn, whips a tarp off the car, and there, on blocks, is a mint-condition '56 Corvette. The guy stammers and stutters, and tries to give her more money, but she just wants rid of it.

You do know that's an urban legend, right? Well, I've got a brewery story that's just as good, about how Chris Ericson, the Lake Placid Pub and Brewery guy, bought the AAA brewery in Plattsburgh. And this one's true.

AAA was a couple of guys who had an odd plan. They were going to crack the Boston craft beer market. That's not odd. What's odd is that they were ignoring the way Mass Bay Brewing and Sam Adams already had it pretty well sewn up, that they were planning to do it from a base in Plattsburgh, and that they were planning on doing it with two Bavarian-style wheat beers. Now, that is odd.

What's truly odd is that they managed to convince people to invest in this. This was in 1996, the last gasp of the big microbrewing boom, and people were still trying to get rich in brewing. Reality set in pretty quickly for these guys, and they went under in less than a year; the power was shut down, they skipped town, and no one went into the place for three years.

Beers brewed: Ubu Ale, 46'er IPA.

The Pick: Ha, I've got a chance to pick *another* of Chris's beers! That's good, because it gives me a chance to pick Ubu. Ubu was named for a huge chocolate Lab that would wander Lake Placid all day, then meet his 6-foot-7 owner, Dan, at P. J. O'Neill's pub every night. "Everyone in town knew him," Chris says, "so we named our huge ale for him." Woof! When you're in an Adirondack bar (and maybe farther afield, once this big place gets rolling), tell the bartender to grab that bone and pour you a glass of this rich, malty ale. It's big stuff for a brewery's best-seller: 7 percent ABV, and you can feel it on your palate when you drink it. There's some tart fruitiness in the finish and just a light touch of anise. Complex, big, and friendly: No wonder it's named for a dog.

Chris remembers the guys. He was telling me the story at the Lake Placid brewpub. "They used to sit right over there," he said, waving an arm toward the corner of the room, "and talk about how they were going to do it. That was about all they did, though: talk."

Then in 2001, Ericson's off-premises beer business grew by 178 percent. He had three brewers working full-time on a 7-barrel system. "If my beer business grew only 5 percent," he said, "I was out of beer." But he remembered those AAA guys, and he took a drive up to Plattsburgh. "I called the realtor," said Chris, "and then the owner. 'Come on up,' the owner says. 'I've got a buyer who wants the building, but I know it has more value as a working brewery.' So I went up to look around."

That's when the guy took the tarp off the Corvette. There was a 21-barrel brewhouse and five fermenters that still had three-year-old beer in them. There was a completely oversized bottling line that Ericson doesn't even intend to use (he's put a smaller line in the warehouse). There was an absolute mountain of bottles these guys had bought in preparation for their success. And there were seven hundred brand new, never-used half-barrel kegs. I swore I wouldn't repeat the price Chris paid, but it was a deal. Add into that the bonus of seven hundred new kegs that usually cost $100 each, and he got an absolute steal.

Dreams do come true. Ericson needed more capacity for Ubu Ale and 46'er IPA, and he got more than he dreamed. He's sitting right across the lake from the mighty and established Magic Hat brewery in Burlington, and now it's going to be Ubu vs. Fat Angel, 46'er vs. #9, in a beer battle for the Adirondacks. A tough fight for the underdog, but Ericson seems to have a lot of luck on his side.

The old brewery is more lively than it's ever been, with a tasting room, gift shop, and tours. It's going to be crazy for the first couple years. Get in quick, before all the evidence of AAA's hubris is gone. It's quite the cautionary tale. Savor the irony as you savor a glass of Ubu.

Opened: August 2002.
Type: Brewery.
Owner: Christopher Ericson.
Brewers: Christopher Ericson, Kevin Litchfield, Matt Ray.
System: 21-barrel Jacob Carl brewhouse, 6,000 barrels annual capacity.
Production: Not available for 2001.
Brewpub hours: Monday through Saturday, 10 A.M. to 5 P.M. You might want to call for updated hours; at press time this was still a work in progress.
Tours: Call for schedule.

Take-out beer: Half-gallon growlers, 5-gallon and half kegs, six-packs and cases.
Special considerations: Kids welcome. Handicapped-accessible.
Parking: Large on-site lot.
Lodging in the area, area attractions, and other area beer sites: See pages 145 and 146.

Red Lion Brewing Company

500 Newell Street, Watertown, NY 13601
315-785-5466

Finding Red Lion Brewing isn't easy. Newell Street is named for Watertown's first brewer, Andrew Newell, who built his 1804 brewery just up the street from Red Lion. Newell runs alongside the Black River, the roaring torrent that sluices through Watertown. But Watertown turned its back on the Black River, which was heavily polluted in the mid-twentieth century, and riverside Newell Street is tucked away from view.

"Putting the water back in Watertown" is one of Mike Bauer's snappy slogans at Red Lion, referring to the way the brewpub celebrates the Black River. The river's been cleaned up and is a favorite of kayakers for its reliable flow. I first visited Red Lion during a drought, and the Hole Brothers, the standing wave rapids behind the brewpub, were still rocking and roaring. You've got a great view of them from the glass-walled dining rooms and back deck, something most Watertowners don't see that often.

Bauer was a lieutenant in the U.S. Army and was assigned to nearby Fort Drum in the early 1990s. After his hitch was up, he decided to settle in Watertown. In a recapitulation of microbrewing's origins, Mike wanted to find the kind of beer

Beers brewed: All beers brewed on the premises. Year-round: Northern Light, Red Lion Lager, Velvet Elvis Stout. Seasonals: Iron Horse Ale, All Saints IPA, The Empire Strikes Bock, Ye Olde Frothingslosh, Dim Wit, Rasta Raspbeery, Summer Lemon Wheat, Mojo ESB, Big Bad Leroy Brown.

he had when he was stationed in Germany. Thwarted by a lack of beer variety, he took to homebrewing, which grew into a job brewing at Stephen Flynn's brewpub in nearby Sackets Harbor.

"I brewed there for three and a half years," Mike told me. "It was good, but it's lots better making my own recipes." To achieve that nirvana, he hooked up with Watertown native Mike Martini to open Red Lion. The name comes from the rampant red lion on Mike Bauer's old battalion crest, a copy of which is on the outside wall of the brewery.

It wasn't easy sailing. Watertown sold them the building for a dollar, and they started clearing out decades of trash. By the time they'd finished out the first two floors, built the mandatory fire escape tower, and poured the slab for the brewhouse twice (the power went off to the heaters the first time, and the slab cracked the pipes underneath), they were about out of money. None was left for outside decoration, leaving Red Lion with a severely plain exterior.

The Pick: Velvet Elvis Stout is what I automatically ordered the first time I returned to Red Lion, before I had even tried the new seasonal. Well, after all, life's uncertain, you never know what beer might be your last, and I'd hate to think I might miss having one more glass of this malty milkshake of a beer, roasty and bitter with a whiff of graham cracker. It's definitely enough to pull you into Watertown from a drive-by on I-81, and maybe enough for a detour all the way off the thruway.

But it is solid as a rock, and it's comfortable inside. One of my favorite things about Red Lion is the sense of humor. For instance, take a look behind the bar, where you usually find a big mirror. That was just a bit too expensive when it was getting close to opening time. So Mike ran down to the store, bought a bunch of cheap mirrors, and hung them on the wall.

Another thing I like is the menu. Red Lion goes for the "slow food" concept, using local and fresh-prepared foods instead of prepackaged foods as much as possible. So you'll find locally made Morgia's pasta featured, and less-than-ordinary items like the flaming goat cheese appetizer, a traditional "ploughman's lunch," and the Red Lion sandwich, Bauer's tribute to his hometown of Pittsburgh's favorite Primanti Brothers' sandwiches, with the french fries and cole slaw tucked right in.

Try the "raft of draft," the beer sampler on its little wooden raft holder. Mike's loving this part, making his own recipes, and you'll like it too. "That's what it's about," he summed up. "I love beer, and I did just want to brew. But I like to eat and drink, and if I can make a living at that. . . ."

With a shrug and a smile, he said it all. If reading this persuades you to make the trek north to Red Lion, I'm happy to have helped him achieve his dream.

Opened: May 2001.
Type: Brewpub.
Owners: Michael Bauer, Michael Martini.

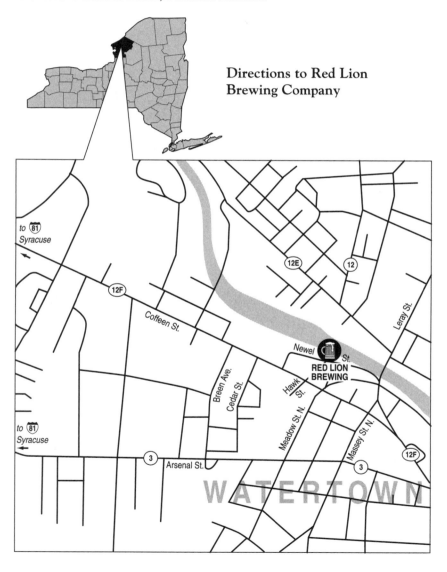

Directions to Red Lion Brewing Company

Brewer: Michael Bauer.

System: 7-barrel Bavarian Brewing System brewhouse, 1,000 barrels annual capacity.

Production: Not available for 2001.

Brewpub hours: Monday, 5 P.M. to 10 P.M.; Tuesday through Thursday, 11:30 A.M. to midnight; Friday and Saturday, 11:30 A.M. to 1 A.M.; Sunday, 1 P.M. to 9 P.M.

Tours: Upon request.

Take-out beer: Half-gallon growlers.

Food: Red Lion's menu features local and fresh-prepared foods as much as possible. I heartily endorse this and urge you to try the local Morgia's pasta. And get the Primanti-inspired Red Lion sandwich, just because it's so much fun.

Extras: Live music on weekends (out on the deck, weather permitting); call for schedule. Mike and Mike's other business, the Watertown Brewing Supply Company, is upstairs to serve your homebrewing needs. It also hosts meetings of the North Yeast Homebrew Club.

Special considerations: Cigars allowed. Kids welcome. Vegetarian foods available. Handicapped-accessible, even the deck.

Parking: Large lot, street parking.

Lodging in the area: The Inn, 1190 Arsenal Street, 315-788-6800; Days Inn, 110 Commerce Park, 315-782-2700; Ramada Inn, 6300 Arsenal Street, 315-788-0700.

Area attractions: The big draw in Watertown is the water. There are outfitters in town that do rafting. **ARO *Adventures,*** an outfit out of Old Forge that does other Adirondack rafting trips, runs four-hour trips down the Black River (800-525-7238). **B.O.B. *Rafting*** (23873 Route 342, Watertown, 315-785-9386) takes rafting trips right through Watertown, and if that doesn't sound like wilderness fun, just remember the Hole Brothers out back of the brewpub. *Hudson River Rafting Company* has an outfitter in Watertown just up the street from Red Lion (424 Newell Street, 315-782-7881). *Do not* mix whitewater rafting with drinking; outfitters will absolutely not take you if you have been drinking. Raft first, visit Red Lion second.

Other area beer sites: A lot of brewery owners try to tell me there aren't any other places in the area for good beer than their pub. Mike Bauer did, and he was almost right: Bars in Watertown can be downright nasty. He did mention **Coleman's Corner,** out by the Jefferson County Fairgrounds (322 Fair Street, 315-782-6888), and it's worth a visit just for the architecture. Coleman's is almost all corners: It's an octagonal building with a high pointed roof, lined with warmly honey-colored wood on the inside and hung with pictures and breweriana. The food's high-quality pub grub, and the bar's got Sackets Harbor 1812 and Guinness. The only other bar I liked in town was **Barkeater's Cafe** in the Salmon Run Mall west of town (315-782-5218): 1812, Sam Adams, and Saranac in an Adirondack-decor bar.

Regional Foods—Red Hots, Greek Sauce, and Fish Fries

Talk about New York and food, and most people will assume you're talking about the restaurant scene in New York City. To be sure, the city's restaurants range from the homiest of hash houses to grandly elevated examples of world-class culinary innovation. But I married a girl from upstate and learned about a whole pastiche of regional food specialties that you'll just have to enjoy with a fresh New York beer in hand.

Any talk of food and New York, be it city or state, has to start with the statewide obsession with hot dogs. I've overheard barroom and church picnic discussions of the relative merits of hot dog packers and their frankfurters that make political discussions seem half-hearted and unimportant. Do you favor skinless or "pop-opens," white hots or red hots, foot-longs or bun-length, Nathan's or Shofar, Tobin's or Zweigle's? Be prepared to defend your choice or be branded a know-nothing!

As if that weren't enough, there's the question of sauce. Call it Coney Island sauce, Texas Hot sauce, Michigan sauce, or Zippy sauce (the generic name is "Greek sauce"), but don't leave it off. This is something that is seen outside of New York—I've seen Greek sauce throughout the northern tier of Pennsylvania, and there's a "Texas Hot Wieners" shop in Hanover, Pennsylvania, near Gettysburg—but it is so widespread in New York as to be unremarkable.

Greek sauce is most likely the source of "chili dogs," though in other parts of the country, chili dogs are topped with actual chili, usually with beans. Greek sauce is based on ground beef, but while it is different at each dog-house, it is beanless and usually does not have much spicy commonality with chili.

The Michigan sauce popular in Plattsburgh is drier and chunkier than most. "It's the sauce that makes it a Michigan," I was told by the waitress at Michigans Plus in the Plattsburgh Plaza (316 Cornelia Street, near the Aldi's, 518-561-0537, or try McSweeny's Red Hots at 600 State Route 3, 518-562-4687), although there's a flaming controversy now in Plattsburgh because the local Bouyea Fassetts bakery has stopped making the special Michigan rolls. Conversely, the sauce from Wellsville's Texas Hot grill (132 North Main Street, right next to

Fisher's Pharmacy, 716-593-1400), where I first met Greek sauce, is more liquid than most Coney Island sauces.

I have an old copy of one of these secret recipes from a still-operating Texas Hot shop, passed down through my wife's Hudson Valley family. The ground beef is boiled, and the sauce contains turmeric and nutmeg, among other spices. (No, I won't pass it on; it's a *secret* recipe. Go find your own!)

It's funny how similar these places are. There's a grill out front, behind the plate glass window, where the grillman has dozens of dogs gently cooking (except in Plattsburgh, where the Michigans are boiled), with the cashier close at hand and a counter running on down the store. When the rush hits and people start ordering "fourteen with everything," the experienced grillmen will line up six or more buns on a forearm and pop them full of dogs. Some quick ladle work lays a thick stripe of sauce on each tube steak, followed by a snowy layer of finely minced onions and a ribbon of yellow or brown mustard (let's not even get started on brands of mustard, since most places doctor it up anyway); the order of sauce, onions, and mustard may change.

It's a happy mouthful of spices, hot meat juices, and the pleasantly bouncy texture of the dog cradled in the soft, absorbent bun, where the juices collect and soak. It's almost required to eat more than one, they're just so good and reasonably sized. At the Famous Lunch in Troy (111 Congress Street, 518-272-9481), the standard order is *four* of their 4-inch double-pencil-width dogs (made at the Troy Pork Store) with Zippy sauce and a can of RC cola for $2.75.

Hot dogs are one of the "meat" possibilities for a classic Rochester "garbage plate" (or "rubbish plate," to use the upstate cant). The garbage plate is a late-night, *après*-bar favorite in Rochester, and originated at Nick Tahou Hots (320 West Main, 315-436-0184). The original Nick's is no longer open late, but there's another Nick's that is, at 2260 Lyell Avenue (315-429-6388). To build a garbage plate, first take a paper plate. Layer home fries, macaroni salad, and a meat (chicken, a burger, or hot dogs) on it, then cover everything with Greek sauce and chopped onions; you can add baked beans to it as well. Most people then slather the whole mess with about half a bottle of ketchup and plenty of hot sauce. You can see how it got its name!

Surprisingly, the garbage plate does *not* include "salt potatoes." This is a delicacy as geographically tied to Rochester as the garbage plate, though it crops up along the beaches of Lake Ontario in the summer. Salt potatoes are simply small potatoes, under 2 inches across, boiled in their jackets in heavily salted water and served drowned in melted butter. They're certainly not something to be eating in front of your doctor, and with all that butter, they're not really great beer food, but they sure are good eating.

Rochester also sits in the middle of the fish fry belt that runs through the northern tier from Buffalo to Albany. Fish fries are a Friday tradition in upstate New York, probably Catholic in origin way back when, but now wholly ecumenical. The semifamous Doug's Fish Fry in Skaneateles (8 Jordan Street, 315-685-3288), where fish fries are best known and may have originated, serves fish fries all week long. It's also smoke-free and serves Middle Ages beer; "Doug loves good beer," Marc Rubenstein told me. There are also franchised Doug's in Cortland, East Syracuse, and Mattydale.

But lots of taverns, diners, and fire halls have a sign out front on Fridays that just says, "Fish Fry Tonight." You can count on french fries, cole slaw, and a slab of fried fish (a generic white fish, but classically it's walleye, or "yellow pike," as it's known in Buffalo), but you may get lucky and get a platter of deep-fried seafood. If you can score a draft Saranac Amber with your fish fry, you're in heaven.

New York is known for its cheese. My wife's family introduced me to the Old York cheese products from the Cuba Cheese Shoppe (53 Genesee Street, Cuba, 800-543-4938, www.cubacheese.com) and I became a believer, especially in the horseradish cheddar cold pack spread. But the product that catches the eye is little plastic bags of cheese curds. They're just what they sound like, lumps of cheese, not pressed into bricks. The trick is finding them fresh, so they squeak.

Really, they do squeak. I thought my wife's family was nuts when they kept talking about "Didja hear that squeak?" Loonies, I figured, or they're messing with the Pennsylvania boy. Then I got some really fresh curds, and by golly, squeeze one between your molars and they do squeak! You can find them in a bunch of different flavors, but the plain old cheddar is great eating with some mustard and pretzels, and a Genny Cream or two on the side.

Did that whet your appetite? Don't eat yet, there's another course to come after the next set of breweries!

Touched by a Glacier
The Finger Lakes

Look at a map of New York. See the stripes across the middle? That's the Finger Lakes. Indian legend says they are marks left by the Great Spirit, who placed his hands on the land to bless it. Geologists say they were created by the action of glaciers in the Ice Ages. I'm backing the geologists for now, but I'm open to persuasion.

Origins don't seem as important as living in the moment and enjoying the Finger Lakes. From the big lakes of Seneca and Cayuga to pristine little Canandice and Hemlock, the lakes are scenic treasures carved into the high plains of central New York. They're carved deep, too. Seneca is over 600 feet deep, one of the deepest lakes in the United States, and was used to test submarines in secret during World War II.

The Finger Lakes are full of parks and waterfalls. The Letchworth Gorge in Letchworth State Park (716-493-3600) is 17 miles of steep-sided gorge, punctuated by three spectacular waterfalls. Camping is available, and some cabins; reservations are needed (800-456-CAMP). Another beautiful falls is found near Trumansburg in Taughannock Falls State Park (607-387-6739). The falls is thin, from a small stream, but 215 feet high, higher than Niagara, and set in a huge bowl that has been cut by the stream over thousands of year. You can hike down to the base of the falls, but it's a long way back up.

Watkins Glen State Park is a mile-and-a-half hike through a wonderland of stream-carved rock, waterfalls, pools and potholes, tunnels and stairways (607-535-4511, closed December through April). Watkins Glen also has the International Race Track (607-535-2481, www. theglen.com), which hosts the NASCAR Winston Cup and a number of Sports Car Club of America races.

Over on Keuka is Hammondsport, home of aviation pioneer Glenn Curtiss, who founded his aircraft company there. The Glenn H. Curtiss

Museum, on the south edge of town (8419 Route 54, 607-569-2160), is in the former hangars of the company. It's an interesting mixture of air-plane, motorcycle, boat, and automobile museum, and well worth an hour or two.

The Finger Lakes are also known for the birth of the great social movement of women's rights and as the home of Harriet Tubman. Tub-man, born in slavery in the South, escaped to freedom in the North. But she decided to go back and bring out more slaves to freedom. Trav-eling the Underground Railroad, she brought over three hundred slaves north. Tubman settled in Auburn after the Civil War, her work done. The home is open for tours (180 South Street, 315-252-2081).

The women's rights movement began in Seneca Falls in 1848, when Elizabeth Cady Stanton put an announcement in the local papers for a discussion on the rights of women. Three hundred people showed up, and a movement was begun. The Women's Rights Visitor Center and Women's Rights National Historic Park celebrate the movement (136 Fall Street, 315-568-2991).

Agriculture is big in this area, where the wide, flat land supports dairy and hog farming, fruit trees, and big fields of buckwheat. Birkett Mills, in Penn Yan on Keuka Lake, is the world's largest processor of this odd little fruit, and sells buckwheat products in a retail shop (163 Main Street, 315-536-3311, www.thebirkettmills.com). There has been a migration of Amish farmers to the area, escaping high land prices and tourists in Pennsylvania, so keep an eye peeled for their horse-drawn buggies as you travel the roads.

A more specialized agriculture is what the Finger Lakes are best known for these days: viniculture. There are forty-five wineries in the Finger Lakes, which account for 85 percent of New York's 30 million gallons of annual wine production. The wineries are here because of the microclimates of the lakes and the drainage of the glacial soil. The huge quantities of water in the lakes heat slowly in summer, then cool slowly in winter, moderating the temperatures on the shore. Also, the steep slopes allow cold, denser air to drain down to the lakes, particu-larly on Cayuga Lake's precipitous shores, avoiding frost on the grapes in the winter.

When the wine's on the table, who cares about cold air drainage? Take a break from beer and tour some wineries while you're here. You can just keep an eye peeled for the Wine Trail signs around Cayuga, Seneca, and Keuka, and drop in on one as the mood strikes, or you can plan a trip with the help of the Finger Lakes wineries website, www.fin-gerlakeswineries.com. If you want it all done for you, guided packages are available from the Finger Lakes Winery Tour Company for groups of any size (www.fingerlakeswinerytours.com, 585-329-0858).

Wine, waterfalls, buckwheat. . . . Who could ask for more? I could, and I do: Where's the beer?! Coming right up. Just a quick note first, for geographical purists. I've expanded the Finger Lakes region a bit to the east to take in the two breweries in Cooperstown. Otsego isn't one of the Finger Lakes, but it is beautiful and glacial. Similarly, I stretched things a bit west to take in Ellicottville Brewing . . . but I don't really think anyone will mind.

Brewery Ommegang

Route 33, Cooperstown, NY 13326
800-656-1212
www.ommegang.com

BREWERY OMMEGANG

Where to begin with Brewery Ommegang? There's so much to cover, and so little space, and Don Feinberg and Wendy Littlefield are so passionate, that we'll never make it. I'll try to summarize.

Don and Wendy were married and living in Belgium, and having the time of their lives. They had discovered Belgian culture, Belgian food, and Belgian beer, and thought that this would be a great product to sell in the States. For over ten years, they imported Belgian specialty beers under the name Van Berg and DeWulf ("Because Feinberg and DeWulf sounded more like an accounting firm," Don noted), starting with Duvel and adding beers like Scaldis, the Boon lambics, and Dupont's saisons.

Then in 1997, they surprised everyone and opened Brewery Ommegang. "If the import business had been bigger," Don explained, "I would have been happy. Inherently, we didn't want to brew. We just wanted to say a very simple, stupid thing: We went to Belgium, we got married, we had a good time in Belgium, we saw things we didn't see

Beers brewed: All beers brewed on the premises. Year-round: Hennepin, Rare Vos, Ommegang, White. Seasonals: Cave-aged Hennepin. There are also "special editions," beers that may be one-offs or special batches, like the Three Philosophers beer they did for a Real Beer Page contest. Note: Don Feinberg pronounces his three beers' names just as they look: Ommegang ("OH-muh-gang"), Hennepin ("HEN-uh-pin"), and Rare Vos ("rare vahss").

here. We want to share. It's kind of like a photo album for us. Our original plan was that the brewery was to help the imports, to be a stepping-stone to the imports."

They were already in Cooperstown for the town's rare blend of rural quiet and relative sophistication. The area's hops-growing heritage was intriguing, and there turned out to be substantial Belgian roots in the area as well. Real roots, too: Don told me that the yellow flowers that cover the hill behind the brewery are a Belgian weed that got here as a stowaway in a ship's ballast. The site they picked is south of town on the east bank of the Susquehanna: a former hops farm. "Where else could we put it?" Wendy asks.

The brewery is gorgeous, a spotless white building with the look of a horse barn. "It's based on a farmhouse schema from Belgium," Don told me. "The center is where the family lives and does business. One wing is for the farm animals and hay, the other wing is for machinery." So in the middle are the offices, on the south end is the brewery, and on the north end are bottling and the warm cellar.

The Pick: This isn't easy when there are only four beers, all from the same brewing tradition. I love drinking Rare Vos in large, quaffing quantities, the kind of drinking it was made for. Hennepin and the new White are wonderfully refreshing at any time of year. But my love has to go to Ommegang, the eponymous beauty that is so beguiling with a wide variety of the foods I love, and equally so all by itself, resting in its own named goblet. The chocolate-dark fruit lushness of this beer is delicious, and it's equally at home on the shaded banks of the Susquehanna, with a reflective mood by the fire, or shared in an intimate moment. It's that good.

That means it's finally time to talk about the beer. Ommegang's beers are all of Belgian stylistic origins. They rely more on yeast and spices for their flavor. There's a small wooden box in the brewery, like a jewelry box. It holds the spices used in brewing these beers. Don laid them out for me: "Put that in your hand and smell it," he said. "That's star anise. Orange peel. Cumin. Ginger. Coriander. That's our palette. Here, this'll blow your mind." He picked out something like a peppercorn. "It's a little bit hot, right? Sort of fruity, almost like a spiced plum? Paradise grains, it's a pepper.

"Now, why would you put pepper in beer?" he asked. "If you think about this kind of quality against something malty, something sweet, now you're getting something refreshing, something alive, and most importantly, a beverage that can be a complement and not a protagonist."

Being complementary is terribly important, because they're crazy about beer and food here. They've started a chapter of the Slow Food movement that celebrates regional foods, they sell food in the gift shop (see the whole list of *stuff* they sell below), they host beer dinners all over the country.

Do they want beer to "be like wine"? The answer is a definite no. "All we're trying to do is expand the definition of beer. Something you drink with good food. Something you take as a present to friends at a dinner or a cocktail party. Something you age. These are definitions we would like to add."

They work at these other angles. The beers come in 12-ounce bottles, but also in 750-milliliter corked and caged bottles, which make an impressive gift. They've demonstrated how well the beer ages with the Cave-aged Hennepin, aged in Howe Caverns for ten months. The aged beer is smoother, with a honeyed aspect. I had a two-year-old brewery-aged Ommegang that was an amazingly expanded beer. "But," Don told me, "don't write, 'You must wait two years to try Ommegang!' That's going to kill my sales!" No problem: Don't wait! Because it's really good fresh, too.

Oh my, I'm out of room, and I've got so much more to write about. You'll want to know how the beers are "warm-aged" for three weeks before release (and how they're first packed into plastic cartons for ventilation during the aging, and then repacked in cases for sale). I haven't told you about the marvelous yeast (picture Don pounding on the tank during our interview, shouting, "People don't understand that this is an *animal*, an animal that works for us!") or the brewery's fantastic festivals (giant puppets, Belgian flag throwers, live falconry exhibits, and lots and lots of *frites* (Belgian french fries) and waffles). There's so much to see, and taste, and hear, and experience—wait: experience. There is one more thing I have to tell you.

Some years ago, I asked Don to justify the costs of his imported beers. "How much are you willing to pay for a beer experience?" he countered. And that's exactly what he and Wendy have created here on the bank of the Susquehanna: a beer experience, just for you.

Opened: October 1997.

Type: Brewery.

Owners: Wendy Littlefield, Donald Feinberg, Brouwerij Moortgat.

Brewers: Randy Thiel (head brewer), Kevin Davis.

System: 40-barrel Falco-Steineker brewhouse, 5,000 barrels annual capacity.

Production: 4,350 barrels in 2001.

Tours: Daily tours, October through May, noon to 5 P.M.; Memorial Day through September, 11 A.M. to 6 P.M.

Take-out beer: The three main beers—Ommegang, Hennepin, and Rare Vos—are available in 12-ounce, 750-milliliter, and (occasionally) 6-liter bottles. There may also be special editions and test beers, such as the Cave-aged Hennepin or Three Philosophers, usually available in 750-milliliter bottles.

Food: Ommegang is not a restaurant, but it does have a lot of food available in the gift shop, which is a celebration of both the local area and . . . er . . . *Belgianosity.* You can find local cheeses, sausages, and mustards (made with Ommegang beer); you'll also find Belgian chocolates, waffle mixes (including the hard-to-find pearl sugar you need for authentic Belgian waffles), jellies, fruit spreads, cookies, candies, and so on. There are also cold juices and bottled water, so you can take your beer and sausage and cheese and have an impromptu picnic. The gift shop also has lots of Belgian cookbooks, tour guides, beer books, Belgian music, and a number of Tin-Tin and Asterix illustrated books (my kids love the Tin-Tin books). There's also the usual brewery assortment of gear and glassware, which is broader in this case: It includes branded Belgian glassware from Littlefield and Feinberg's beer import company, Van Berg and DeWulf.

Special considerations: Kids welcome. Handicapped-accessible.

Parking: Large lot behind the brewery, just drive right through the building and turn right.

Lodging in the area: The White House Inn, 46 Chestnut Street, 607-547-5054; Overlook B&B, 8 Pine Boulevard, 607-547-2019. There are two state parks in the area that offer camping: Glimmerglass State Park, on the northeast corner of Otsego Lake, and Gilbert Lake State Park, near New Lisbon, west of Milford, where there are also cabins for rent. Campsites and cabins can be reserved by calling 800-456-CAMP or at www.reserveamerica.com.

Area attractions: Ommegang itself is quite an attraction. They host a number of annual events, including the "Belgium Comes to Cooperstown" festival in July, the one with the waffles and *frites* and Belgian flag throwers, a fascinatingly athletic and beautiful experience. The giant puppets (and more waffles) are at Ommegang's annual birthday party in October, the (what else?) Waffles and Puppets Festival. Check the website for dates and other events.

The baseball attractions are listed on p. 168, but there's a lot more to Cooperstown than just baseball. This is, after all, *Cooperstown,* as in James Fenimore Cooper; the town was founded by his father. Cooper's books *The Deerslayer* and *The Pioneers* are set here. **Otsego Lake** is Natty Bumppo's Glimmerglass, and you'll find references to the books in the area, just as the reader familiar with

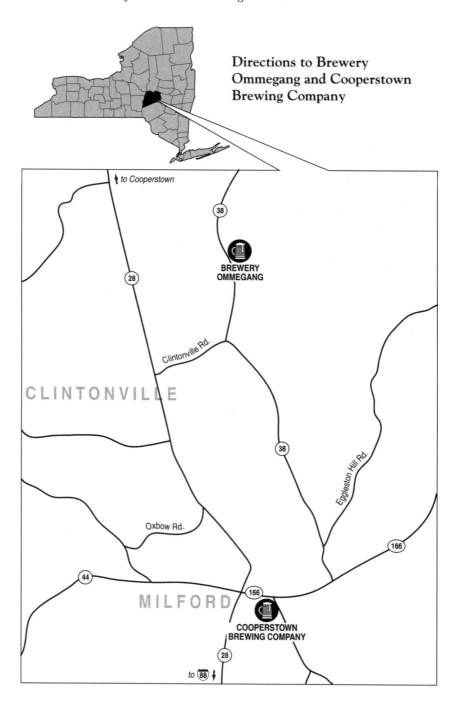

Directions to Brewery Ommegang and Cooperstown Brewing Company

Cooper's work will find many familiar vistas and vantages even today: The rock at the south end of the lake, right by the source of the Susquehanna, is one, and Hawkeye's cave can still be found up on the eastern shore of the lake.

The Farmer's Museum is on what is known as the Fenimore Farm, a farm that was owned by James Fenimore Cooper. Now it is a farming museum, with over twenty-three thousand artifacts that are displayed in the Main Barn exhibits, a re-created nineteenth-century village, and a working farm with heritage vegetables and breeds of livestock (open April through November, 1 mile north of Cooperstown on Lake Road, 888-547-1450). *The Fenimore House Museum* (607-547-1700) is just across Lake Road from the Farmer's Museum and is stuffed with folk art and Native American art: flat art, sculpture, and practical crafts, one of the best collections in New York. *The Glimmerglass Opera,* a semi-open-air opera hall (Route 80 by the lake; box office is at 18 Chestnut Street in Cooperstown, 607-547-2255), puts on ambitious programs that have greatly pleased the critics. Ommegang's beer cellar is a very popular tourist attraction: *Howe Caverns,* near Cobleskill, is a huge system of immense caves, so big that weddings have taken place in them. There is an elevator and a boat ride on an underground lake.

Other area beer sites: Wendy gave me an interesting list of restaurants with good beer selections. *The Autumn Cafe* in Oneonta (244 Main Street, 607-432-6845) is an excellent place to start your exploration of the area, a favorite of the college faculty in town. Good drafts, Ommegang and Belgian bottles, and a relatively large wine list accompany an interesting menu. Also in Oneonta are the *Italian Kitchen* (66 Church Street, 607-432-2776) and its upscale sister restaurant, *Stella Luna Stazione* (58–60 Market Street, 607-433-7646), both serving innovative Italian food and Ommegang beers. The tiny *Alex and Ika Restaurant* is over in tiny Cherry Valley (11 Main Street, 607-264-9315) and they're only open three days a week, but they have an extremely adventurous menu and a powerful little beer list. *The Blue Mingo Grill* at Sam Smith's Boatyard (6098 State Highway 80, Cooperstown, 607-547-7496) is right on the water; you can bring your boat up and dock. You can also see the more traditional beer listings on pages 168 and 169.

Cooperstown Brewing Company

110 River Street, Milford, NY 13807
607-286-9330
www.cooperstownbrewing.com-ctownbrew

Let's get one thing clear right away: Cooperstown Brewing Company is not in Cooperstown. It's down Route 28 in Milford. But it's not Stan Hall's fault, and he's hardly keeping it a secret, with a beer named Pride of Milford on the market. "We had property in Cooperstown," Stan told me, somewhat wearily. "But the town wouldn't allow a production business." He laughed. "No one makes anything in Cooperstown except baseball bats. We'd sell more if we were there, but Milford is great."

It's Cooperstown's loss. Stan and his family make good beer, some great beer, and proudly put vintage baseball-related labels on them. Most of the bars in Cooperstown are happy to serve the Halls' beers even if they wouldn't let them make it there. They also serve the beers from the other brewery "in" Cooperstown, Brewery Ommegang, which is located on a beautiful back road between the two towns. The two breweries get along fine, by the way, and sponsor a Brewery to Brewery Run every year.

Stan and his son-in-law Daniel Barry chose the Pugsley Partners brewing system, the Peter Austin brewhouse that uses the proprietary Ringwood yeast. "We visited Pugsley, DME, the whole gamut," Stan said. "We liked this because it was very hands-on and they offered a lot of support. We haven't had a problem since we started, and we still keep in touch with Alan Pugsley."

The building was an old milk station, where the dairy farmers in the region would bring their milk for trucking to dairy or cheesemaker. "We liked the tile floors and good drainage," Stan pointed out. "We did as much work as we could ourselves: plumbing, carpentry, wiring. We went

Beers brewed: All beers brewed on the premises, year-round: Old Slugger Pale Ale, Nine Man Ale, Benchwarmer Porter, Strike Out Stout, Back Yard IPA, and Pride of Milford Strong Ale.

The Pick: It's not just because I like Stan Hall that I picked the beer with his picture on it, the Pride of Milford Strong Ale. The Pride has become my favorite Cooperstown beer over the past two years, a big beer that showcases the beautiful character of the Yorkshire yeast. It's malty, cookie-sweet, and touched with the fruity esters and Ringwood nuttiness I love. Well named, this one.

through a hundred tubes of caulk in one day sealing up the building to keep the wind out."

They didn't plan to do quite so many different beers, but demand drove seasonals to year-round status. Truth is, they didn't plan to bottle them, either, but quickly realized that New York distributors just weren't interested in a draft-only brand at that time. They came up with a barely used bottling line Boston Beer had bought as a pilot and used once. It fits snugly in the western bay of the building, and I can only imagine what bottling days must be like.

The brewery flagship is Old Slugger, the brand you see most often in bars. (The ballplayer on the Old Slugger labels and taps is the famous Golden Age player Nap Lajoie.) The pale ale pours a reddish gold color; "That's the color beer should be," Stan remarked as he tapped a glass for me. Benchwarmer Porter joined Old Slugger in the year-round roster as a regular dark beer, then the tourists coming through kept asking for a lighter beer. Stan came up with Nine Man Ale, a light golden ale.

If you visit at the right time, you'll see the hop vines growing on the building. This area was once the country's hops center before cultivation moved west. Stan's grandfather was a hops farmer, and he's followed that to a small degree. The Cascade and Willamette hops growing on-site are used as finishing hops in Cooperstown's Backyard IPA, a nice local touch.

Take a look at Pride of Milford, the brewery's 7.7 percent strong ale. It's a beautiful beer, but it's the label I want you to notice. That smiling face is Stan Hall in a high school picture. The beer and the label were a Christmas surprise for him that the rest of the family slipped into the production schedule. Again, it proved so popular that it "moved up to the majors," and I'm glad it did.

This is one of the most quiet and laid-back tours on the circuit. Stan lays it out for you, then sits back and lets his beer do the talking. Wise man, it's an articulate brew. Stop in, get him to sign your book, and maybe he'll autograph his label for you, too.

Opened: April 1995.
Type: Brewery.
Owners: Stanley Hall, Jewel Hall, Sandra Hall Barry, Henry Schecher III.
Brewer: Daniel Barry.
System: 20-barrel Peter Austin brewhouse, 3,120 barrels annual capacity.
Production: 1,800 barrels in 2001.

Tours: Seven days a week, hourly from 11 A.M. to 5 P.M. (no tour at noon).

Take-out beer: Bottled beer available in singles, six-packs, twelve-packs, gift packs, and cases, half and quarter kegs.

Special considerations: Kids welcome. The World Series Sarsaparilla is a favorite of my son. Handicapped-accessible.

Parking: Plentiful parking at the brewery.

Lodging in the area: The restored and splendid Otesaga Hotel is high-end, but worth it, 60 Lake Street, Cooperstown, 800-348-6222; Tunnicliff Inn, 32–36 Pioneer Street, Cooperstown, 607-547-9611; Leatherstocking Lodge, 4909 State Highway 28, south of Cooperstown, 607-544-1000; the Lake Front Motel serves an excellent fish fry in its restaurant, 10 Fair Street, 607-547-9511; Stony Brook Motel is an older motel with a huge front porch and a quiet location, 232 Main Street, Richfield Springs, 315-858-9929.

Area attractions: *The Baseball Hall of Fame.* This is it—the reason Cooperstown draws people. And it's fantastic. I will admit, I'm not a big baseball fan, but I loved this museum (25 Main Street, 607-547-7200). It is America's pastime, and this is American history. Want more sports? *The National Soccer Hall of Fame* (18 Stadium Circle, Oneonta, 607-432-3351, www.soccerhall.org) is an ambitious project that young soccer players will love. Not just a museum, the Hall of Fame features the "Kicks Zone," a combination of computer simulations and hands-on, feet-on, heads-on challenges to get your game up.

Back in Cooperstown, the *Chief Uncas* is docked down the hill from the Hall of Fame. This trim little wooden boat was brought to the lake by the Busch family as their private excursion vessel. Now it runs regular tours, and is a perfect way to see the lake in an hour-long narrated cruise (607-547-5295). *The Leatherstocking Historical Railway Society* runs the Cooperstown–Charlotte Valley Railroad from Milford to Cooperstown through the beautiful Susquehanna Valley. Not only is it scenic, it's a great way to beat the parking in Cooperstown, an easily walkable town. There's also a "Blues Express" on Friday and Saturday evenings, featuring live bands and a full bar. The depot is right behind the brewery (607-432-2429).

Other area beer sites: *The Elm Inn* is up toward the middle of Milford (104 East Main Street, 607-286-9903), and it reminds me of some of my favorite country hotel bars in Pennsylvania. Not too fancy, not hurried at all, just friendly, relaxed bar company with a tap or two of hometown beer. *The Doubleday Cafe* has one of the smallest bars I've seen, only eight stools, but there's good food (great breakfasts, by the way) served in this attractive brick-walled space, with Old Slugger on tap, and Cooperstown and Ommegang beers in bottles. *"The Pit"* (34–36 Pioneer Street, 607-547-9611), as the basement bar in the Tunnicliff Inn is known locally, has two Cooperstown beers on draft, a classic back bar and wooden-door coolers, and a low ceiling. *The Bold Dragoon* (49 Pioneer Street, 607-547-9800) is refreshingly *normal*. There's not a bunch of baseball stuff here, just Old Slugger, Saranac, and Genny Cream. A good place to hide when you've finally had enough of baseball.

Wagner Brewing Company

9322 Route 414, Lodi, NY 14860
607-582-6450
www.wagnervineyards.com/wag2_brew.html

There are a few drives I really enjoy. One is rolling down through Franconia Notch in New Hampshire, through the steep, dark valley and along the mountains. Route 28 through either the Catskills or the Adirondacks is a roller-coaster ride, in and out of shadow, roaring down the valleys and winding up the grades. One of the best is Route 44 from Carter Camp through the Appalachians to the turnoff to Woolrich in the northern tier of Pennsylvania, a road that does everything but loop the loop.

Driving in the mountains is great. But few things are finer than running over the highlands between Cayuga and Seneca Lakes on a bright, sunny day with puffy, white cumulus overhead and a brisk wind buffeting through your window. You can see for miles across the farmland, the lakes tease you with distant vistas, the sky is the limitless blue of your childhood.

As if that weren't enough, there's a brewery up here, too. The Finger Lakes are best known for

Beers brewed: All beers brewed on the premises. Note: The brewery is Wagner Brewing Company, but the beers are bottled under the Wagner Valley brand. Year-round: Dockside Amber Lager (GABF Gold, 1998), Mill Street Pilsner, Grace House Honey Wheat, Seneca Trail Pale Ale, Captain Curry ESB, Caywood Station Oatmeal Stout, Sled Dog Doublebock (TAP NY Gold, 2002). Seasonal: Sugar House Maple Porter (TAP NY Silver, 2002).

vineyards, and rightly so; 85 percent of New York's wine comes from here. But one of the vineyards, Wagner, decided to add another string to its bow and brought Andrew Cummings in to start a brewery. William Wagner has a little something for everyone at this spot southwest of Lodi.

So does Andrew. He came to Lodi in March 1997 to install Wagner's HDP brewhouse and was persuaded to stay on as the brewer. It was a lucky move for Wagner's. He's a gifted brewer who's been crafting and perfecting a fairly wide range of ales and lagers to his own high standards. Chances are you've never had them or even heard of them, but that might be about to change.

"We've hired a salesman," he told me, "and he's heading out into upstate and the Hudson Valley." The brewery is really a separate entity from the winery, despite the obvious proximity. "All we really share is the steam plant and the forklift," said Andrew. The one thing he doesn't want the winery and the brewery sharing is yeasts, which would have a nasty effect on both products. Proper precautions are in place to prevent wandering yeasts.

The interesting thing to observe is the other thing the brewery and the winery share: the customers. Andrew learned early that wine people do *not* like hoppy beers; it's a range of flavors and aromas they're not used to, and they perceived them as unpleasant. "Wine people tend to like the bigger, more complex beers," he noted.

That's probably why his Sled Dog Doublebock went from being a seasonal to a year-round beer, and then became the best-seller, possibly a first for an American brewery. "They like it," Andrew says of the wine people who drift over to the brewery and try the doublebock. "It can and does age well, a lot of people like the sweeter beers, and some of them like it because it's 8.5 percent ABV." Party on, wine folk!

Contrary to intuition, there have been no fruit beers made here yet. I didn't really expect a brewer with standards like Andrew's to crank out a quickie fruit-essence-in-light-ale sparkler. He's working on something much more ambitious: grape- and cherry-infused pseudo-lambics, an homage to the spontaneously fermented beers of Belgium. He gave me a sample of a cherry that I'm supposed to cellar for a year. He's thinking like a wine guy already.

Directions to Wagner
Brewing Company

Take the drive, make the stop, and don't forget your wallet. You'll want to take some of these home for your cellar.

Opened: August 1997.
Type: Brewery.
Owner: William Wagner.
Brewer: Andrew Cummings.
System: 20-barrel HDP brewhouse, 3,500 barrels annual capacity.
Production: 690 barrels in 2001.
Tours: The tasting room, which includes a self-guided tour of the brewery, is open Monday through Saturday, 10 A.M. to 5 P.M.; Sunday, noon to 5 P.M.
Take-out beer: Half-gallon growlers, six-packs and cases of 12-ounce bottles. Pints and pitchers are also available for immediate consumption.

Special considerations: Cigars not allowed. Kids welcome. Handicapped-accessible.
Parking: Large on-site lot.
Lodging in the area and area attractions: See page 175.
Other area beer sites: Other than the brewery, if you're in Lodi, you
pretty much have to go somewhere else for a good beer. Like the
Crooked Rooster in Watkins Glen (303 North Franklin Street,
607-535-9797) for its beer selection, great open-air dining, and pub
atmosphere. I'm also going to stick in two Keuka Lake bars just
because they rule and I can't put them anywhere else. *The Village
Tavern* in Hammondsport (30 Mechanic Street, 607-569-2528)
has a fine tap selection and good bottles, as well as an exceptional
array of Finger Lakes wines and great food. *The Switzerland Inn*
(1249 East Lake Road, 607-292-6927) doesn't have any of that, and
the beer's boring except for Guinness. Okay, they do have really
good pizza. But the place is wonderfully atmospheric, and the view
of the lake from the dock is great at night, and the staff and the
patrons are friendly. Places like that should be shared. Andrew recommends the **Inland Reef** in Geneva (500 Hamilton Street, 315-
789-2704). See the Ithaca bars, too: pages 175 and 176.

Ithaca Beer Company

606 Elmira Road, Ithaca, NY 14850
607-273-0766
www.ithacabeer.com

Ithaca Beer Company is a romantic story of microbrewing. Not romantic in the sense of hearts and flowers—at least, not that I know of—but
in the sense of a romanticized idea of a small brewery being integrated
with the community and doing things the way they want, combining
art and brewing and fun. It all started really small and really local, and
it grew in a way that is wonderfully Ithacan.

Dan Mitchell was tending bar in Ithaca while attending Cornell
part-time. Cornell's getting to be a real beer school, by the way: It was
the school where the Coors men traditionally got their engineering

degrees, and it's developing a Vinification and Brewing Technology Laboratory, with two pilot breweries at the Geneva campus. Anyway, Dan saw the way people took to the beer at the Chapter House, saw the success of its fling with craft brewing, and decided he'd give brewing a shot.

His first thought was for a brewpub, but if there's one problem in Ithaca, it's parking. A microbrewery doesn't have the immediate cash flow of a brewpub, but there's a way around that: contract brewing. Dan signed up to have his Ithaca Beer brewed by Steve Dinehart's Chicago Brewing Company.

It was not a happy decision. Ithacans are kind of particular about using the town's name on a product not made right there, so there was resistance to the words "Ithaca Beer" on the labels. The only Ithacan thing about the beer was the smiling face of Cayuga Lake on the labels, done by Ithaca graphic artist Jeff Miller. But more to the point, Dinehart was not up to the rough and tumble of Chicago's beer business, and Chicago Brewing folded in 1997.

Beers brewed: Year-round: Amber Ale, Nut Brown Ale, Pale Ale, Apricot Wheat Ale. Seasonals: Anniversary Stout, Flower Power IPA.

The Pick: I really liked the Anniversary Stout and hope it gains the popularity it deserves. It's rich and obviously an ale, with estery notes perking off it (like so few stouts achieve). This is luscious stuff. Day to day? The Nut Brown is the way to go. It's sweet and creamy, smooth and drinkable, everything you could want in a British-style brown ale.

Mitchell realized he had to bring his beer home. He rounded up some investors and opened a brewery in December 1998, with Jeff Lonvel as the brewer. Actually, Dan and Jeff were the entire brewery for a while, with Jeff brewing and Dan making sales calls and deliveries in his pickup truck.

That's when everything really came together. Ithaca liked the local production idea, and word spread quickly. Jeff started a homebrewing club that met in the brewery, figuring that would help create a wider, better-educated clientele (it also created a market for homebrew supplies in the brewery gift shop). Art began popping up in the brewery, as part-timers on the bottling line wanted to liven up the cinder-block walls.

Then art began appearing on the barrels themselves. Gift shop operator/tour guide/woman-of-many-hats Amanda Eckler explained that the kegs were painted for a very simple reason: "There are a lot of these kegs being used by small breweries and homebrewers. We painted them so people would know right away that they were ours. A lot of the unique things we do are really just necessity."

Four year-round beers is hardly unique, but it's a necessity if you want to sell mixed cases. Ithaca's Nut Brown is the big seller, accounting for 45 percent of sales, but the other three beers are solid performers

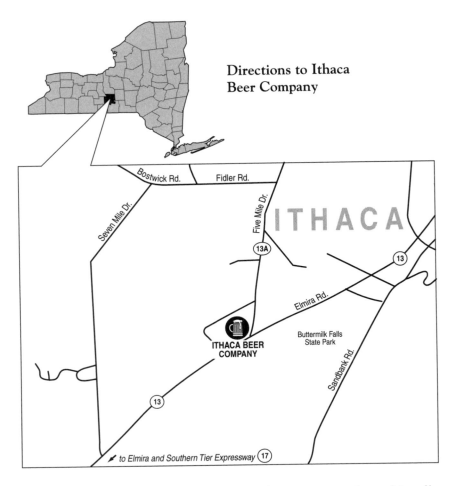

Directions to Ithaca Beer Company

as well. Jeff has started to stretch a bit with some seasonals, and I really like the direction he's taking. The Flower Power IPA jumps with East Kent Goldings aroma and was a big hit with drinkers; the Anniversary Stout, my Pick, is deliciously rich, and defiantly an ale, possessing the alefruit so infrequently found in stouts.

Coming home was the right thing to do for Ithaca Beer. Come visit, take one of Amanda's tours, and you'll agree.

Opened: December 1998.
Type: Brewery.
Owner: Dan Mitchell.
Brewer: Jeff Lonvel.
System: 20-barrel Criveller brewhouse, 8,000 barrels annual capacity.

Production: 2,000 barrels in 2001.

Tours: Tuesday through Saturday, 11 A.M. to 6 P.M.

Take-out beer: Six-packs, cases, growlers, and quarter and half kegs. Homebrew supplies are also for sale.

Special considerations: Kids welcome. Handicapped-accessible.

Parking: On-premises lot.

Lodging in the area: Holiday Inn Downtown, 222 South Cayuga Street, 607-272-1000; Super 8, 400 South Meadow Street, 607-273-8088; La Tourelle Country Inn, 1150 Danby Road, 607-273-2734; Taughannock Farms Inn, 2030 Gorge Road, Trumansburg, 607-387-7711.

Area attractions: Ithaca is very much a college town. You see students and faculty everywhere, and their needs and desires are reflected in the town's offerings. Of course, they have nothing to do with **Ithaca Falls,** a striking waterfall that plunges through the town from the corner of Falls and Lake Streets. On the other hand, the **Sciencenter** (601 1st Street, 607-272-0600) is all about the Cornell engineering and science people who built a lot of the exhibits: a camera big enough to stand in and learn about lens and focal lengths, an oversize open-backed combination lock that shows how these mysterious things work, powerful magnets. Cool stuff. **The Commons** is very college, several blocks of pedestrian area dotted with fountains and plantings. One of the best attractions is **Moosewood** (215 North Cayuga Street, 607-273-9610), a world-renowned vegetarian restaurant. Don't expect haute cuisine: Moosewood is simple and natural and reasonably priced.

  Bellwether Cidery is up on the western shore of Cayuga (1609 Trumansburg Road/Route 96, Ithaca, 607-27-CIDER) and seems to be a natural for this book. Bill Barton makes apple and pear ciders that are not the sweet soda-poppy stuff you'll find most places. Take a trip up and sample; you'll be impressed. This is good stuff.

Other area beer sites: I can't tell you how many people I know who have told me, unprompted, that the **Rongovian Embassy to the U.S.A.** (1 West Main Street, Trumansburg, 607-387-3334) is "the best #*%&! bar in the world!!!" I have to admit, it's one hell of a bar. Good beer, but that's just the start. Great Mexican food, fantastic live music, wild decor, and an authoritatively solid bar . . . and you still don't get it. It's the vibe, a vibe that has lasted for thirty years. Go get some. **The Chapter House** would have been in this book a few years ago (400 Stewart Avenue, Ithaca, 607-277-9782). It had a brewery (and was linked to the seminal Vernon Valley brewery, like Ramapo Valley and Hyde Park) and made what was by all reports a killer blonde doublebock. But the Chapter House's brewing equipment is gone, and now it's just fifty-one taps of great imports and craft-brewed beer, knowledgeable staff, and a solid beer-hall atmosphere. **Maxie's Supper Club and Oyster Bar** (635 West State Street, Ithaca, 607-272-4136) is mostly about great eats, but the beer selection's no slouch. Ommegang for dessert, anyone?

Custom Brewcrafters, Inc.

93 Papermill Street, Honeoye Falls, NY 14472
585-624-4386
www.custombrewcrafters.com

Mike Alcorn was telling me about how he started Custom Brewcrafters: "My original idea, way back when, was to make good beer for Rochester." Mike feels as though he was lured to Rochester under false pretenses. He was working (and drinking great beer) in California, and when he came to the Flour City to interview, he happened to stay in the hotel that had the now-closed Shannon brewpub on the first floor. "I thought that was normal here," he said. "So I moved." The awakening was sudden and disappointing.

Mike persevered until 1994, when he figured it was time to leave the corporate life. "My first thought was brewing," he said. What he came up with was, in the reaction of Institute of Brewing Studies president Dave Edgar, "an original idea." Custom Brewcrafters (CB) makes 7.5-barrel batches of over fifty different unique recipe beers for sale under private labels by taverns and restaurants. That's original, all right.

I don't believe any other brewery in the country is doing this. There are brewers who make private labels, but nowhere near this many, and not as the main thrust of their business. It's incredible, and it's a tribute to Mike's sales abilities that he was able to put the idea across to such a notoriously conservative bunch as tavern owners. But they've lined up in Rochester and in Buffalo, to the point where CB had to open a refrigerated storage area in Buffalo to handle the volume.

How does it work? Head brewer Jason Fox talks over the beer with the tavern owner, then goes and formulates it, does a test batch, and sends it out. That sounds simple, but consider that those beers really do taste different, and then consider that Jason Fox is working with only one yeast, an ale-lager hybrid of British origin. "I use a lot of different fermentation regimens," he said earnestly, referring to the use of various fermentation temperatures and temperature cycles. He also has a malt room bulging with specialty malts and a rainbow of hops.

"I like my beers to be clean," Jason said, and from what I've tasted, he hits that mark. Even the NoCeeMe malt liquor he brews for the California Brew House in Rochester is clean. At 7 percent and full of corn and Saaz hops, the NoCeeMe is surprisingly bitter and full in the mouth, truly unlike any beer I've ever had. Likewise with the Jeremiah's Anniversary Amber, a rye amber beer with big Mt. Hood hops aroma and a crisp rye-tinged finish: another cleanly drinkable, tasty beer.

Actually, he's brewed a lot of them. As Mike Alcorn said, "It keeps the brewing interesting to keep all those beers constant. I figured that would be a drawing point for brewing talent." He laughed. "What good brewer wants a simple job?"

Jason is a good brewer. For example, look at on-premises sales. CB is tucked away on a back street in a small, out-of-the-way town, yet it does 25 percent of its business in growler sales. It's a testimony to the quality and variety of the beer. "People have made it a regular stop," Mike said, "some from an hour away. We can't sell by the glass, so we just give samples and sell growlers."

Beers brewed: All beers brewed on the premises. Custom Brewcrafters has two year-round beers on their house label that are always available at the tasting room for growler sales: CB's Private Stock English Pale Ale and CB's 19th Hole Ale. House label seasonals: Christmas Ale, St. Paddy's Irish Red, Spring Fever Bock, Raspberry Wheat, Hop Harvest (a single hop varietal stock ale), Wee Heavy. The rest of the beers they make are all at the different accounts in Rochester and Buffalo, and they are all different beers; Jason and Mike swear to it and showed me the file of formulations. A randomly chosen two taps of these beers are always on at the tasting room. The best way to see what's where is to go to the Custom Brewcrafters website, where all the accounts with unique beers are listed, with addresses and beer descriptions. Finally, the Hogan's Park Avenue Ale won GABF Bronze in 1998, and Silver in 2000. You'll find it at Hogan's Hideaway, 197 Park Avenue, in Rochester (585-442-4293).

You can tell the habitual growler guys. They're the ones drinking out of the nice little glass sampling mugs, a step up from plastic cups for regulars (and beer writers). It's another original idea, from a microbrewing maverick.

Opened: August 1997.

Type: Brewery.

Owners: Mike and Luanne Alcorn.

Brewer: Jason Fox. Assistant brewer, Jeff Snell.

System: 10-barrel Criveller brewhouse, 3,000 barrels annual capacity.

Production: 1,900 barrels in 2001.

Brewpub hours: The tasting room is open for sampling and growler sales Monday through Thursday, 5 P.M. to 8 P.M.; Friday, 3 P.M. to 8 P.M.; Saturday, 11 A.M. to 6 P.M.; and Sunday, 12 P.M. to 5 P.M.

Tours: Saturday and Sunday at 1, 2, 3, and 4 P.M.

Take-out beer: Growlers, half kegs, 5-gallon kegs.

Special considerations: Cigars not allowed. Kids welcome. Handicapped-accessible.

Parking: Large on-site lot.

The Pick: Obviously, I couldn't taste more than a fraction of the beers Custom Brewcrafters makes. The one I kept running into, though, and enjoying a lot when I did, was the Inferno Pod Ale they do for the Pizza Plant in Buffalo. You'll also find it in Rochester at Monty's Krown; at least, I did. It's a sizzling IPA, very crisp and piney, but not over the top with it, and manages a complex synergy of hop effects that is more interesting than the solid straightforward slam of some IPAs. The light golden color is appealing as well, visually lightening your perception of the beer.

Directions to Custom Brewcrafters, Inc.

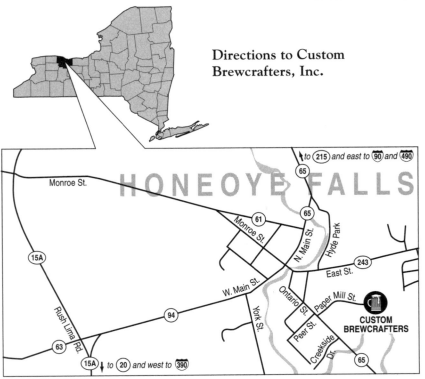

Lodging in the area: Microtel, 905 Lehigh Station Road, West Henrietta, 585-334-3400. See Rochester suggestions, page 11.

Area attractions: The falls (it's Honeoye *Falls,* remember?) is rather stunning, visually, particularly when the water's high. It's no Niagara, but it's worth a look. But it you want to see *real* falls, **Letchworth State Park** is not far (see page 158, 585-493-3600). There's also a bunch of golf courses nearby; Mike Alcorn said that Monroe County has more golf courses per capita than any other county in the country.

Other area beer sites: *The Brewery,* in Honeoye Falls, is a bar, not another brewery, though they do have four CB beers on tap (8 West Main Street, 585-624-7870). See the beer suggestions for Rochester, pages 12 and 13.

Market Street Brewing Company and Restaurant

63–65 West Market Street, Corning, NY 14830
607-936-2337 (BEER)
www.936beer.com

When I was a boy, we used to vacation in New York's southern tier. My father was an earth sciences teacher, so when we went to Watkins Glen, we got lectures on the sedimentary rock formations and erosion that created the glen and never got near the racetrack. When we visited Corning, we toured the Corning glassworks and never, ever went into any of the Market Street bars.

Okay, I was twelve. But Market Street has an amazing collection of bars for such a small town and such a relatively short street, and it's not even what it used to be. There were times in the 1800s when there were ninety bars in three blocks of Market Street, and Corning claimed the highest concentration of booze joints in the world. C'mon, Dad, that's educational!

Beers brewed: All beers brewed on the premises. Year-round: Mad Bug Lager, Brisco Bridge Blackberry Lager, Wrought Iron Red, Pot Belly Pale Ale, D'Artagnan Dark. Seasonals: Hibernator 12-Grain Wheat Ale, German Wheat, Oktoberfest, Nut Brown Ale, Stout, Christmas Ale.

I was making up for lost time when I dropped in on the Market Street Brewing Company. It was snowing, it was a Tuesday, but Market Street was humming. Uncle Don and I had already sampled our way up and down the street, visiting the convivial people at Boomers', Wet Goods, the Glory Hole, and Pelham's Upstate Tuna Company.

Pelham is Pelham McClellan, who is also behind Market Street Brewing Company (his wife, Theresa, actually owns it). He's been a restaurateur for years, and also a homebrewer. That's how the Upstate Tuna Company came to have such an impressive beer selection, the best for miles around.

The Pick: Surprise—I liked the Brisco Bridge Blackberry! You just don't see blackberry beers that often, and that intrigued me. It's a berry I like, the beer was crisp and tartly quenching, and I don't know what more you could want from a fruit beer. It's an honest one, not just another "I did it because we gotta have a fruit beer" raspberry wheat ale.

"The Tuna Company came first," Pelham said, "in 1989, and that's what got us into beer. We started an around-the-world beer club at the Tuna and found people really liked them, and that there was a market. I was already a homebrewer and restaurateur." He chuckled. "Being insane as we are, we decided to open a brewpub."

The Criveller brewhouse sits right in the front window on Market Street. Once you come in, the bar's the first thing you see, and that's how this beer lover likes it. You can walk in and belly right up to it. Check out the chalkboard tap selections behind the bar and order up your pleasure. You also have the option of sitting out on the patio or up on the second-floor deck when the weather's nice.

Things can get pretty crazy when the weather's nice. Outdoor recreation has assumed an ever-greater importance in the town's tourism fortunes, from the LPGA Corning Classic in May right through the fall foliage season and on into an expanding winter sports season. The glassworks is still a major draw, thanks to a $50 million renovation of the museum and exhibits. Market Street can get downright crowded as tourists stroll the tree-lined sidewalks, thronging the art-glass galleries, shops, and restaurants.

Pelham sees the seasons in beer turnover. "Winter is slow, regardless of what you do," he said. "There's just not a lot of visitors." Beers sometimes stay on tap longer than he'd like. "But in summertime, it's tough to keep up with demand with a 7-barrel system." Fast turnover is good news for you, of course.

And do bring the kids. I've always liked the glassworks and it's even more fun these days. But when you're done, hop the shuttle bus and take them to Market Street!

Opened: June 1997.

Type: Brewpub.

Owner: Theresa McClellan.

Brewer: Pelham McClellan.

System: 7-barrel Criveller brewhouse, 550 barrels annual capacity

Production: 365 barrels in 2001.

Brewpub hours: Seven days a week, 11:30 A.M. to 1 A.M. (closed Sundays, November through April).

Tours: On request.

Take-out beer: Half-gallon growlers.

Food: Watch out—they like their spicy food hot here, so when you order the buffalo wings or shrimp, or the jerk chicken sandwich, be sure you're ready for it. Even the bowls of bar mix are fiery. But the signature MSBC Soup, a cream-based soother of artichokes, rosemary, and lemon, is a surprisingly mellow mouthful. There's an international flair to the menu, with Thai scallops and cream curry pasta, but you can also get the house-made beer sausage and a regional favorite, bumble-berry pie, a kitchen-sink kind of fruit pie.

Extras: Live music Friday nights (call for schedule); patio and deck seating in season.

Special considerations: Cigars allowed on the deck, in season. Kids welcome. Vegetarian foods available. Handicapped-accessible, except the upstairs deck.

Parking: Plentiful street parking, except on weekends. Large parking garage behind brewpub.

Lodging in the area: Rosewood Inn, 134 East First Street, 607-962-3253; Comfort Inn, 66 West Pulteney Street, 607-962-1515; Gate House Motel, 145 East Corning Road, 607-936-4131.

Area attractions: The big attraction is CMOG, the **Corning Museum of Glass** (151 Centerway, the route is well marked, 800-732-6845, www.cmog.org), and it is some attraction. There are glassblowing demonstrations going on constantly, and there is a huge gift shop with everything from bags of marbles to year's-salary glass artwork; not a place where you'd want to let a three-year-old run loose. The museum has interactive exhibits, displays of glassware going back thousands of years, and interfaces with the working Steuben glass factory. There's a lot to see. You can hop a shuttle bus every twenty minutes to get over to Market Street, maybe for lunch (and a beer). Even though Corning Glass has recently taken a whupping

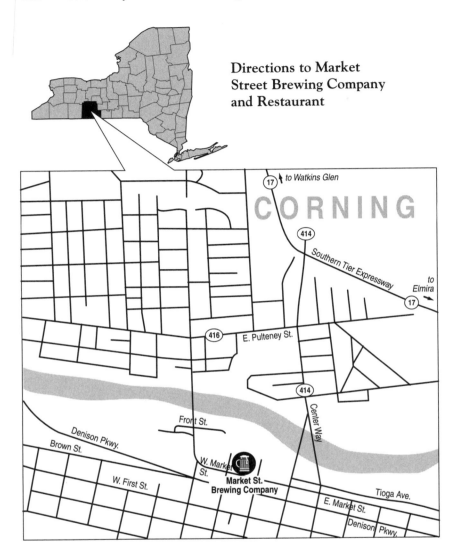

Directions to Market Street Brewing Company and Restaurant

in its glass fiber telecommunications business, it remains committed to this small town and this museum, and that's rare these days.

Look, up in the sky! You might see any kind of interesting air machine. You're near Elmira, one of the great soaring centers of the world, and not far from Horseheads, newly home to the **National Warplane Museum's** collection of World War II and Korean War airplanes. **The National Soaring Museum** (Harris Hill Road, 607-734-0641) is a look back at the history of soaring (gliding), with a rare collection of antique sailplanes. You can get a ride in a sailplane at the **Harris Hill Soaring Center** (beside the museum, 607-734-0641), a twenty-minute silent thrill over hills and fields. **The National Warplane Museum** recently relocated from Geneseo to Horseheads (17 Aviation Drive, Elmira-Corning Regional Airport, 607-739-8200). The museum's collection includes warbirds like a B-17, PBY-6A Catalina, MiG-17, MiG-21, B-25, B-26, and a number of Korean-era Navy jets, all at or intended to enter flight-ready status.

Other area beer sites: **Boomers'** (58 West Market Street, 607-936-1408) is right across Market Street from the brewpub (in fact, all these bars are easily walkable from the brewpub) and serves up Bellwether Hard Cider and Ithaca Nut Brown Ale; it gets a little crazy when the students crowd in, but it's very nice in the early evening. **Wet Goods** (54–56 West Market, 607-936-4493) is an old hotel, and you can feel the age in the stone walls, iron spiral staircase, and the copper bar. A pretty good beer selection makes it good, live music on Fridays makes it interesting. **The Glory Hole** (74 East Market, 607-962-1474) gave me a start until I remembered it was a glassblower's term for the hot orifice of the kiln where molten glass is dipped for blowing. There's glassblowing memorabilia on the walls and ceiling, and there are good taps behind the bar, the best tap selection in town. Be sure to read the "glass blower's misconceptions" in the men's room; it's priceless. **Pelham's Upstate Tuna Company,** Pelham McClellan's first endeavor in Corning, is across from the Glory Hole (73 East Market, 607-936-8862). The taps aren't much, but this is easily the best bottled beer selection in town, with some excellent imports and micros. The bartender told me the building used to be a Tucker automobile dealership.

Ellicottville Brewing Company

28A Monroe Street, Ellicottville, NY 14731
716-699-2537
www.ellicottvillebrewing.com

Here's a good marriage of town and brewery. Ellicottville used to be a lumber town, harvesting the timber from the surrounding hills. But as the timber ran out and the leisure budgets of people grew, Ellicottville reinvented itself as a year-round vacation destination, with a great array of stuff to do on long weekends. Two ski areas right outside of town benefit from abundant snow, which they supplement with lots of snow-making capability. There are trails for hiking, mountain biking, and cross-country skiing, and a festival of some sort almost every month of the year.

Ellicottville Brewing is right in the middle of that, a fun place that goes year-round, indoors and outdoors, and participates fully in all the festivals. As soon as weather permits, you can take your beer out in the beer garden and relax in the cool, shaded, flagstone area, surrounded by potted plants and trees. If it's cold, stay inside and feel the camaraderie of that *après*-ski glow . . . whether you're *après* or not.

And if you don't feel like hanging around the brewpub, if you've got fun stuff to do back at your rental space that maybe requires a little privacy, that's no problem. Take a keggy, and the brewpub goes with you.

Keggy? Ellicottville Brewing is the "home of the keggy," a little self-contained, self-pressurized, self-tapping keg that holds about a case and a half of beer. "We license them from a German outfit," owner Peter Kreinheder explained. "We do a big business in them with weekend guests." All it needs is refrigeration; all you need is a deposit . . . and a thirst. When you're done with the beer, take the keggy back to the brewpub for your deposit. It's bigger than a growler, and you don't even have to clean it.

Beers brewed: All beers brewed on the premises. Year-round: Lennon's Light Lager, Two Brothers Pale Ale, Ellicottville Amber Ale, Buchan Nut Brown. Seasonals: Belgian-style Wit, Allegany Alers Stein Beer, A-big-ale's ESB (Extra Special Baby), Black Jack Dry Stout, Winter Lager.

The Pick: For a brilliant execution of a concept I'd like to see more brewers take up, I give the nod to the Black Jack Dry Stout. What's the concept? This beer is only 2.9 percent ABV, yet it is jet black and full of flavor, a real pintful of beer. I've often said of stronger beers, "Wow, this beer is really good; I wish it were lower in alcohol so I could drink it all day!" With Black Jack, you can.

Kreinheder sells beer in keggys to outside accounts, along with regular kegs. He sells quite a bit, actually; about half the brewery's output. I've seen Ellicottville beer as far away as Rochester, the Catskills, and even at festivals in Pennsylvania.

It's a good thing, too, because it would be a shame to keep beer this good penned up in one little town. If you're a regular Newcastle drinker, don't try the Buchan Nut Brown: It's a lot more flavorful, full of malty, nutty goodness, and you'll never be happy with Newkie again. If you're a hophead, don't look for an IPA: The pale ale is plenty hoppy, stuffed with piney Cascade aroma. ("We did an IPA once," Peter told me. "It would have burned your mouth.") The Pick, the Black Jack Stout, is black, full of flavor, creamy with nitro, and you'd never know it was only 2.9 percent ABV. Now that's an all-day sucker!

If you're going to Ellicottville, come prepared. Bring your skis, bring your stumpjumper, bring your snowboard, bring your hiking boots. Most of all, bring your thirst. You're going to need it.

Opened: September 1995.

Type: Brewpub and brewery.

Owner: Peter Kreinheder.

Brewer: Andy Arena.

System: 10-barrel Bohemian Brewing system, 1,200 barrels annual capacity.

Production: 950 barrels in 2001.

Brewpub hours: Seven days a week, 11:30 A.M. to midnight. Closed in April and first two weeks of May.

Tours: By appointment.

Take-out beer: Growlers, quarter and half kegs, and "keggys."

Food: You'll find typical American grill food here, with a nice flair to the daily specials. The menu is largely sandwiches and salads, but there are steaks and pasta dishes as well.

Extras: There's a beautiful beer garden on the side, with a flagstone floor and lots of shade from trees and vines. Rooms are available for private parties.

Special considerations: Cigars not allowed. Kids welcome. Vegetarian foods available. Handicapped-accessible.

Parking: Parking is tough in high season. The street fills up fast, as does the lot across the street. Luckily, it's a nice town for walking.

Lodging in the area: Inn at Holiday Valley, 716-699-2537, www.holiday valley.com (Holiday Valley also offers a rental agency for condo, townhouse, and country home rentals); R&R Dude Ranch, 8940

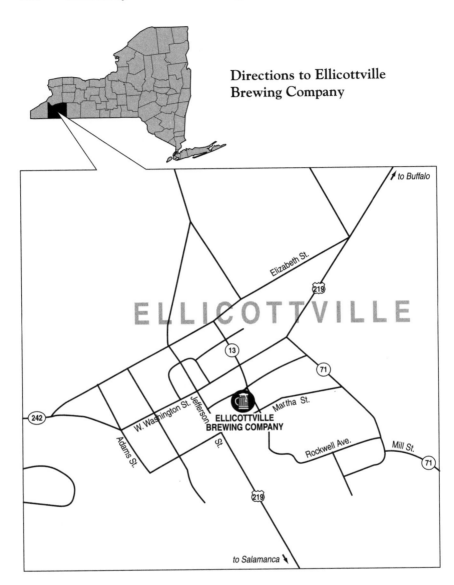

Directions to Ellicottville Brewing Company

Lange Road, Otto, 716-257-5663, www.rrduderanch.com; Best Western Bradford Inn, 100 Davis Street, Bradford, Pennsylvania, 800-344-4656.

Area attractions: Ellicottville used to be all about lumber, and you can still see some of that. But now the town's about having fun. There are outdoor activities year-round, starting in winter, with an average of 180 inches of natural snow in a season. You can cross-country ski, snowmobile, and ice-fish at nearby **Allegany State Park** (716-354-9121). In the summer, you can swim, fish, bike, and camp and there are game lands for hunting as well. Check out the skiing at **HoliMont** (half a mile west out Washington Street/Route 242, 716-699-2320, www.holimont.com) during the week; it's members-only on the weekends. There's a 700-foot vertical drop, "wall-to-wall, top-to-bottom" snowmaking, and a half-pipe and terrain park for snowboarding. **Holiday Valley** (Route 219, 716-699-2345, www.holidayvalley.com) offers a 750-foot vertical drop, fifty-two trails (thirty-nine set for nightskiing), and two half-pipes and terrain parks for snowboarders, as well as an eighteen-hole, par-seventy-two golf course, swimming, and mountain bike riding in the summer. **The R&R Dude Ranch** in Otto (716-257-5663) offers horseback riding, biking, four-by-four trails, hunting and fishing on over 300 posted acres with stocked streams, and a very outdoorsy atmosphere. For a different kind of brewery-related experience, check out the **B&B Buffalo Ranch** on Horn Hill Road, 716-699-8813, a few miles from the slopes at Holiday Valley. It's a working ranch with a gift shop, a sampling room, and three hundred head of buffalo, fed partly on Ellicottville's spent grain.

There are events year-round in Ellicottville: the Christmas Stroll in December, the Winter Blues Festival in January, the Mardi Gras Parade and Winter Carnival, the Jazz Festival in May, July's Summer Arts Festival, Taste of Ellicottville in August, the Rock 'n' Oldies Weekend in September, and the biggest of all, the Fall Festival in October when tens of thousands of leaf peepers descend on the town. Get dates and details at www.ellicottvilleny.com, or call the Chamber of Commerce at 800-349-9099.

Other area beer sites: The Gin Mill is right on the main drag (20 Washington Street, 716-699-2530), and it's a winner. Check out the old Bevador cooler dressed up in Rolling Rock livery, the mounted game trophies, and those old wooden beer coolers behind the bar: This is cool. There are plenty of video games to entertain the kids while you check out the sixteen taps and eclectic spirits selection. **Madigan's** (36 Washington Street, 716-699-4455) is open seven days a week for lunch and will get you grooving with live R&B on weekends. Look for the soup can. **Mother Murphy's** (26 Monroe Street, 716-699-4533) is a comfortable joint next to the brewpub on Monroe Street that serves a great jar of Guinness and a wide selection of spirits. The soup's pretty good, too.

Regional Foods—Spiedies, Weck, and Wings

This half of my tribute to New York's regional foods focuses on foods that definitely originated in New York: Binghamton's spiedies, western New York's beef on weck, and the enormously popular Buffalo wings.

There's no brewery in Binghamton anymore, since the unlamented Parlor City Brewing closed, but the Ale House ("The Beer Joint of Your Dreams") is right there in Vestal (3744 Vestal Parkway, 607-729-9053, www.beerjoint.com) with plenty of good beer, so there's an excuse to head down there for the local delicacy: spiedies. To make a spiedie, you marinate chunks of meat (originally lamb, but now everything from chicken to venison) for at least twenty-four hours in a marinade of olive oil, vinegar, garlic, and a variety of spices. Thread the meat on small skewers, grill it, and lay the skewers on a slice of Italian bread. Grip the meat with the bread and pull the skewer out, and devour a deliciously spicy and juicy spiedie.

The beauty in this is that spiedie marinade—lots of different spiedie marinades—are readily available in local supermarkets, along with precut meats and even premarinated meat chunks. You can get your marinated meat and skewers, drop by Sam the Beer Man (1164 Front Street, Binghamton, 607-724-5225) and pick up some cold Saranac, then go home and fire up the grill: Spiedie feast coming right up! Just don't expect to find them more than 20 miles from Binghamton. As an enthusiastic (but poorly spelled) e-mail to a spiedie tribute website put it, "I am never gonna leave Broome County becuases I cant get fresh speedies anywhere else." The only other place I have found them is at Troy Brewing, and they're pretty good with a pint of Trojan Pale Ale.

Move west, and you get into beef on weck territory. Let me describe a classic weck house. First, it is old, but it is not decrepit; it is established. It is dark, not dark like a nightclub, but dark with subdued lighting and wood paneling. The dining room is quiet but for the conversation of the guests and perhaps some soft background music—swing, or Mantovani.

The waitresses, the bartenders, and the busboys all wear whites, not the dingy whites of a labcoat, but the crisp, proud whites of a Navy uniform. The waitresses smile, but do not tell you their names. The bartenders are omnicompetent, but deferential to the counterman. The busboys are quiet, quick, and nimble. The counterman wears whites also, but ones that are even more impressive, with neatly rolled sleeves and a tucked tie. He is large and broad-shouldered, and he may have a mustache, and the mustache must be full. The counterman slices the beef.

The beef is large and steaming, and proudly displayed at the counter. It is a center-cut round roast, sliced with a razor-sharp carving knife, to order and only to order. It is juicy, and it is not tough. Once it is sliced and placed on the kümmelweck, pan juices are ladled over it—not so much that the roll is soaked, not so little that the roll is not moist. The kümmelweck is a roll the size of a large hamburger roll, and it is crusted with salt crystals on the outside and fresh and soft on the inside; it is made with caraway seeds. There is horseradish on the table, grated and not creamed, and it is hot and flavorful.

I don't know about you, but I'm drooling. What I've described is Schwabl's, at the corner of Union and Center, in West Seneca (789 Center Road, 716-674-9821), the best weck house I found in Buffalo, the home of weck. Schwabl's dates from 1837 (when it was a small brewery that started serving food with its beer), and the place has got it right. As for the beer these days, well, take my advice: Skip the so-so draft beer and get the draft birch beer, unless you're lucky enough to visit in the winter. Yes, I said lucky, in the winter, in Buffalo, because from December to February at Schwabl's, you can get a hot Tom 'n' Jerry in a little mug, a delicious hot whiskey, citrus, and thick meringue concoction that is just the thing for cold weather.

I know you're wondering when I was going to get to Buffalo wings! This is one New York food that has become popular everywhere, but not the way it is in its hometown. You can't go in a bar in Buffalo that serves food that doesn't serve wings. Can you have a bar in Buffalo and not serve wings? I asked every bar owner I met, and all but one said no. He said, "Sure, you can do it." Then he smiled and added, "For about two months. Then you'll be out of business."

Hot wings, mild wings, atomic wings, suicide wings, barbecue wings, garlic wings, I even saw Thai lemon grass wings on one menu. But as any wing aficionado knows, there's one place you have to go for wings in Buffalo, heck, one place in the world: the Anchor Bar (1047 Main Street, 716-886-8920, www.anchorbar.com). License plates adorn the walls, along with other knickknackery, and check out the full-size Ducani motorbike over the door. You're presented with a big, square bar in the front room. Sure, there's beer here, like McSorley's and Genny

Cream, but this is about *wings*. This is where wings were invented back in 1964.

The story's well documented elsewhere; suffice it to say that wings were a late-night invention for famished friends of the Bellissimo family, owners of the Anchor. Where the inspiration for celery and blue cheese dressing came from, I've no idea, but it was genius; they really do cut the heat of some of the more outrageous wings. The Anchor serves about 70,000 pounds of chicken wings a month, and it gets kind of crazy on July 29, which is Buffalo Wing Day in Buffalo.

But honesty compels me to admit that of the wings I've had, and particularly of the wings I've had in Buffalo, some of the very best were out at the Buffalo Brewpub (see page 227). They were a little crispy on the outside and greasy and tender on the inside, and the hot sauce coating was just this side of brutal. You can always tell good wings by the way their aroma spreads through the room when they're served; it's a tangy, nose-opening, vinegar-and-hot-peppers shock that wings without that right spunk just don't have. They're Buffalo's gift to a . . . well, we're not really a hungry nation, just a nation that wants something to eat with its beer.

Man, I'm hungry now. Let's go get a beer and some wings. But don't get any sauce on the book!

Lake Effect

N ew York is washed by three great bodies of water. The Atlantic's vastness stretches away from Long Island and New York Harbor, but in the north and the west, the vistas across the fresh waters of great Ontario and Erie are just as limitless to the human eye.

From Barker Brewing, way out in Fredonia by Lake Erie, to Sackets Harbor, at the eastern extremity of Lake Ontario, New York's breweries dot the land along the lakes. I've included cities like Rochester and Syracuse in this section because of the well-known "lake effect," the driving, moisture-laden wind that can bury these towns in snow.

Buffalo is the hinge pin of this territory, lake port and international gateway, situated on the Niagara River, which links the two lakes. Once a roaring dynamo of industrial energy, fed first by the Erie Canal and then by lake-borne commerce symbolized by looming grain elevators, these days Buffalo is largely an overlooked city, the butt of jokes (and most of the good ones are told by Buffalonians), and often a "drive-by" for people on their way to Niagara Falls or Toronto. I've lost count of how many times I drove through Buffalo before I finally got off I-90, had a beer, and looked around.

What I found made me curse my wasted opportunities. Buffalo is a friendly place, full of people ready to talk to travelers, and overflowing with historic and beautiful buildings from its glory days. The huge expansion of the city's street grid brought on by the Pan-American Exposition of 1901 left a legacy of long, open vistas. In the tighter confines closer to the lake, the Allenwood district is dotted with small clubs, art galleries, a variety of shops, and plenty of bars. Geeks will like the Colter Bay Grill's twenty-four taps (561 Delaware Avenue, corner of Delaware and Allen, 716-882-1330).

For the beer traveler, Buffalo is worth a stop if only to pay homage to the temple of bar food, the Anchor Bar (1047 Main Street, 716-886-8920, www.anchorbar.com), where Buffalo wings were invented. If feeling that way gets me in trouble with beer geeks, so be it; these zesty, eye-popping mouth-maulers taste just as great with an IPA as they do with a Bud, so enjoy. But be sure to try them at the Buffalo Brewpub, which makes some of the best, and gives you over thirty drafts to pair them with.

Niagara Falls is situated between the two lakes and is New York's biggest natural tourist attraction. The wisdom for years was that the Canadian side was more attractive for visitors, but the New York side is undergoing a major renovation and should be much more tourist-friendly. The beer traveler should nip over to the Canadian side, though, just to pick up some bottles of Niagara Falls Brewing Company's justly celebrated Eisbock at the brewery (6863 Lundy Lane, Niagara Falls, Ontario, 905-356-2739).

The Erie coast southwest of Buffalo is wine country, which can be fun for a change. The views along Route 5 through the lakeside vine-yards are worth the drive, especially when you know Barker Brewing's halfway along the coast, and you can always go a few miles farther down into Erie and hit Erie Brewing (1213 Veshecco Drive, 814-459-7741) and Porter's Pub.

East of Buffalo, you hit Rochester, Buffalo's big upstate rival in industry, culture, and prestige. At least, that's how Rochester sees it. How Buffalo sees it might be best expressed by the joke they tell about how it takes 25,001 Rochesterites to screw in the requisite lightbulb: one to put the bulb in and 25,000 to comment on how much brighter and prettier it is than the lightbulbs in Buffalo. Sibling rivalry! For the multitap fans, Rochester wins hands-down as the home of the Mac-Gregor's chain: The three Rochester-area MacGregor's alone have almost three hundred taps among them, and they're not repeats or mainstream lagers, either; they're interesting beers.

The average traveler may not be aware of Rochester's attractions, including the High Falls of the Genesee River, which makes a very impressive sight from the Pont du Rennes footbridge, just downstream of the falls. The footbridge leads right into the back lot of the High Falls brewery, though that is not the preferred entrance for visitors. The other, western end of the bridge leads to the Center at High Falls (60 Brown Street, 585-325-9810), an educational center built around the mills that have harnessed the power of the falls. The center also hosts entertainment and a regular laser and fireworks display in warm weather (call for schedule).

Known as Salt City for the brine boiled from Lake Onondaga, Syracuse is home to the rabid sports fans who worship the Orangemen at Syracuse University's Carrier Dome. It is also right next to the Onondaga

Indian Reservation, tribal center for the Iroquois tribes. Upstaters know this primarily as a place for cheap gas and smokes, but the Onondaga Reservation is a place of great natural beauty, as well as a bone of contention in treaty negotiations. There has been Indian unrest here in past years as the tribes work out their future with the state.

Syracuse is also home to Armory Square, one of the best concentrations of good beer in the whole state, or anywhere. Within four blocks you'll find Empire Brewing, Syracuse Suds Factory, Kitty Hoyne's Irish Pub (301 West Fayette Street, 315-424-1974), the huge spirits selection and great beer chasers at Awful Al's Whisky and Cigar Bar (321 South Clinton Street, 315-472-4427), and two wholly excellent beer bars, the Blue Tusk (165 Walton Street, 315-472-1934) and Clark's Ale House (122 West Jefferson Street, 315-479-9859). You can walk from Kitty Hoyne's to Clark's in less than ten minutes, though with stops of properly appreciative length, it could take you days.

The lake coast ends at Sackets Harbor, just south of the start of the St. Lawrence River and the Thousand Islands. This area is rich in history from both colonial days and the lake battles of the War of 1812. You can tour the Sackets Harbor Battlefield state historical site, where reenactors have an encampment every weekend in June and July (315-646-3634). You can also catch the ferries from Cape Vincent to Wolfe Island and then on to Kingston, Ontario, to see how the British did it at Old Fort Henry (800-437-2233), a fully restored fortress from the war that features daily parades of military drill and music.

New York's interior coastline is beautiful, dotted with parks and beaches and marinas. The people may complain about the weather—often overcast, tons of snow—but they're friendly and hard-working, and they make really good beer. Pick a spot and set sail for it.

Barker Brewing Company

34 West Main Street, Fredonia, NY 14063
716-679-3435
www.barkerbrewco.com

Way out on the edge of New York, past Buffalo even, lies the little college town of Fredonia. Unless you're a student, there are really only two reasons to stop in town: The White Inn, a famous restaurant and inn, was noted by Duncan Hines in his restaurant guide and has been a regional favorite for decades. The other is the Barker Brew Company.

Brewer-partner Joe Rogers and his beers are half the draw. He is fanatical about his beers and will research a style and mess with his formulation until he's happy with it. He was obsessing about the Scotch Ale when I was last there (before that, it was the ESB). "I'm going to make it more regularly," he confided. "It's an obsession. If it doesn't come out exactly the way I want it, then I have to live with it for the next couple weeks."

He then lectured me for ten minutes on how scotch ale was supposed to be brewed and how so few pros and homebrewers did it right. He talked about how he uses mostly Thomas Fawcett malts, from England's only family-owned floor maltings, even for his base malt. To be fair, it was an enlightening and fascinating lecture; Joe's an articulate and passionate speaker.

Unlike a lot of fanatical brewers, though, Joe makes beers that are quite accessible, not screaming hop monsters or huge head-knockers. Take the Scotch Ale as an example. It's malty but not heavy, and a deep, dark amber in color. There are layers of flavor that your tongue discovers as you sip, expand, and swallow, and not a touch of peat smoke in it, a bad habit of American brewers. Cookie sweet and not cloying, this is an easy-to-drink beer, though at 6.75 percent ABV you wouldn't want to have too many.

Beers brewed: All beers brewed on the premises. Joe renames his beers every time he puts a new batch on, purely by whim, so it's best to just go with style names. Year-round: Porter, Pale Ale. Seasonals: Scotch Ale, ESB, Brown Ale, Hefeweizen, American Wheat, Honey Blonde, Amber, Oatmeal Stout, Dry Stout, Irish Red. Some beers are available as real ale on a handpump.

He's a fanatic about some other things, too. I asked him what people did for fun in Fredonia, and he mentioned the outdoor recreation, particularly boating and fishing on Lake Erie. I asked if it was good fishing on the lake. He got a sudden gleam in his eye and rushed off without a word, leaving me with my glass of porter, mystified. Suddenly, the door behind the bar opened, and Joe slammed 3 feet of frozen muskie down on the bar. "I got *that* out of the lake," he said triumphantly. "Usually I catch and release, but he bit me on the ankle when I got him in the boat. I wasn't going to let that go by!" Now that's fishing!

The Pick: The Porter is always on and is great; I won't visit Barker without having a glass of it. But the ESB is a wonderful, very special beer, with a beauty to its every aspect that left me smiling. It is a beautiful beer to look at, an orange-amber color, and it has a nose of solid British malt and lightly citric, floral hops (Santiam, a new American strain that Joe really likes for this beer). The body is light but not skinny, the hop flavor is solid and just what the aroma promised, and the malt flavors are complex and drinkable. "Mostly," I wrote in my notes, "it tastes like *more*."

The other draw at Barker is the music series. It's all about jazz and blues performances, and the brewpub manages to get national touring acts to come to Fredonia. Barker is getting quite a name for jazz; people come from Buffalo, Erie, and even Cleveland for the shows. Surprisingly, one of the willing helpers in the community has been the local Anheuser-Busch distributor, who has been very supportive of things like the homebrew and blues competition-festival Barker organized in town. That's what small towns are all about.

The reputation and wide appeal of the beer and the music are driving the possibility of a second Barker Brew in the Buffalo area, a bigger place with more room for music and a bigger brewhouse. I asked Joe if he was looking forward to that, and he was ambivalent. "One of the good things about the small brewhouse is that the beer's always fresh," he said. "When you only have three and a half barrels to go through, it doesn't get a chance to get old."

And a batch you're not completely, obsessively happy with isn't staring you in the face for long, I guess. Joe's obsession is our reward.

Opened: April 2000; restaurant opened in 1994.
Type: Brewpub.
Owners: Bobbi Pike, Joe Rogers.
Brewers: Joe Rogers. Assistant brewer, Loran Peterson.
System: 3.5-barrel HDP brewkettle and dairy equipment, 300 barrels annual capacity.
Production: 250 barrels in 2001.

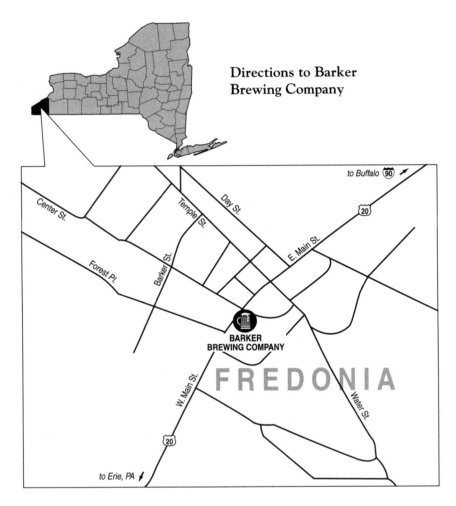

Directions to Barker
Brewing Company

Brewpub hours: Monday through Saturday, noon to 2 A.M.; Sunday opens at 3 P.M.

Tours: On request.

Take-out beer: 2-liter growlers.

Food: "A small-town restaurant has to be diverse," Joe Rogers says. "You can't afford to specialize." The sauces, salsas, and dips are all made in-house. They aim high, too: Take a look at the French-cut rack of pork with ancho chile and honey sauce, a stunning dish. There is a good selection of lake fish and seafood dishes, including a delicious fish fry with homemade slaw and potato salad. The white chili and blackened chicken salad are great for lighter meals, and there are a lot of great Mexican dishes made from passed-down family recipes. There are a number of innovative vegetarian dishes, and the kitchen is happy to prepare other dishes in vegan fashion. Finish up with a slab of Kentucky bourbon pie.

Extras: Serious live music, major jazz acts, and other college bands on a regular basis. Check the website for the jazz schedule, or call for all acts. There is a regular chess session on Sundays.

Special considerations: Cigars allowed at the bar. Kids welcome. Vegetarian foods available. Handicapped-accessible, first floor only.

Parking: On-street.

Lodging in the area: The White Inn, 34 West Main Street, 716-672-2103; Four Points Sheraton Harborfront, 30 Lake Shore Drive, Dunkirk, 716-366-8350; Comfort Inn, 3925 Vineyard Drive, 716-672-4450.

Area attractions: As Joe said, the fishing on the lake is great (wear sturdy boots!). The other draw in the area is the vineyards and wineries along the coast. Chautauqua is the largest grape-growing county outside of California. So where's all the wine from the 20,000 acres of grapes? Heh. Ever heard of Welch's? About 90 percent of the grapes grown here are Concords, headed for the Welch's plant in Westfield, which unfortunately does not offer tours. There are a number of wineries that do, though, including **Woodbury,** just outside of Fredonia (3230 South Roberts Road, 716-679-9463). You can find all the area wineries offering tours at the New York Wine and Grape Foundation's "Uncork New York!" website (www.nywine.com/winecountry/ lakeerie). Just driving along the coast on Route 5 is pretty scenic, too, on the right day. Just relax and enjoy.

Other area beer sites: Folks, there just isn't much else here that isn't a college bar full of smoke and mainstream lager, and you can find them on your own. However, you can always go a few miles farther, down into Erie and hit **Erie Brewing** (1213 Veshecco Drive, 814-459-7741) and **Porter's Pub** (123 West 14th Street, 814-452-2787).

Sackets Harbor Brewing Company

212 West Main Street, Sackets Harbor, NY 13685
315-646-2739
www.1812ale.com

Stephen Flynn is a native of the Sackets Harbor area who got out—way out, to southern California. He was writing software in a building that happened to be across from a brewpub. He had developed a taste for good wines in California, and good beer seemed like a natural jump from there. He got to know the owner and started thinking about running his own. "That's when I decided," Stephen told me, "to quit the rat race . . . for a bigger rat race: owning a business!"

He made his way back across the country, stopping in brewpubs as he went, and by the time he got to Sackets Harbor, he was ready. He set up shop in what was the old New York Central railroad depot, a waterfront property right on Main Street in this little resort town. Ulysses S. Grant may have once stood on the very spot; he was stationed at nearby Madison Barracks in 1852, though at that time, Sackets Harbor was considered a stark and frigid outpost.

The brewpub opened in 1996. Things went well, and Stephen soon got the idea to push one of his beers out the door: the War of 1812 Ale, a malty amber ale. He picked up accounts at bars and restaurants in the area, doing so well that the brewpub system couldn't keep up. For a while, 1812 Ale was contract-brewed at Middle Ages Brewing in Syracuse, then Stephen moved production to Mendocino Brewing in Saratoga Springs, where it remains in production in draft and bottle.

"I do the 1812 for the sales, but also for the exposure," Stephen explained. "It's in three thousand supermarkets and three hundred on-premises accounts; we've expanded into Rochester and Buffalo. People see 'Sackets Harbor' on every label, and it prompts some of them to visit. We get a lot of boaters from the lake cities, Toronto, Buffalo, Kingston." The marina right across from the brewpub's dock offers tie-ups for everything from kayaks to big sailboats.

Stephen believes in giving something back to the community, and you can tell that it's real with him, not just something that's good press for the business. He has a deal with a local bakery to make "beer bagels" and "beer bread" from the brewery's spent grain (with a portion of the sales going to the Children's Miracle Network). The Blues and Chowder Fest in the spring and the Oktoberfest in the fall are both benefit events.

That kind of responsible attitude, coupled with the success of 1812 Ale, were factors in Stephen's being named the 2000 Small Business Person of the Year for New York, and the brewpub's being noted as the Adirondack North Country Association's 2001 Small Business of the Year. Those kinds of awards are not easy for breweries to win these days, when the public impression of breweries is no longer so rosy.

Stop by, and you'll pick up on what Stephen's doing right. Sit at the bar and receive the smooth attentions of Mark Ralston, the brewpub's head bartender and Stephen's right-hand man. Try some of the biscuity 1812 Ale, or dive headfirst into a Sackets Harbor IPA, a fruit bowl of great hop flavor with a long hop finish. If you're having seafood, you should have a glass of St. Stephen's Stout, an eponymous brew that's smoky, roasty, and a bit on the rich side.

Look around at the brewpub, and imagine the depot as it was when people arrived in the 1800s to take carriages to the hotels. Take your beer down to the dock and watch the play of the sun- or moonlight on the waves. It's a long way from the hardship post Grant suffered through with his family, and I have to believe Grant would have enjoyed a glass or two of the brewpub's Grant's Golden if he'd had the chance.

Beers brewed: Bottled beers and some draft beer brewed at Mendocino Brewing. All beer served at the brewpub is brewed on the premises. Year-round: Lake Effect Lager, War of 1812 Ale, Railroad Red, Grant's Golden, St. Stephen's Stout. Seasonals: Adams Center Abbey, Alex's Apricot, Apple Spice Ale, Battlefield Brown, Black River Rye, Black Watch Scottish, Blackberry Ale, Blitzen Ale, Cranberry Ale, Dunkel Weizen, Featherhammer Maibock, Ginger Ale, Ginger Pear Ale, Heather Loch Beer, Independence Wheat, Maple Peach Ale, Millennium Beer, Old Style Alt, Ontario Octoberfest, Pickering Pale Ale, Pillar Point Porter, Pumpkin Spice Ale, Raspberry Wheat, Red White and Blueberry, Root Scootin Raspberry, Sackets Harbor IPA, Smoked Porter, Strawberry Blonde, Swashbuckler Hefeweizen, Watertown Cream Ale, and Winter Weizenbock.

Opened: August 1995.
Type: Brewpub and contract brewery.
Owner: Stephen Flynn.
Brewer: Stephen Flynn.
System: 7-barrel DME brewhouse, 750 barrels annual capacity.
Production: 750 barrels in 2001.

Brewpub hours: Hours vary with the season, and a bit with the manager's whim. In the summer, the place is open seven days a week for lunch and dinner, then the bar's open till "closing," which might run as late as 2 A.M. In the winter, it's open at 4:30 P.M. Tuesday through Saturday for dinner only, then till "closing," which might be as early as 10 P.M. if no one's in. Given the vagaries of the season in Sackets Harbor, you're best off calling ahead.

Tours: None.

Take-out beer: 2-liter and half-gallon growlers.

Food: The menu at Sackets Harbor changes often, but along with several shellfish "tap'petizers" and soups, you can count on some of chef Karen Cornish's innovative dishes appearing along with the salads, pizza, and pasta—grilled ratatouille salad, steak chimichuri (grilled Argentina-style, with black beans

The Pick: I'll bow to the inevitable: Let's pick the 1812 Ale. It's a good beer, malty and biscuity, with a nice dryness on the end that pulls you into the next sip. I have to admit, I like having this on tap all over the area. I also liked the Adams Center Abbey, a sweet and just a little funky dubbel-ish kind of abbey-style ale with lots of alefruit: peach, melon, a little orange.

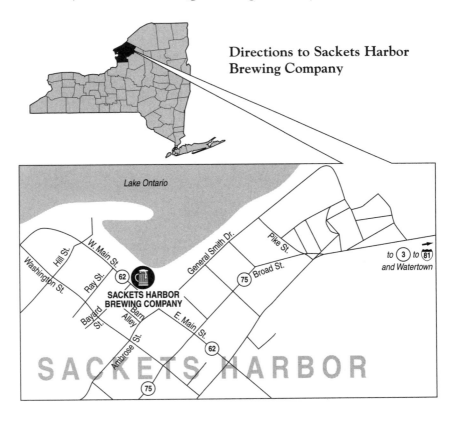

Directions to Sackets Harbor Brewing Company

and rice), and scallops, artichoke, and chorizo hash. There's also a more casual pub menu, served till 11 P.M. on weekends, with burgers, wings, nachos, and the like. You might want to get to Taco Tuesday, too: two tacos for $2 and $2 pints. All menu entries have suggested beer pairings.

Extras: Outside dining on the deck in summer; regular live music (call for schedule). The brewpub sponsors a popular annual Oktoberfest that brings in other New York brewers. They also participate in Sackets Harbor's Blues and Chowderfest, an annual celebration of clam chowder ("There's a *lot* of chowders!" Stephen said), with music, and all the other stuff that shows up at festivals like that. It's held the last weekend in April to benefit the North Country Children's Clinic. Call for dates and information for either event.

Special considerations: Cigars allowed. Kids welcome. Vegetarian foods available. Handicapped-accessible.

Parking: On-site lot, street parking, other lots on block.

Lodging in the area: Sackets Harbor B&B, 102 West Main Street, 315-646-1718; Jacob Brewster House B&B, 107 South Broad Street, 315-646-4663; Ontario Place Hotel (right next to brewpub), 103 General Smith Drive, 315-646-8000; Old Stone Row Country Inn, 85 Worth Road, Madison Barracks, Sackets Harbor, 315-646-1234.

Area attractions: Sackets Harbor itself is an attraction: Stroll its tree-lined streets and take in its historic homes and the stone buildings of **Madison Barracks.** As a border port, Sackets Harbor played a major role in the War of 1812, and markers are scattered about to note individual actions. You can get information about reenactments and other events from the **Sackets Harbor Battlefield State Historic Park Office** (505 West Washington Street, 315-646-3634). Get out on the lake and go fishing with Captain Bob Dick: The walleye, trout, salmon, and bass are waiting to taunt you (353 Pike Road, 888-232-2827, www.imcnet.net/mobydick). "Old McDonald has a farm . . . and it's in Sackets Harbor!" That's what the signs say, and it's true: **Old McDonald's** is a 1,200-acre working farm where kids can see pigs, cows, goats, sheep, horses, and even reindeer (North Harbor Road, just follow the signs, 315-583-5737). There is a **Farmers' Market** in town on Market Square on Friday afternoons, June through September. Call 315-646-1700 or 315-646-8174 for details.

Other area beer sites: **The Boathouse** is right next door to the brewpub in that Quonset building (214 West Main, 315-646-2092): It's a locals' hangout that never stops in the off-season. Stephen's other restaurant and bar, **Good Fellos** (202 West Main, 315-646-2345) is a wine bar, and it's a beauty, with a big, old brick pizza oven right in the front room. There's a lot of good wine, almost all available by the glass and carefully chosen with Stephen's California-trained palate, plus Guinness and Sackets Harbor beers. **The Lake Ontario Playhouse** (103 West Main, 315-646-2305, www.playhousecomedy.com) has a bar, a restaurant, a big comedy club that gets serious stars during the summer, and a bartender who knows how to pour a truly proper jar of Guinness.

Empire Brewing Company, Syracuse

Armory Square, 120 Walton Street, Syracuse, NY 13202
315-475-2337
www.empirebrewco.com

I'm sure you know people like Michael Hodgdon and Dave Katleski. They're the ones who always had paper routes, who sold the most candy in the fund-raiser and got the bicycle, who had parties in college and made money on them (but no one minded because the parties were so good). They were the ones your parents always looked at fondly and cast up to you as examples. You thought they weren't having any fun because they were always working.

Hey, guess what? Your parents were right, because now Michael and Dave are Empire Brewing and own two big, successful brewpubs. But no one minds, because the brewpubs are so good, and everyone's having fun, even Michael and Dave.

"Most American guys fantasize about owning a bar," Michael said, laughing. "We weren't any different. Dave and I had hosted parties and events in college to make money for school. After we got out, we stayed in touch and dreamed a little about doing that to make money for life."

Then in 1990, Michael took a job in Northampton, Massachusetts. "It was the first week I was there," he recalled, "and I wandered into this place called the Northampton Brewpub. It was cool, all the design in place, and the brew-house in sight. I walked up to the bar and ordered a beer, and got the whole story from the bartender. He knew all about the beer. It was a completely new experience, and I fell in love with it."

Hodgdon thought he'd found the right project for himself and Katleski. "The more I researched it," he said, "the more I saw that the revolution was under way in the West, and you didn't need a crystal ball to see that the East would follow. We educated ourselves and wrote a business plan, but it took four years to raise the money. No one knew what a brewpub was; we had no experience at all in brewpubs or restaurants. It was tough to find anyone who was willing to loan us money. I'd have liked to have been out there in 1992," he admitted, "but 1994 in Syracuse was the right place at the right time. It was exploding."

Empire Brewing Syracuse opened in the sub-sidewalk level of an old grocery warehouse that was being used as office space. "We called it the subter-ranean space," Michael told me with a chuckle. "It was a lot of square pegs in round holes from the perspective of fitting the kitchen and the brewery in there, but from a customer's viewpoint, it's warm and inviting." True; I love that low-ceilinged, stone-walled rathskellar look to the place; it has a feel like some of the old European house breweries. I keep hoping that someone's going to break out into song and the whole place will join in, harmonizing and thumping their glasses on the tables.

Beers brewed: Most beers brewed on the premises; some beers brewed at Empire's Rochester brewpub. Year-round: Skinny Atlas Light (GABF Gold, 1997, 1998, and 1999; Bronze, 2001), Amber Ale, Black Magic Stout (GABF Silver, 2000), Hefe-weizen (GABF Bronze, 1995). Seasonals: Purgatory Pale Ale, Downtown Brown Ale (GABF Bronze, 1998), Barley Wine, "various" fruit beers, Bock, Maibock, Doppelbock, Munchener Helles, October-fest, Platt Street Pilsner, Vienna, Schwarzbier, White Christmas, Berliner Weisse, Bodacious Blonde, Dunkel Weizen, Great Pumpkin Ale, Honey Ginger Ale, Gruit Ale, Heather Ale, Imperial Stout, Porter, Rauchbier, Red Mulli-gan, Rye Ale, Scotch Ale, and Winter Elixir. More will follow. "We brew about thirty differ-ent beers every year," Michael Hodgdon told me.

A lot of those glasses are filled with Skinny Atlas Light, Empire's most popular and most award-winning beer. "Skinny Atlas" is a refer-ence to nearby Skaneateles Lake and its namesake town. Don't let the "Light" blind you: This is a great kölsch-type beer, clean and soft, with a little twist of graininess and just a hint of alefruit and hops, delicate and subtle. It also won the gold medal at the Great American Beer Festival three years in a row, no small feat.

I asked Michael an awkward question: Syracuse versus Rochester, which is the better beer town? He hesitated, and I jumped in to remind him of the incredible concentration of great beer bars in Syracuse around Armory Square. "Armory Square is amazing," he said quickly. "With our place and the Blue Tusk right across the street, Awful Al's and Clark's, the concentration is there. But the sheer numbers are bigger in Rochester." Tough question, one I wouldn't want to be pinned down on!

There's no competition between the two brewpubs in the two towns. It's all cooperation toward the goals of good food, good beer, and good times, the goals Michael and David have been headed for over the past decade. Your parents always knew they'd make it.

The Pick: How to pick from so many?! First, don't overlook the Skinny Atlas Light. Kölsch is a delicate style, when done right, and this is a great quencher, particularly with Empire's spicier foods. But I can't help it: When faced with an array like this, I like to go with what I know, and that's the Black Magic Stout. It's a classic Irish dry stout, noticeably roasty in the nose and mouth, and just drinkable as hell. This one will wear out your elbow.

Opened: October 1994.

Type: Brewpub.

Owners: Michael Hodgdon, David Katleski.

Brewers: Andrew Gersten.

System: 7-barrel Pub Brewing brewhouse, 1,500 barrels annual capacity.

Production: 700 barrels in 2001.

Brewpub hours: Seven days a week, 11:30 A.M. to "closing," which varies depending on business; it's usually between midnight and 2 A.M.

Tours: By appointment only.

Take-out beer: 2-liter growlers, half kegs.

Food: Empire's menu shows a number of influences: southwestern, Asian, southern . . . it's best summed up as "eclectic." There are some New Orleans–flavored entrees, like the Big Mamou Platter of jambalaya, gumbo, and crawfish. Vegetarians will find a particularly good selection. For an appetizer, try the sesame tofu with Javanese vegetables, then fill up with the Bodega del Sol, a po' boy roll stuffed with grilled vegetables and cheese, or the big burrito, jammed full of vegetables, pesto, and red beans. Don't fret, carnivores: There are also plenty of burgers, chicken, and a 14-ounce New York strip steak.

Extras: Empire offers live music on weekends (call for schedule), and plenty of well-situated TVs at the bar.

Special considerations: Cigars allowed. Kids welcome. Vegetarian foods available (exceptional selection). Handicapped-accessible.

Parking: There are a number of reasonably priced lots and garages nearby; Armory Square is a popular destination.

Lodging in the area: The Dickenson House on James, 1504 James Street, 315-423-4777; Hawthorne Suites, 416 South Clinton

Street, 315-425-0500; Hotel Syracuse, 500 South Warren Street, 315-422-5121.

Area attractions: ***Armory Square*** isn't just about beer, although beer joints *do* dominate it, by golly. It's also got a bunch of shops—some counterculture-ish, some not—and restaurants and coffeehouses and all that. You can take a cruise on the Erie Canal with **Mid-Lakes Navigation** (800-545-4318); cruises go from four hours to three days. **The Erie Canal Museum** (318 Erie Boulevard East, 315-471-0593) is housed in the Weighlock Building, which is what it sounds like: a scale for weighing full, entire canal boats; fascinating mid-nineteenth-century technology. See some twentieth-century technology at the **Museum of Automobile History** (321 North Clinton Street, 315-478-CARS). Over ten thousand items celebrate the history of cars, trucks, and motorcycles, with plenty of the advertising that sold them to us: billboards, radio jingles, posters. Catch a game at ***P&C Stadium*** (1 Tex Simone Drive, 315-474-7833, www.skychiefs.com) and cheer on the Syracuse SkyChiefs, a Toronto Blue Jays AAA farm team. Syracuse hosts a huge free jazz festival in June and a blues festival in July (315-470-1910 for schedules).

Other area beer sites: Welcome to Syracuse, home to the Incredible Walkable Triumvirate of Bars. Start at the ***Blue Tusk*** (165 Walton Street, 315-472-1934), across the street from Empire Brewing. The Blue Tusk is simply awesome, easily one of the top-ten beer bars in the state: sixty-nine excellent taps, cask ale, great food, plenty of space, incredibly beer-savvy bartenders (they almost knew as much as I do!), a Belgian beer bar and cafe quietly tucked away in one end of the area, and thoroughly civilized and clean bathrooms. If you can tear yourself away, walk over to ***Awful Al's Whiskey and Cigar Bar*** (321 South Clinton Street, 315-472-4427), across from the Suds Factory and lose yourself in contemplation of hundreds of bottles of spirits. Come back to your senses and realize that there are some great taps of beer here as well, a big old humidor, and big couches and armchairs to relax in while you enjoy your smoke and whiskey. This is civilization. Then lever yourself up out of there and waddle down to ***Clark's Ale House*** (122 West Jefferson Street, 315-479-9859), where it's twenty-two taps and one sandwich (there actually are some other sandwiches these days, but for years it was roast beef or nothing, and it's still the best). Clark's has different beers than the Tusk or Al's, cask ale, fun bar games, a very cosmopolitan feel, and plenty of room for overflow upstairs.

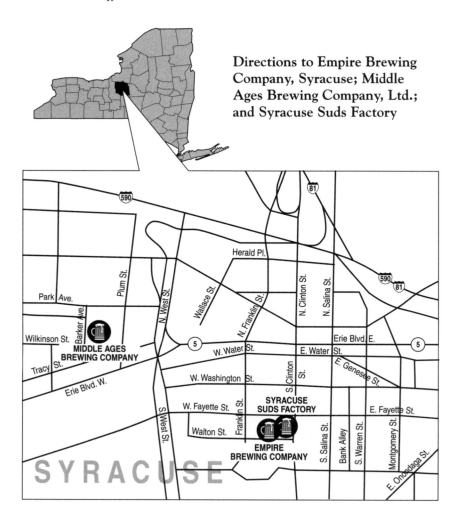

Directions to Empire Brewing Company, Syracuse; Middle Ages Brewing Company, Ltd.; and Syracuse Suds Factory

Three *great* bars, and they're not only in the same town, they're easily walkable. Syracuse rules!

You can also walk to **Kitty Hoyne's Irish Pub** (301 West Fayette Street, 315-424-1974), an Irish place with a great tap selection and some fantastic whiskeys. It's good-looking, too, with a double-sided backbar that serves both sides, a rare bit of bar architecture. **Coleman's Authentic Irish Pub** (100 South Lowell Avenue, 315-476-1933) gets rave reviews as an Irish joint, a friendly one with great Guinness pouring . . . and a full-featured little "leprechaun door" beside the main entrance. Cute. If you're really hungry, it's got to be **Dinosaur Bar-B-Que** (Franklin and

West Willow Streets, 315-476-4937) for a big chunk of deliciously barbecued meat done the right way: long and slow over hickory wood. That's barbecue; sauce is just sauce. Luckily, someone at Dinosaur is a beer lover, because there are good beers here, including the house Apehanger Ale made at Middle Ages. Parking is nearly impossible, but it's worth every single erg of hassle to eat here. And as if they didn't have it good enough here, there's a **MacGregor's** in Syracuse (253 East Water Street, 315-425-7740), lucky stiffs: plenty of excellent taps, good service, good beer knowledge, that's MacGregor's.

Middle Ages Brewing Company, Ltd.

120 Wilkinson Street, Syracuse, NY 13204
888-289-4250
www.middleagesbrewery.com

"Real ale."

If you know what that means, you're probably thirsty now. Real ale, or cask-conditioned ale, is how all beers used to be consumed: right from the barrel, unfiltered and "alive." The brewery fills the cask with uncarbonated, unfiltered beer straight from the tanks, with the live yeast still in it, doses it with a small amount of sugar or fresh wort, and hammers home the bung to seal the cask. The beer will come to peak condition in the cask as it waits at the tavern.

By the time the beer is tapped, it is lightly carbonated by a secondary fermentation done by the still-live yeast, fueled by the addition of sugar or wort. The cask has been sitting quietly, giving the yeast a chance to drop to the bottom of the cask. An ideal tapping will produce a clear glass of cellar-temperature (about 55°F), lightly carbonated ale that has a fresh, estery aroma and flavor that cannot be matched by any other method.

Beers brewed: All beers brewed on the premises. Year-round: Grail Ale, Syracuse Pale Ale, ImPaled Ale, Beast Bitter, Duke of Winship Porter, Old Marcus, Black Heart Stout, Highlander. Seasonal: Apricot Ale, Druid Fluid, Wizard's Winter Ale, Ye Olde Kilt Tilter, Triple Crown British Triple.

That's how they liked it in the Middle Ages, and that's how they like it at Middle Ages Brewing in Syracuse. Brewer-owner Marc Rubenstein and assistant Tim Butler brew their beer for bottling and for "regular" kegging, to be sure, but it's clear that their real passion is reserved for the lucky pints of their beer that will be served as real ale.

When I visited the brewery and sampled Marc's excellent line of beers, even though I praised them (and got a couple growlers to take along), he wasn't really happy until he had called the bartenders at the Blue Tusk, over on Armory Square, and set me up for a pint of cask-conditioned ImPaled Ale. "You don't have to have the cask," he assured me. "You can have whatever beer you want. But I'd really like you to try it."

The Pick: Let's go with the Big Beer: Druid Fluid. I mean, I like the ImPaled Ale just fine, and the Duke of Winship Porter's great, but sometimes you just gotta be a geek! Druid Fluid is powerful stuff, way too much malt, over-the-top hops, and that's the kind of beer we geeks love, because sometimes too much is just enough. Get some of this and age it, too: I had a two-year-old bottle I kept in my basement in the dark, and it was phenomenal.

As if I'd want anything else! The cask ImPaled Ale they served up at the Tusk was delicious, with the soft carbonation I've become fond of. The real beauty of cask ale is that the cool serving temperature and the lack of fizziness lets more of the hidden flavor of the beer come through.

And there's plenty of flavor in Middle Ages' beers. They're brewed with the Ringwood yeast, a proprietary strain supplied by Alan Pugsley of Shipyard Brewing in Portland, Maine. That's who Marc bought the brewhouse from. Ringwood is a heritage yeast, the kind used in classic Yorkshire ales in England, and it gives a beer a characteristic nutty flavor.

Tim Butler loves the yeast, as most experienced Ringwood brewers do, citing how robust and easy to work with it is. But a lot of beer geeks have preconceived notions about it. "You can't change their minds," he says, shaking his head. "They'll come in here, try the beers, they'll love the beers, then they find out it's Ringwood and they just walk right out." Their loss, I'd say.

Ringwood works well in Middle Ages' cask beer program. "That's what Ringwood was bred for," Marc told me. "It settles quickly in the cask; it drops like a rock." Rather than take chances with bars that can't handle cask ale properly, Marc and Tim condition the beer at the brewery, leaving only tapping for the bars. All the work is done for us; we just have to enjoy it.

My medieval history professor used to paraphrase Hobbes's *Leviathan* and say that life in the Middle Ages was nasty, brutish, and short. Too bad he never knew about the Middle Ages that comes in a 20-ounce imperial pint glass and is anything but.

Opened: May 1995.

Type: Brewery.

Owners: Marc and Mary Rubenstein.

Brewers: Marc Rubenstein, brewmaster; Tim Butler, brewer.

System: 30-barrel Peter Austin brewhouse, 6,200 barrels annual capacity.

Production: 4,000 barrels in 2001.

Tours: Saturday, 1:30 P.M. and 3:30 P.M. (call ahead; no tours on festival weekends)

Take-out beer: Half-gallon and quart growlers, six-packs, cases, half and quarter kegs.

Special considerations: Kids welcome.

Parking: On-street parking's pretty easy; there's also a small lot.

Syracuse Suds Factory

320 South Clinton Street, Syracuse, NY 13202
315-471-2253
www.sudsfactory.com

Don't you love the name? "Syracuse Suds Factory." Kind of brings to mind a picture of beer somehow being welded, riveted, and pressed into being. But this is no industrial space. This spacious brewpub on the corner of South Clinton and Walton Streets, by Armory Square, is smooth and comfortable, a real bar of a brewpub, more a place for the second shift to come and spend their wages rather than earn them.

Al Smith, the young guy who owns the Suds Factory, is brimful of confidence. There's neither uncertainty nor conceit in his makeup, just easy good humor over a solid core of purpose. Al also does general contracting, so he's no stranger to hard work and project schedules. So why a brewpub? He worked his way through Syracuse University with jobs in bars and restaurants. "I figured if I can eat a burger, I can run a bar," Al said, compressing whole schools of business thought into one sentence.

The Suds Factory started as an idea for a place on Cape Cod. But Al's partner backed out of that deal, so Al decided to finish school in Syracuse. He

Beers brewed: Pale Ale, Brown Ale, Stout, Weizen, Black Cherry Lambic, Honey Light. The brewpub also brews its own root beer.

still thought a brewpub would be "a cool thing to do," but he was looking for the right opportunity. It came when the Chapter House people, from Ithaca, tried to open a brewpub on Syracuse Hill. When it didn't work out, Al stepped in, assumed payments on the equipment, and moved it to a location two blocks north of the current one.

The Suds Factory opened there in January 1993, though it was three months before the first batch of beer was brewed. "It took a while to get the paperwork pushed through," said Al, laughing. "We weren't used to that much of it!" Al's brewer, Norman Soine, had worked at Matt's, in Utica, and quickly got the place up and running once all the licensing was set. Norman also works as Al's general manager at the pub.

The Pick: Norman grows his own hops for the pale ale right here in Onondaga County. Maybe they're what makes the Pale Ale far and away the best beer at the Factory, in this man's opinion. This "pale ale" would be an IPA in some brewpubs, with a nice hoppy flavor and a good bitter finish with notes of citrus, spice, and earthiness.

The brewpub was moved to its present location in October 1998, which is less than 50 yards from Empire Brewing's Syracuse location. How does that work, two brewpubs that close? "It works okay," Al said breezily. "It's the difference between the two places. You can't please everyone. That's why we carry 150 beers besides our own. I get people who can't stand our beer, I get some who won't drink anything else. It's all about difference." The guy's willing to accept that people might not like his beer. Like I said: confidence.

Even if they don't like the beer, they ought to like the food. The Suds Factory has three weekly specials. Thursday nights is fresh roasted turkey day—real turkey, not turkey roll, and it's served as turkey dinners, turkey sandwiches, turkey soup, and open-faced turkey-and-gravy sandwiches. Every Friday is a fish fry, complete with the Factory's acclaimed New England–style clam chowder. And Saturday night is prime rib dinners. That's serious, no-kidding food. It's a full menu all the time. "We do a little bit of everything," Al said.

Al seems the most pleased to have been one of the first restaurants in the area. "When we started up, there weren't many places here," he said. "Now there are twenty-two restaurants; that's good for business." There's that confidence again. It's something that's obviously gotten Al Smith (and isn't that a great name for a brewery owner in New York?) a long way and will likely keep him right up there.

Opened: Original location, 1993; present location, October 1998.
Type: Brewpub.
Owner: Al Smith.

Brewer: Norman Soine.

System: 7-barrel Pub Brewing System brewhouse, 550 barrels annual capacity.

Production: 250 barrels in 2001.

Brewpub hours: Seven days a week, 11 A.M. to 2 A.M.

Tours: By appointment.

Take-out beer: Half-gallon growlers, half, quarter, and 5-gallon kegs.

Food: "Our buffalo chicken tenders are something people come in for all the time, our biggest seller," says Al Smith. Grab a spinach salad or a Greek salad, pair it with one of the Factory's big, juicy sandwiches: prime rib melt, the Suds Bomber cheese steak, or a buffalo tender sandwich. Don't forget the turkey, fish fry, and prime rib nights on Thursday, Friday, and Saturday.

Extras: Pool table, dartboards, golf game, 16 TVs. Live music on occasion.

Special considerations: Cigars allowed. Kids welcome. Vegetarian foods available—take a look at the grilled vegetable skewers and daily specials. Handicapped-accessible.

Parking: Street parking, pay lots in area.

Lodging in the area, area attractions, and other area beer sites: See pages 204–207.

Empire Brewing Company, Rochester

300 State Street, Rochester, NY 14614
585-454-2337
www.empirebrewco.com

The Pont du Rennes footbridge spans the gorge just downstream of the High Falls in Rochester. Stand in the middle and look south at the roaring spectacle of the Genesee River hurling itself over the cliff, a half-scale Niagara. Sometimes I think Rochester takes the power of the Genesee for granted. But to the visitor, its presence is awesome, almost shocking. The rushing river forces its rapid way through the town as if it can feel the nearness of Lake Ontario, its downhill goal.

Standing on the bridge looking at the falls presents you with a choice. If you turn left, you'll walk right into the back of the High Falls Brewing Company's complex of huge buildings, outdoor fermentation tanks, and loading docks. If you turn right, you're walking toward the other end of the brewing scale: the open, airy spaces of Empire Brewing, where the entire brewhouse would handily fit inside one of the tanks at High Falls.

I asked Empire partner Michael Hodgdon how that felt, being linked to such a huge brewery (High Falls has a capacity of 4 *million* barrels a year). "I don't know what to make of it," he answered. "Mostly we think it's amusing. People often comment on it in terms of what they do, and how in comparison we're very small." It's not a big deal: High Falls doesn't serve food, and Empire doesn't put beer in cans. Every brewery follows its bliss.

Empire is located in the old Rochester Button Factory. I learned that from brewer Greg Smith, who told me that there was an absolute rain of buttons during the renovation. "All the buttons that ever got lost, went missing, rolled down a crack. . . ." He laughed. "When we started tearing things apart, they all came out!"

Happily, they didn't really tear things apart. This is a solidly impressive old factory space that reminded me of a beerhall I'd visited in Lisbon called Cerveceria Real Fabrica, set in an old silk factory with the thick brick support pillars and geared power trains still in place. Too often, as we're criticized for by Europeans, Americans use a building, then tear it down and put up something faster, uglier, and shoddier. That's not, I'm pleased to say, something that usually happens with brewpubs.

Empire has put its stamp on the space with clever, consistent design. The lowercase sans-serif "e" that adorns the handles on the distinctive tap towers is worked in elsewhere, as are the beige-black-white and indigo-black color combinations. It's Empire's space, and that's subtly impressed on you everywhere you look.

One place that's not Empire's space, evidently, is Buffalo. Hodgdon and partner David Katleski opened a third brewpub in Buffalo that failed.

Beers brewed: All beers brewed on the premises. Year-round: Skinny Atlas Light (GABF Gold, 1997, 1998, and 1999; Bronze 2001), Amber Ale, Black Magic Stout (GABF Silver, 2000), Hefe-weizen (GABF Bronze, 1995). Seasonals: Purgatory Pale Ale, Downtown Brown Ale (GABF Bronze, 1998), Barley Wine, "various" fruit beers, Bock, Maibock, Doppelbock, Munchener Helles, Octoberfest, Platt Street Pilsner, Vienna, Schwarzbier, White Christmas, Berliner Weisse, Bodacious Blonde, Dunkel Weizen, Great Pumpkin Ale, Honey Ginger Ale, Gruit Ale, Heather Ale, Imperial Stout, Porter, Rauchbier, Red Mulligan, Rye Ale, Scotch Ale, and Winter Elixir. More will follow. "We brew about thirty different beers every year," Michael Hodgdon told me.

Michael actually brought it up in our interview: "When are you going to ask me about Buffalo?" He's heard the question a lot, I imagine. "We thought," he explained, "people know about us in Buffalo, they've heard about us, some of them have come to the Rochester restaurant. We figured we'd go into downtown Buffalo, it's the same western New York market, we'll do fine.

"Well," he sighed, "we did what we did here, and we had some business and regulars, but not enough to support what we had put in. We struggled for a year, and then just had to cut our losses, lesson learned. It was humbling, and we're still licking our wounds, mentally and fiscally. But we know we're good at what we do."

The success of the Syracuse and Rochester brewpubs prove that. Will they take another shot somewhere else? Michael wouldn't rule it out but said that the challenge in upstate is to find another market big enough to support the kind of high-end operation Empire is. "Where else would we go?" he asked. Perhaps the future lies in a different direction. "We still harbor the dream of getting our beers on the shelves," he told me, "but that's a totally different business. We're just trying to do the best we can do in these two places."

And doing a fine job of it, I'd say. The guys at the other end of the footbridge don't have anything to worry about from Empire in terms of size, but don't count them out on quality, service, or spirit.

The Pick: Greg Smith and I had a real nice chat at the bar at Empire in Rochester and became fast friends, all thanks to a couple glasses of Empire's excellent Barley Wine. We became such good friends that he insisted I take a liter growler of it, with which I made *more* friends when I got home. This is *big* beer, weighing in around 13 percent ABV, with a ton of mouthfeel. Plenty of hops, but not overwhelming, plenty of alefruit, but not sappy. The Barley Wine is brewed in January and released on Election Day, an Empire tradition.

Opened: January 1996.
Type: Brewpub.
Owners: Michael Hodgdon, David Katleski.
Brewers: Greg Smith.
System: 15-barrel Criveller brewhouse, 3,000 barrels annual capacity.
Production: 1,250 barrels in 2001.
Brewpub hours: Seven days a week, 11:30 A.M. to "closing," which varies
    depending on business; it's usually between midnight and 2 A.M.
Tours: By appointment only.
Take-out beer: 2-liter growlers, half kegs (call for availability).
Food: See page 204.
Extras: Pool table, dartboard, bar-area TVs.

Special considerations: Cigars allowed. Kids welcome. Vegetarian foods available (exceptional selection). Handicapped-accessible.

Parking: On-street parking is pretty easy, but don't even think about using the Kodak lot across the street.

Lodging in the area, area attractions, and other area beer sites: See pages 11–13.

Rohrbach Brewing Company

3859 Buffalo Road, Rochester, NY 14624
585-594-9800
www.rohrbachs.com

You could almost cry when you think about it. I understand some people did. The old Gregory Street location of Rohrbach's, just down the block from MacGregor's original (and still best, by a nose) multitap bar, closed down in the fall of 2001. No more hot nights in the basement of the old German House, cooled by plentiful drafts of Gregory Street Lager and Highland Amber, no more traipsing down to MacGregor's for one last half-pint of stout, no more Rohrbach's.

Well, yes, actually, more Rohrbach's. A second Rohrbach's had already been opened, out on the west side of Rochester on Buffalo Road. "The lease came up on the first place," brewer Jim McDermott told me. "We had issues with the building anyway, so we got out while we could. I prefer to think of it as a consolidation."

It's easy to understand why, from Jim's viewpoint. The 7-barrel system at Gregory Street and the big 20-barrel Criveller at Buffalo Road were sharing a malt mill, which meant constant trucking back and forth. Now the mill, the big system, and the tanks from both systems are all housed in the back brewhouse at Buffalo Road.

Beers brewed: Year-round: Highland Lager, Scotch Ale, Pale Ale, Porter. Seasonals: Bluebeary Ale, Red Wing Red, IPA, Imperial Stout, American Lager (TAP NY Bronze, 2002), Barley Wine (GABF Bronze, 2001). Note: Rohrbach's beer list is still somewhat in flux after the closing of the Gregory Street operation.

Rohrbach may not be brewing at Gregory Street anymore, but the brewer's still around. Bruce Lish does the specialty brews, like the recent 10th Anniversary Ale, a boldly Belgianish beer with a big dash of hops. Jim does the big brews of the regulars, the Highland Lager, Scotch Ale, and Red Wing Red, the beers that go out the door. "We sell off-premises to about sixty or so accounts," Jim said. "We're still technically two separate companies."

They sell a lot of Red Wing Red over at Frontier Field, the home of Rochester's International League AAA baseball team, the Red Wings. "We're the best-selling draft beer there," partner John Urlaub told me. "People these days may only have one or two beers, so they have something good. That's us."

The Pick: I have in my notes that the Scotch Ale is "velvet hammer stuff." That's because this smooth, cookie-sweet, and impressively clean ale that is purely quaffable hides a bottom line of 6.5 percent ABV. That's truly impressive work, a stealthy strong ale. Consider yourself forewarned. I'd also tip my hat to the 10th Anniversary Ale, a one-shot commemorative brew full of hops and funky esters that I hope enough people acclaimed so that Bruce Lish is forced to brew it again.

John said, "I like to lead. I came home to Rochester because upstate needed good beer." He had a strategy for making and selling beer from the beginning that's working out well. "We didn't do a microbrewery because of the slow start they get," he said. "We did the pub instead. You get a cash flow immediately. Ten years later, outside sales are over half the beer we brew, and it's all draft."

Like McDermott, John's not altogether unhappy with the "consolidation." The Buffalo Road location has a big advantage over the old site: room. "One location is good," John said. "We can expand here, and when we do, we expand the whole business at once. We can just build more of the same out back." There is an empty lot behind the brewpub, all part of the parcel of land.

But for now, Rohrbach's is standing pat. They've got a good thing here, loyal regulars, two good brewers, and popular beers. They're starting to experiment with cask conditioning, and Bruce continues to stretch the patron's palates with new beers. The restaurant is a big part of the business, sporting an adventurous menu and a separate dining room.

The last time I talked to Jim McDermott, the gang at Rohrbach's was gearing up for the Flour City Fest, an annual beer festival in early August (contact the brewpub for annual information). John does like to lead: He started the fest eight years ago. Traditions live on, whether in familiar haunts or on new ground, and Rohrbach's will be there to celebrate them.

Directions to Rohrbach Brewing Company

Opened: July 1995. (The Gregory Street location of Rohrbach opened in 1992 and closed in the fall of 2001.)

Type: Brewpub and brewery.

Owners: John Urlaub, Steve Brooks.

Brewers: Jim McDermott, Bruce Lish.

System: 20-barrel Criveller brewhouse, 2,100 barrels annual capacity (this is a rougher figure than most, because of Rohrbach's mix of ale and lager brewing and unusual flexibility with tank space).

Production: 1,500 barrels in 2001.

Brewpub hours: Monday through Thursday, 11 A.M. to 1 A.M.; Friday, 11 A.M. to 3 A.M.; Saturday, 11:30 A.M. to 3 A.M.; Sunday, 4 P.M. to midnight.

Tours: Saturdays at noon, and on request, at brewer's discretion.

Take-out beer: Growlers, kegs.

Food: An upgraded pub-style menu with a German influence, including plenty of serious sandwiches like the Heart Stopper Burger, topped with cheese, bacon, and a fried egg, and big meat dishes: beef and porter stew, beer-braised baby back ribs, pork schnitzel. There are also some interesting surprises, like the Seven Lily Soup, made with Spanish and red onions, garlic, shallots, leeks, scallions, and chives—all members of the lily family.

Extras: Monthly "beer and food pairings" (call or check website for schedule). Outside seating in good weather.

Special considerations: Cigars not allowed. Kids welcome. Vegetarian foods available. Handicapped-accessible.

Parking arrangements: Plentiful on-site parking.

Lodging in the area, area attractions, and other area beer sites: See pages 11–13.

The Distillery

1142 Mount Hope Avenue, Rochester, NY 14620
585-271-4105
www.thedistillery.com

No, The Distillery is not one of the tiny handful of new distillery pubs that have started to spring up around the country, unfortunately. The name actually predates the 1997 addition of the Micropub International brewhouse in the front of the bar. Get used to this kind of confusion; there are lots of bars out there with "brewery" or "brewing company" in their names that have never reeked of sweet mashing malt.

The Distillery is a sports bar, a serious one with lots of TVs and different satellite dishes to cover all the games. (It also offers various satellite feeds for catered business meetings in private rooms.) It's been rated the best sports bar in Rochester by several local polls, and the fans have always been pretty absorbed when I've stopped in.

Like I said, it's a Micropub International system: prepackaged malt extract is heated in the brewkettle and fermented in the tanks downstairs. They don't do quite as good a job with the beer here as Lou DiPronio does at Eddie's, but the house beer's okay. There's a fun promotion with the house beers: They are deeply discounted whenever it rains. "When it rains, we pour," the promotion goes.

There are a large number of guest beers. Most of them are mainstream lagers, but you'll find some Saranac beers and a couple of bigger micros. The food's great pub grub, and it comes fast and friendly. Check out the wings; they'll make you sweat.

This is a nice side of town, and you're not far from Beers of the World or the MacGregor's on Jefferson Road. Stop in, catch the game (maybe it will rain!), get some wings to go, and pick up a six-pack on the way home. There are worse ways to spend an afternoon.

Beers brewed: , Hyland Amber, Raspberry Wheat, Irish Red, British Ale. Seasonal: Octoberfest.

The Pick: The Raspberry Wheat, surprisingly, had the most character here, a tart quenching beer that's refreshing in the summer.

Opened: Brewery added in early 1997.
Type: Brewpub.
Owner: Peter Psyllos
Brewers: Steven Smith, Mark Lewis.
System: 9-barrel Micropub International brewhouse, 930 barrels annual capacity.
Production: 450 barrels in 2001.
Brewpub hours: Monday through Saturday, 11 A.M. to 2 A.M.; Sunday, noon to 2 A.M.
Tours: N/A; brewhouse is in plain view from bar area.
Take-out beer: N/A.
Food: The Distillery's menu is a sports bar menu: a variety of sandwiches, deep-fried snacks, and a lot of things covered with cheese.
Extras: The Distillery has a ton of TVs with plenty of sports and other satellite feeds; they also have dartboards.
Special considerations: No cigars. Kids allowed. Vegetarian foods available. Handicapped-accessible.
Parking: Large on-site lot.
Lodging in the area, area attractions, and other area beer sites: See pages 11–13.

Eddie's Brewery and Grill

4244 North Buffalo Street, Orchard Park, NY 14127
716-667-2314
www.eddiesgrill.com

A brewpub in a bowling alley: Why didn't someone think of this before?! Actually, someone has: The Water Tower brewpub in Eden Prairie, Minnesota, has a bowling alley and thirty-six pool tables. But that's a big Brunswick outfit, a corporate experiment. Eddie's Brewery (and I love that name) is homegrown, just some guys with a bowling alley and a restaurant in Orchard Park who wanted to have something a little different.

The guys are Jim Clinton, the owner, and Lou DiPronio, Jim's manager and brewer (Eddie was Jim's father, who owned the bowling alley). Lou did not come to brewing through the usual path of coursework, apprenticeship, or homebrewing. He got there by brochure. Jim got a mailing from Micropub International, a Rochester-based company that sells small footprint extract brewing systems for restaurants that want to add fresh beer to their menus.

Beers brewed: All beers brewed on the premises. Year-round: Altbier, Simon Amber, Ed's Light, Pilsner, Munich Helles, Raspberry Wheat, Aussie Lager, Czech Pilsner, IPA, Porter, Special Bitter. Seasonals: Munich Dunkel, Nut Brown Ale, Rudolf's Red Nose Ale.

"I got the brochure in the mail, and it looked interesting," Jim said. "So I gave it to Lou and told him to take it home and take a look at it. Then, after he leaves, I'm thinking, he's already managing the place, cooking, he's not gonna want to do this too! He came back the next day and tells me, hey, this looks good. So we did it." And it was as simple as that.

The Pick: The Nut Brown Ale did it for me. Frankly, I'm amazed that Lou can coax this kind of malt character out of such a simple extract brewery. This beer has a light malt-cookie aroma, and a lightly malty smoothness that slides into a pleasingly clean finish. A real drinker, this one, the kind of beer that can give you some elbow exercise.

Well, maybe not quite that simple. When the brewery was installed, Lou brewed a few batches. Micropub makes it as simple as possible for brewers, with prehopped malt extract you can just add to hot water. But that wasn't good enough for Lou. He did a full boil on the extract, added extra hops, kept the carbonation low to bring out the flavor, and generally messed around with the brewing process to get the most out of it. I'll be honest, I was surprised at the beer he wrings out of this system. It's easily the best beer I've ever had from a purely extract brewhouse.

Jim and Lou have a good thing here, because they figured out right away something it takes other brewpub guys years to get. "The beer puts us a step above," Lou explained. "The bars around here don't have anything other than Sam Adams and Guinness for a guy who's interested in beer. The brewery in the window is a novelty, and if there's one microbrew drinker in the car when they're trying to decide where to go, they'll come in. If there's one thing a microbrew drinker likes, it's trying a beer he hasn't had yet."

I call this the "CB X+1 Theory." Once you try a craftbrew and like it, you'll have it again. But as you get to really like it, this CraftBrew X, you start to think, hey, I never knew beer like this existed. Wonder what else I'm missing? And instead of wanting another CraftBrew X, now you want a new CraftBrew: CraftBrew X+1. Jim and Lou have a whole row of taps full of X+1s.

No one believes me when I tell them how good the beer is at Eddie's. "That's extract beer," they say with a sneer. Okay, so it is. But Lou DiPronio puts a lot of soul into this beer, and I swear you can taste it.

There's one other thing I want to say about this place. I went to Buffalo looking for a bar out of *The Last Fine Time*, Verlyn Klinkenborg's outstanding book that explains Buffalo's character and soul in terms of bars and people and fish fries. Eddie's, this little brewpub, is the closest I found, right down to the butterflied shrimp. There's something archetypical about this bar. Go and find it.

Opened: Brewery opened September 1999.
Type: Brewpub.
Owner: James Clinton.
Brewer: Lou DiPronio.
System: 4-barrel Micropub International brewhouse, 104 barrels annual capacity.
Production: 104 barrels in 2001.
Brewpub hours: Seven days a week, 11:30 A.M. to "closing" (varies depending on crowd, usually after midnight).
Tours: The little Micropub system is right in the front of the bar; you can take a look anytime you want. If Lou's handy, he'll explain things to you.
Take-out beer: Growlers (the containers are not sold; bring your own).

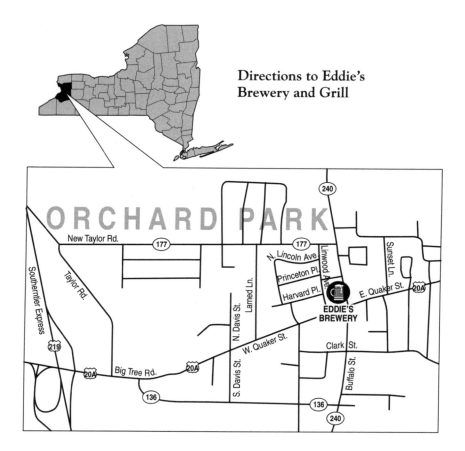

Directions to Eddie's Brewery and Grill

Food: Eddie's menu has northern Italian influences and a big chunk of German entrees—the "brewmaster's international fare." This is the beauty of nonchain restaurants: Where else would you find stuffed banana peppers both as an entree and as a pizza topping? Get the spinach bread, garlic bread stuffed with seasoned spinach and cheeses, or a huge portion of cheese and bacon fries. Still hungry? Tuck into a pizza, or a variety of steaks, chops, and seafood (try the butterflied shrimp on Friday, or get the fish fry any day). There are plenty of meatless pasta dishes, including stuffed shells Florentine style.

Extras: Eddie's is right in a bowling alley, so it's not too hard to slip on the shoes and bowl a few frames. In the bar are a pool table, a good jukebox, video games, and the New York State Lotto and Quick-draw games.

Special considerations: Cigars allowed. Kids welcome. Vegetarian foods available. Handicapped-accessible.

Parking: Large lot for the bowling alley behind building, some street parking as well.

Lodging in the area: Econo Lodge South, 4344 Milestrip Road, 716-825-7530. Also see on page 224.

Area attractions: Schwabl's, the weck place mentioned in the Regional Foods section (see p. 188), is not far from Eddie's, and definitely worth a visit. You can try to get a ticket to a Bills game at **Ralph Wilson Stadium** (716-649-0015 or at www.buffalobills.com). **The Bob-o-Link Golf Club** (4085 Transit Road, Orchard Park, 716-662-4311) and the **South Shore Country Club** (5076 Southwestern Boulevard, Hamburg, 716-649-6674) are both public courses that Jim recommends. See other suggestions under Flying Bison Brewing Company.

Other area beer sites: Right around the corner from Eddie's, the **Big Tree Inn** (4277 Abbott Road, 716-649-9892) is a busy, friendly sports bar, largely blue-collar, clean and comfortable . . . and insane during Bills games.

Flying Bison Brewing Company

491 Ontario Street, Buffalo, NY 14207
716-873-1557
www.flyingbisonbrewing.com

Flying Bison's beers are not what you'd expect. Come into a city cold these days and find out that there's a new packaging microbrewery in town, and you could almost bet that it's going to be making either timid stuff to appeal to a broad market or "manly" hoppy beers because some hophead finally got enough money together to make "the kind of beer people should like." Surprise! Flying Bison's flagship Aviator Red is a malty Irish red ale that throws geeks for a loop and catches mainstream beer drinkers off guard with its sweet smoothness.

Flying Bison owner Tim Herzog isn't your usual brewery guy either. Oh, he's a beer geek, no doubt about that, but he's an uncommonly articulate one who has an encyclopedic knowledge of Buffalo. He was good enough to take me bar-hopping around Buffalo, and everywhere we went, every street, every corner, he pointed out where old breweries once stood, or the grounds of the Pan-American Exhibition, or the old Pierce-Arrow plant. Not bad for a guy from Rochester.

Beers brewed: All beers brewed on the premises. Year-round: Dawn Patrol Gold, Aviator Red, Blackbird Oatmeal Stout. Seasonals: Buffalo Destroyers Brown, Barrel Roll Bock, Barnstormer Pale Ale, Baron Von Bisonfest, Skye Pilot Scotch Ale.

Tim came to beer from off the mainstream. "I never liked beer," he told me, freely admitting that he'd tried it underage. "But when I was eighteen, I tried a Guinness. I figured if that was what beer tasted like, I could drink it."

That became the kind of beer Tim always drank, so it was natural that after he got married in 1980, his father-in-law thought of Tim when he read in the paper about a California chef who had moved to Buffalo and was homebrewing because he couldn't get beers like the ones in California. Tim thought that sounded interesting, so his wife got him a kit.

As Tim was telling me the story, he stopped at that point and motioned around us at the brewhouse, tanks, and keg filler. "And here I am," he said with a mustachioed grin, "after twenty years of sliding down that slippery slope."

Tim thought a lot about opening a brewery. The path became clear after a trip to England with his best friend and partner Red Mrozek, a homebrew shop owner. "We went over and drank cask ale for six days," Tim recalled. "One place made four very different beers with only three malts, one hop, and one yeast. We learned a lot about brewing simply." They decided to open a microbrewery and wrote a detailed business plan.

Tragically, Red was killed in a traffic accident in 1997. Tim gathered up his resolve, raised more money, and went on. "At some point," he said, "you set yourself, say 'I'll show them!' and that's at least 50 percent of making it." He wasn't going to fail at that point. After lots of work, Flying Bison opened in May 2000.

Making it in Buffalo isn't easy. Wholesaler consolidation has made for a tough market to crack, forcing Tim to go to self-distribution. "Some places like the fact that we're not with a distributor," Tim said. "But the toughest job is convincing people that Labatt is not the local brewery." Indeed, Labatt Blue is the biggest-selling beer in Buffalo.

Tim's up to the challenge. After all, he makes the beers he makes because, he says, "no one else will." The beers do sell if people just try them. I saw it happen at the Old Toad in Rochester. They had just put a cask of Tim's Blackbird Oatmeal Stout on when I got there, and I immediately ordered the first pint. As the barmaid handed me the coal black beer and I sipped it with obvious relish, everyone around me, literally everyone, looked at the beer, and they all ordered one. Then we all had another.

Tim's right. I showed them. And that's at least 50 percent of it. Look for the blue propeller tap handles and show them yourself.

Opened: "Incorporated July 1995, opened May 2000 . . . it's a long story."
Type: Brewery.
Owners: Tim Herzog, Phil Internicola.
Brewers: Tim Herzog, Phil Internicola.
System: 20-barrel Criveller brewhouse, 2,000 barrels annual capacity.
Production: 700 barrels in 2001.
Tours: Friday, 4 P.M. to 7 P.M.; Saturday, 11 A.M. to 4 P.M.; or by appointment.
Take-out beer: Half-gallon growlers, 5-gallon, quarter, and half kegs.
Special considerations: Kids welcome. Not handicapped-accessible.
Parking: Plenty of parking out back; watch your step.
Lodging in the area: Sheraton Four Points, 2040 Walden Avenue, 716-681-2400; Holiday Inn Downtown, 620 Delaware Avenue, 716-886-2121; Lord Amherst Motor Hotel, 5000 Main Street, Amherst, 716-839-2200.
Area attractions: I think Tim would want you to start at the **Buffalo and Erie County Historical Society** (25 Nottingham Court, 716-873-9644) if only because it is housed in the only remaining building from the 1901 Pan-American Exposition (because it's the only one that wasn't built from plaster on lath and chicken wire!). The exposition was a big watershed in Buffalo history and affected how the city grew, saw itself, and was perceived by America and the world. The society's exhibits look at that, and other developments of Buffalo's history. **Shea's Performing Arts Center** dates from

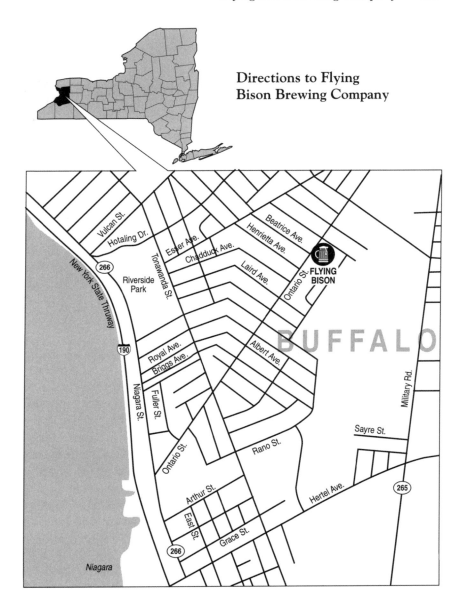

Directions to Flying
Bison Brewing Company

1926, a gorgeous old building (646 Main Street, 716-847-0850, call for schedules). ***The Albright-Knox Art Gallery*** (1285 Elmwood Avenue, 716-882-8700) is exceptionally strong in its collection of twentieth-century American and European art: Pollock, Mondrian, Picasso. It is the art museum of a larger city, and Buffalo is justly proud of it.

Naval and Servicemen's Park (1 Naval Park Cove, 716-847-1773) is a waterside park with three decommissioned warships that are accessible for boarding: USS *Little Rock*, a 1960s-era guided missile cruiser; SS *Croaker*, a World War II submarine; and the famous USS *The Sullivans*, the World War II destroyer named for five brothers killed in action in the Pacific Theater. There are also land exhibits: a PT boat and an F-101 Voodoo jet fighter.

Sports! Buffalo's nuts about it. Here are your contact numbers: Bills football (716-649-0015 or visit www.buffalobills.com); Sabres ice hockey (716-855-4100); Bisons AAA baseball (716-878-8488); Bandits lacrosse (716-855-4444 ×82); Buffalo Destroyers arena football (716-881-4444; get Flying Bison's Destroyer Brown at the arena!)

And since you're so close, you should go see **Niagara Falls.** There's a lot to see and do; get all the information at these two websites: the Niagara Falls Visitor and Convention Bureau site (American side: www.nfcvb.com/attractions/index.html) and the Niagara Falls Live site (an exceptionally complete commercial site: www.niagarafallslive.com).

Other area beer sites: This is a great town for beer bars. Buffalo didn't have a single bar to match the mighty multitaps of Rochester, Syracuse, Albany, or New York; nothing even came close. But there was such a good selection of beer in so many places, places that obviously cared about the beer, that Buffalo more than holds its own. Let's start at the place with the biggest beer selection, **Alternative Brews** (3488 Sheridan Drive, Amherst, 716-446-0424), where you'll find twenty drafts and a hundred bottles, and not too much of it mainstream. This place rocks on Friday and Saturday, when a growing blues scene takes over. Other times, it's center stage for beer and cigars. One of my favorite places was **Papa Jake's Saloon** (1672 Elmwood Avenue, 716-874-3878), a real neighborhood taproom with an exceptional selection of brews and outstanding food: The grilled meatloaf sandwich on French bread is immense, a slab of meatloaf the size of a Steven King paperback, and it's delicious. **The Sterling Place** (1487 Hertel Avenue, 716-838-2448) has a small and extremely selective set of taps (I wept to see Foster's there and thought of what it might be keeping away), a small menu (ten items), and a heart the size of a whale. Stop in and make some friends.

Ulrich's Tavern is Buffalo's oldest bar (674 Ellicott, 716-855-8409). During Prohibition, it was Ulrich's Deli; the bar continued to do business upstairs as The Hassenpfeffer Club. Check the wooden coolers and the old stained-glass beer signs. And it carries Flying Bison beers! **Colter Bay Grill** (561–565 Delaware Avenue, 716-882-1330) has twenty-four taps (quite a few mainstreams) and free wings during happy hour! There are some good beers here, and a lively crowd. One of the most exclusive tap selections I saw in Buffalo was at the **Pizza Plant** at Walker Center (Walker Center Plaza, 5110 Main Street, Williamsville, 716-626-5566), a Buffalo phenomenon where the Pod is king. Pods are like calzones, but the Pizza Plant stuffs anything in them, and they're good. This is where Custom Brewcrafters' Inferno Pod Ale was born. They have that, of course, and eight great others, plus Middle Ages on cask.

Cole's (1104 Elmwood Avenue, 716-886-1449) is a sophisticated place, with a scull hanging over the dining room, fancy old chandelier-style light fixtures, and an unfortunately high concentration of yuppie types. It's worth it for the tap selection and smooth bartenders. The bartender at **Buffalo Tap Room** (1009 Niagara Falls Boulevard, Amherst, 716-832-6054) was quick, sly, and hilarious as he poured from *ten* taps of Custom Brewcrafters beers and two Flying Bison taps. There's a good vibe here; it's a happy place with a good social range of clientele. And those ten taps make a tempting tap dance.

Buffalo Brewpub

6861 Main Street, Williamsville, NY 14221
716-632-0552
www.buffalobrewpub.com

Buffalo Brewpub is the oldest brewpub in New York, dating its brewing operations from 1986. It's just *barely* a brewpub—the house beers are brewed by adding hot water to hopped malt extracts in a ferment tank, then yeast is added when the mix cools. But malt, hops, water, and yeast are all involved, they come together there at the pub, and beer is produced: It's a brewpub.

It's also a great place to go. Even if they didn't have the house beers, this would be a great place for a beer geek. The pub sports thirty taps of guest beers, including taps of Saranac, Flying Bison, and Ellicottville beers. If you can't find something you like here, you're just not trying.

If you like it enough, you can join the mug club. Be forewarned, though: Joining the mug club here at Buffalo Brewpub is a serious commitment. Other brewpubs have mug clubs with two hundred, maybe five hundred members. "We have between two and three thousand active mug club members," said manager and beermaker Tom Rosenthal. Tom's rightly proud that out of the fifty original members, only two are no longer active, and they're both dead. That doesn't always stop things, either; people have willed their mugs to friends and relations.

There's a whole room behind the bar dedicated to the mug club, shelf after shelf of clean glass mugs, neatly stacked and numbered, with notebooks full of names and addresses. "It was only going to be fifty mugs," Tom told me just a bit sheepishly, "and then it got out of hand." No sweat, Tom. Fanaticism in the cause of good beer is no sin.

Speaking of fanatics, what comes to mind when you think of Buffalo fanaticism? Okay, besides Bills fans. That's right, Buffalo wings, and the Buffalo Brewpub has some of the best in the city. That's not just my opinion; I'm hardly qualified to judge. That's the opinion of Buffalonians. Poll after poll consistently places these wings in the top five in the city, and that's some kinda wings, baby.

I brought my uncle Don along to Buffalo to use his asbestos palate to judge wings. Tom brought us a fresh and steaming plate of his best. They were the reddish orange color that Nature uses to warn animals of dangerous toxins: perfect. They were enveloped in a stinging cloud of vinegar and capsaicin that abraded nasal tissue: divine. They had a crispy layer of greasy skin and razor-textured hot sauce on top of soft, tender tidbits of chicken: outstanding. Three of them and I was gasping. Don thought they were "pretty good; could be hotter." Don also thought the "atomic" wings at the Anchor Bar "could be hotter."

The pub is a big place, with flagstone floors, dark wood, and plenty of glass around the outside. When it gets rocking at night, this is one heck of a fun place to be, beer in your hand, wings on your table, friends at either side. Oh, go on—join the mug club. You know you'll be back, you might as well have a mug waiting for you.

Beers brewed: All beers made on the premises. Year-round: Amber Ale, Red Ale, Buffalo Lager, Pale Ale, Oatmeal Stout, Golden Ale. Seasonals: Autumn Alt, Kringle Beer, Nickel City Dark, Buffalo Bitter.

The Pick: Let's be honest—as purely extract beers, these beers are not the peak of the brewer's art. With that said, the Pale Ale is the best of the lot (though the Amber is the best-seller). There's actually some hop here to balance the malt sweetness, a bit of backbone.

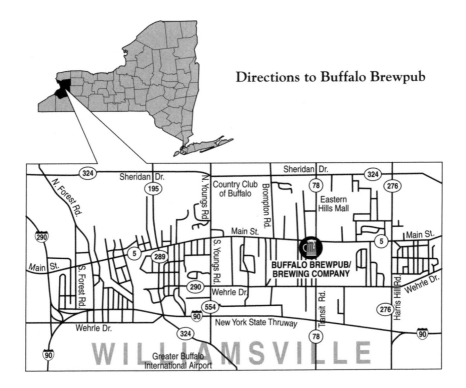

Directions to Buffalo Brewpub

Opened: November 1986.

Type: Brewpub.

Owner: Kevin Townsell.

Brewer: Tom Rosenthal.

System: All-extract system, mixed in ferment tank; no kettle.

Production: 480 barrels in 2001.

Brewpub hours: Sunday through Thursday, 11:30 A.M. to 2 A.M.; Friday and Saturday, 11:30 A.M. to 4 A.M.

Tours: Tuesday through Thursday, noon to 5 P.M., as brewer is available.

Take-out beer: None.

Food: Plentiful peanuts (shell 'em right on the floor) and popcorn make for good bar snacks, but what you must get at the Buffalo Brewpub is the wings. In a town where wings were invented, the Brewpub's wings consistently come up on top-five lists, and I have to agree: There's that sinus-dilating hot-sauce-and-vinegar nose rush, a great crispness to the skin, and just the right amount of endorphin agitation to the sauce. There's a full pub menu, but the wings get top billing.

Extras: Darts (including league play), regular live music, and a regular bank of TVs over the bar. The focus here is really on beer, not just house beer. There are thirty-plus taps of guest beers, including Buffalo's local micro, Flying Bison, and Ellicottville Brewing. There's also the mug club.

Special considerations: Cigars not allowed. Kids welcome. Handicapped-accessible.

Parking: Large on-site lot.

Lodging in the area: The Econo Lodge, right behind the brewpub, can get hand-carried deliveries of wings during Buffalo's fierce snowstorms—something to consider when you're choosing a January stayover (7200 Transit Road, 716-634-1500). Also see lodging on page 224.

Area attractions and other area sites: See pages 224–227.

Pearl Street Grill and Brewery

76 Pearl Street, Buffalo, NY 14202
716-856-2337
www.pearlstreetgrill.com

Pearl Street Grill and Brewery is right in downtown Buffalo, near the lakeshore. It could as easily have been called Seneca Street Grill and Brewery; it sits on the corner of the two streets. Because of the way Buffalo's street grid is laid out, all roads lead to Pearl Street. A map of Buffalo's streets looks kind of like the rays of a sun setting in Lake Erie, radiating out to the suburbs. Follow any of the major arteries toward the lake, or take the light rail, and you'll pop out within a block of the pub.

And that's lucky, because this is a good place to be. Put aside your mug of that surprisingly interesting Seneca Saaz for a second, put the spoon back in the smoked Gouda ale soup, and look around. You've got the big plate-glass windows if you want to people-watch those poor devils on the street who aren't in here. Look at all those overhead fans; notice anything? That's right, they're all running off one long serpentine belt that dates back to when this was a sewing factory, 130 years ago. Scope the bar—no, not the bartender, she's out of your league—those mirrors and solid wood.

Oh, you're not in the main bar? Maybe you're downstairs in the Ratskeller, with those big pool tables, rock walls, the classic old Bevador coolers (those were made in Buffalo, you know), and black-and-white tile floor. Maybe you're listening to a band on the stage, eh? Or maybe you're serious about your pool and you're upstairs, where eight full-size tables share space with a small art collection (it seems to have a lot of nudes; coincidental, I'm sure) and another small bar.

Beers brewed: All beers brewed on the premises. Year-round: Seneca Saaz, Trainwreck Alt, Lake Effect Pale Ale, Burnie's Brown, Canal Street Stout. Seasonals: Viceroy Imperial Stout, Tommy Bock, Waterfront Wheat, Köhlerfest, Lord Stanley's Scotch Ale, Santa's Space Heater. When Paul feels like it, he also throws in American Beauty Bitter and Pearl Street Porter. You'll also find a guest tap of Flying Bison's Aviator Red.

This is a big place with lots going on, and I didn't even mention the main dining room or the big upstairs banquet room, or the brewhouse, there in the corner of the dining room. You've got plenty of room to spread out and enjoy big Paul Koehler's beers, like the impeccably balanced Trainwreck Alt or the great hops synergy of Lake Effect Pale Ale, and to relax and enjoy some of what Pearl Street calls "urban comfort food."

On nights when the Sabres skate, the Bandits whip the lacrosse ball, the Bisons swing the bats, or there's a concert at the HSBC Arena, it's jam-packed in here, six deep around the bar. You don't want to come by then. But on other nights, it's different. So go ahead and finish your soup, and hoist the mug again. Maybe I'll join you and we'll go find some bars later. Or maybe we'll just stay at Pearl Street. This is a pretty good place to be.

Opened: November 1997.
Type: Brewpub.
Owners: Consortium of local investors.
Brewer: Paul Koehler.
System: 15-barrel Specific Mechanical brewhouse, 1,500 barrels annual capacity.
Production: 650 barrels in 2001.
Brewpub hours: Sunday through Thursday, 11 A.M. to 10 P.M.; Friday and Saturday, 11 A.M. to midnight.

Tours: Paul Koehler happily gives brewery tours "by appointment or chance encounter."

Take-out beer: Half-gallon growlers, half kegs (subject to availability).

Food: The Grill characterizes its menu as "urban comfort food." Comforting is the word for dishes like pot roast and those brown sugar–brined pork chops. Start with a bowl of smoked Gouda ale soup, then spice it up with Cajun

The Pick: Sometimes I pick the big beers, and sometimes it's the unusual beers, but this time it's the pint-pounding Seneca Saaz. Paul takes what is usually the "Bud substitute" at brewpubs and shakes it up with that sharp buzz of Saaz hops, crisp and floral, with a bitter finish that sets up the tongue for another. Inspired brewing.

Directions to Pearl Street Grill and Brewery

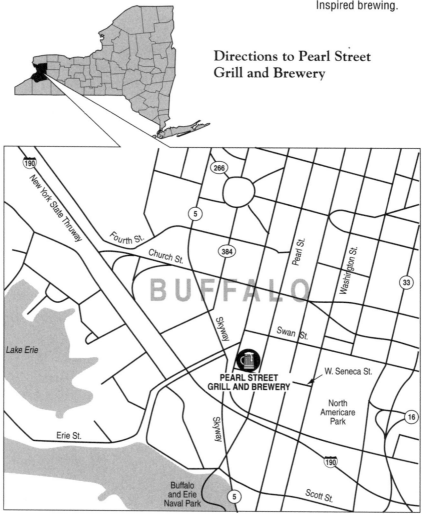

catfish and the ubiquitous Buffalo wings. Add the variety of daily lunch and dinner specials, and you can see why Pearl Street is a popular dining destination.

Extras: There's a poolroom upstairs, with eight tables and some arresting sculpture, and a large banquet area. The Ratskellar, below street level, has three more full-size pool tables. Downstairs is where the live bands play, framed by the stone and brick walls.

Special considerations: Cigars not allowed. Kids welcome. Vegetarian foods available. Handicapped-accessible.

Parking: Street and pay-lot parking. There is free parking in the lot behind the brewpub after 4 P.M. Monday through Friday, and all day on the weekend.

Lodging in the area, area attractions, and other beer sites: See pages 224–227.

BEERWEBS

The Web has become a great place to share beer and bar information. But as with anything else on the Web, you have to use a little wisdom. Beer websites can be out of date, intensely subjective, poorly edited, and just plain wrong. Let the surfer beware.

Here are the websites I use to find beers, bars, and breweries in New York and across the country. If I have any reservations about them, I've stated them. You'll also want to check my own website, **www.lewbryson.com** featuring online updates to this book and my previous book, *Pennsylvania Breweries*, plus news on future guides in the series.

www.pubcrawler.com Pubcrawler is simply the best brewery and bar locator website in the world. No other site has its combination of completeness, search tools, longevity, and objectivity. You can search over 4,000 North American breweries, brewpubs, and bars by name, city, state, zip code, or area code, and every entry has a map link for directions. The entries have phone numbers, addresses, links, logos, and, most importantly, years of patron reviews. You can leave your own as well; you'll find quite a few of mine. My only reservations here are that some of the reviewers are obviously biased, and that sometimes even Pubcrawler is not as complete as it could be. I do my best to keep it up to date in New York, Pennsylvania, Virginia, Delaware, and Maryland.

www.citysearch.com CitySearch is a national search site for entertainment, dining, nightlife, shopping, attractions . . . and bars. They're not anywhere near as beer-aware as they could be, but I've gotten quite a few good leads here. The patron reviews aren't as good as those at Pubcrawler, but the editorial reviews are quite good.

hbd.org/mbas/beer.html This is Bill Coleman's "New York City Beer Alert!" page. Bill does his best to post current tap selections and freshness reports on his favorite bars in Manhattan and Brooklyn, and he's got quite a few. Bill's also responsible for the beer music CDs in various jukeboxes in those bars, and for the "Salty Dog" beer cartoon in *Ale Street News*.

abc.state.ny.us/index.html The New State Liquor Authority website. Mostly dry and dull, this site does have one useful thing: a searchable database of every bar license in the state, with address and phone number for each one.

www.murphguide.com/beerlove/htm The MurphGuide website has a lot of wacky New York City stuff, pulses with advertising, can be sadly out of date in some spots. It also does a great job of finding some spots other sites just never seem to mention.

www.execpc.com/~tjcasey/pubguide.html A personal site, a guide to Irish pubs in New York City, and there are a ton of them! If this is your bag, this is the best guide I found to them.

GLOSSARY

ABV, ABW. Alcohol by volume, alcohol by weight. These are two slightly different ways of measuring the alcohol content of beverages, as a percentage of either the beverage's total volume or its weight. For example, if you have 1 liter of 4 percent ABV beer, 4 percent of that liter (40 milliliters) is alcohol. However, because alcohol weighs only 79.6 percent as much as water, that same beer is only 3.18 percent ABW. This may seem like a dry exercise in mathematics, but it is at the heart of the common misconception that Canadian beer is stronger than American beer. Canadian brewers generally use ABV figures, whereas American brewers have historically used the lower ABW figures. Mainstream Canadian and American lagers are approximately equal in strength. Just to confuse the issue further, most American microbreweries use ABV figures. This is very important if you're trying to keep a handle on how much alcohol you're consuming. If you know how much Bud (at roughly 5 percent ABV) you can safely consume, you can extrapolate from there. Learn your limits.

Adjunct. Any nonbarley malt source of sugars for fermentation. This can be candy sugar, corn grits, molasses or other nonstandard sugar, corn or rice syrup, or one of any number of specialty grains. Wheat, rye, and specialty sugars are considered by beer geeks to be "politically correct" adjuncts; corn and rice are generally taken as signs of swill. However, small amounts of corn used as a brewing ingredient for certain styles of beer is slowly gaining acceptance in craft-brewing circles, and I had a "pre-Prohibition doublebock" made with 25 percent rice that was fantastic. So keep an open mind.

Ale. The generic term for warm-fermented beers. (See "A word about . . . Ales and Lagers" on page 92.)

Alefruit. My own invention, so far as I know. I use this term to signify the juicy esters produced by some yeasts, aromas, and flavors of a variety of fruits: pear, melon, plum, peach, lemon drop, pineapple. I use "alefruit" when I can't tease out the exact fruits (or when I can but don't want to sound pretentious).

ATF, or BATF. The federal Bureau of Alcohol, Tobacco and Firearms, a branch of the Treasury Department. The ATF is the federal regulatory arm for the brewing industry. The ATF has to inspect every brewery before it opens, approve every label before it is used, approve all packaging. The ATF is also the body responsible for the fact that while every food, even bottled water, *must* have a nutritional information label, beer (and wine and cider and spirits) is *not allowed* to have one, even though it is a significant source of calories, carbohydrates, and in the case of unfiltered beers, B vitamins and protein. The problem is that sometimes every ATF agent and bureaucrat seems to have a different interpretation of the regulations, and some have a very negative attitude toward the beverages they're regulating. As a brewer once told me, "I'd enjoy this a lot more if the ATF didn't make me feel like I was dealing in controlled substances."

Barley. A wonderfully apt grain for brewing beer. Barley grows well in relatively marginal soil and climate. It has no significant gluten content, which makes it largely unsuitable for baking bread and thereby limits market competition for brewers buying the grain. Its husk serves as a very efficient filter at the end of the mashing process. And it makes beer that tastes really, really good. Barley comes in two types: two-row and six-row, named for the rows of kernels on the heads of the grain. In days past, two-row barley was plumper and considered finer. Six-row barley was easier to grow, had a better yield per acre and higher enzymatic power, but had a somewhat astringent character. These differences have been lessened by cross-breeding. Most barley grown in North America is six-row, for reasons of soil and climate. (Incidentally, the grain's kernels, or corns, are the source of the name "John Barleycorn," a traditional personification of barley or beer.)

Barrel. A traditional measure of beer volume equal to 31 U.S. gallons. The most common containers of draft beer in the United States are half and quarter barrels, or kegs, at 15.5 gallons and 7.75 gallons, respectively, though the one-sixth-barrel kegs (about 5.2 gallons), known as sixtels, are becoming popular with microbrewers. See also *hectoliter*.

Beer. A fermented beverage brewed from grain, generally malted barley. "Beer" covers a variety of beverages, including ales and lagers, stouts and bocks, porters and pilsners, lambics and altbiers, cream ale, kölsch, and wheat beer, and a whole lot more.

Beer geek. A person who takes beer a little more seriously than does the average person. Often homebrewers, beer geeks love to argue with other beer geeks about what makes exceptional beers exceptional. That is, if they've been able to agree on which beers are exceptional in the first place. A beer geek is the kind of person who would buy a book about traveling to breweries . . . the kind of person who would read the glossary of a beer book. Hey, hi there!

Bottle-conditioned beer. A beer that has been bottled with an added dose of live yeast. This living yeast causes the beer to mature and change as it ages over periods of one to thirty years or more. It will also "eat" any oxygen that may have been sealed in at bottling and keep the beer from oxidizing, a staling process that leads to sherryish and "wet cardboard" aromas in beer. Bottle-conditioned beer qualifies as "real ale."

Brewer. One who brews beer for commercial sale.

Breweriana. Brewery and beer memorabilia, such as trays, coasters, neon signs, steins, mirrors, and so on, including the objects of desire of the beer can and bottle collectors. Most collectors do this for fun, a few do it for money (breweriana is starting to command some big prices; just check eBay), but the weird thing about this for me is the number of breweriana collectors—about a third, from my experience—who don't drink beer.

Brewhouse. The vessels used to mash the malt and grains and boil the wort. The malt and grains are mashed in a vessel called a *mash tun*. Brewhouse size is generally given in terms of the capacity of the brewkettle, where the wort is boiled. A brewery's annual capacity is a function of brewhouse size, fermentation and aging tank capacity, and length of the fermentation and aging cycle for the brewery's beers.

Brewpub. A brewery that sells the majority of its output on draft, on the premises, or a tavern that brews its own beer. Either of these may sell other brewers' beers, and often do. In my opinion, it would be a good thing for the industry in general if more New York brewpubs had a guest tap or two from other New York breweries.

CAMRA. The CAMpaign for Real Ale. A British beer drinkers' consumer group formed in the early 1970s by beer drinkers irate over the disappearance of cask-conditioned ale. They have been very vocal and successful in bringing this traditional drink back to a place of importance in the United Kingdom. CAMRA sets high standards for cask-conditioned ale, which only a few brewers in the United States match.

Carbonation. The fizzy effects of carbon dioxide (CO_2) in solution in a liquid (e.g., beer). Carbonation can be accomplished artificially by injecting the beer with the gas or naturally by trapping the CO_2, which is a by-product of fermentation. There is no intrinsic qualitative difference between beers carbonated by these two methods. Brewer's choice, essentially. Low carbonation will allow a broader array of flavors to come through, whereas high carbonation can result in a perceived bitterness. Most American drinkers prefer a higher carbonation.

Cask. A keg designed to serve cask-conditioned beer by gravity feed or by handpump, not by gas pressure. These casks may be made of wood, but most are steel with special plumbing.

Cask-conditioned beer. An unfiltered beer that is put in a cask before it is completely ready to serve. The yeast still in the beer continues to work and ideally brings the beer to perfection at the point of sale, resulting in a beautifully fresh beer that has a "soft" natural carbonation and beautiful array of aromas. This is a classic British-style "real ale." The flip side to achieving this supreme freshness is that as the beer is poured, air replaces the beer in the cask, and the beer will become sour within five days. Bars should sell the cask out before then or remove it from sale. If you are served sour cask-conditioned beer, send it back. Better yet, ask politely for a taste before ordering. Cask-conditioned beer is generally served at cellar temperature (55–60°F) and is lightly carbonated. Cask-conditioned beers are almost always ales, but some American brewers are experimenting with cask-conditioned lagers.

Cold-filtering. The practice of passing finished beer through progressively finer filters (usually cellulose or ceramic) to strip out microorganisms that can spoil the beer when it is stored. Brewers like Coors and Miller, and also some smaller brewers, use cold-filtering as an alternative to pasteurization (see below). Some beer geeks complain that this "strip-filtering" robs beers of their more subtle complexities and some of their body.

Contract brewer. A brewer who hires an existing brewery to brew beer on contract. Contract brewers range from those who simply have a different label put on one of the brewery's existing brands to those who maintain a separate on-site staff to actually brew the beer at the brewery. Some brewers and beer geeks feel contract-brewed beer is inherently inferior. This is strictly a moral and business issue; some of the best beers on the market are contract-brewed.

Craft brewer. The new term for microbrewer. Craft brewer, like microbrewer before it, is really a code word for any brewer producing beers other than mainstream American lagers like Budweiser and Miller Lite. (See "A word about . . . Micros, Brewpubs, and Craft Brewers" on page 18.)

Decoction. The type of mashing often used by lager brewers to wring the full character from the malt. In a decoction mash, a portion of the hot mash is taken to another vessel, brought to boiling, and returned to the mash, thus raising the temperature. See also *infusion*.

Dry-hopping. Adding hops to the beer in postfermentation stages, often in porous bags to allow easy removal. This results in a greater hop aroma in the finished beer. A few brewers put a small bag of hop cones in each cask of their cask-conditioned beers, resulting in a particularly intense hop aroma in a glass of the draft beer.

ESB. Extra special bitter, an ale style with a rich malt character and full body, perhaps some butter or butterscotch aromas, and an understated hop bitterness. An ESB is noticeably bitter only in comparison to a mild ale, a style not often found in America.

Esters. Aroma compounds produced by fermentation that gives some ales lightly fruity aromas: banana, pear, and grapefruit, among others. The aromas produced are tightly linked to the yeast strain used. Ester-based aromas should not be confused with the less subtle fruit aromas of a beer to which fruit or fruit essences have been added.

Extract. More specifically, malt extract. Malt extract is kind of like concentrated wort (see below). Malt is mashed and the resulting sweet, unhopped wort is reduced to a syrup, which is packaged and sold to brewers. In extract brewing, the extract is mixed with water and boiled. Specialty grains (such as black patent or chocolate malts, wheat, roasted barley) and hops can be added for flavor notes and nuances. It is actually more expensive to brew with extract, but you need less equipment, which can be crucial in cramped brewing areas, and less training, which makes it a lot easier. But the quality of the beer may suffer. Some people claim to be able to pick out an extract brew blindfolded. I've had extract brews that had a common taste—a kind of thin, vegetal sharpness—but I used to have excellent extract brews at the Samuel Adams Brew House when it was open in Philadelphia. My advice is to try it yourself.

Fermentation. The miracle of yeast; the heart of making beer. Fermentation is the process in which yeast turns sugar and water into alcohol, heat, carbon dioxide, esters, and traces of other compounds.

Final gravity. See *gravity*.

Firkin. A cask or keg holding 9 gallons of beer, specially plumbed for gravity or handpump dispense.

Geekerie. The collective of beer geeks, particularly the beer-oriented, beer-fascinated, beer-above-all geeks. They sometime can fall victim to group thinking and a herd mentality, but they are generally good people, if a bit hopheaded and malt-maniacal. If you're not a member of the geekerie, you might want to consider getting to know them: They usually know where all the best bars and beer stores are in their town, and they're more than happy to share the knowledge and even go along with you to share the fun. All you have to do is ask. See the Beerwebs listing for links to the better beer pages, a good way to hook up with them.

Gravity. The specific gravity of wort (original gravity) or finished beer (terminal gravity). The ratio of dissolved sugars to water determines the gravity of the wort. If there are more dissolved sugars, the original gravity and the potential alcohol are higher. The sugar that is converted to alcohol by the yeast lowers the terminal gravity and makes the beer drier, just like wine. A brewer can determine the alcohol content of a beer by mathematical comparison of its original gravity and terminal gravity.

Great American Beer Festival (GABF). Since 1982, America's breweries have been invited each year to bring their best beer to the GABF in Denver to showcase what America can brew. Since 1987, the GABF has awarded medals for various styles of beer; fifty-five styles were judged in 2001, three medals for each style. To ensure impartiality, the beers are tasted blind, their identities hidden from the judges. GABF medals are the most prestigious awards in American brewing because of the festival's longevity and reputation for fairness.

Growler. A jug or bottle used to take home draft beer. These are usually either simple half-gallon glass jugs with screwtops or more elaborate molded glass containers with swingtop seals. I have traced the origin of the term *growler* back to a cheap, four-wheeled horse cab in use in Victorian London. These cabs would travel a circuit of pubs in the evenings, and riding from pub to pub was known as "working the growler." To bring a pail of beer home to have with dinner was to anticipate the night's work of drinking and became known as "rushing the growler." When the growler cabs disappeared from the scene, we were left with only the phrase, and "rushing the growler" was assumed to mean hurrying home with the bucket. When Ed Otto revived the practice by selling jugs of Otto Brothers beer at his Jackson Hole brewery in the mid-1980s, he called them growlers. Now you know where the term really came from.

Guest taps/guest beers. Beers made by other brewers that are offered at brewpubs.

Handpump. A hand-powered pump for dispensing beer from a keg. Either a handpump or a gravity tap is always used for dispensing cask-conditioned beer; however, the presence of a handpump does not guarantee that the beer being dispensed is cask-conditioned.

Hectoliter. A hectoliter (hcl) is 100 liters, a metric measure of volume used by some brewers with European- or Canadian-manufactured brewing systems. One hectoliter is approximately 0.85 barrels; 27 hectoliters is just about exactly 23 barrels. There are also "half-hec" kegs that hold 50 liters, or about 13.3 gallons, compared to the 15.5 gallons in a half keg.

Homebrewing. Making honest-to-goodness beer at home for personal consumption. Homebrewing is where many American craft brewers got their start.

Hops. The spice of beer. Hop plants (*Humulus lupulus*) are vines whose flowers have a remarkable effect on beer. The flowers' resins and oils add bitterness and a variety of aromas (spicy, piney, citrus, and others) to the finished beer. Beer without hops would be more like a fizzy, sweet, "alco-soda."

IBU. International bittering unit, a measure of a beer's bitterness. Humans can first perceive bitterness at levels between 8 and 12 IBU. Budweiser has 11.5 IBU, Heineken 18, Sierra Nevada Pale Ale 32, Pilsner Urquell 43, and a monster like Sierra Nevada Bigfoot clocks in at 98 IBU. Equivalent amounts of bitterness will seem greater in a lighter-bodied beer, whereas a heavier, maltier beer like Bigfoot needs lots of bitterness to be perceived as balanced.

Infusion. The mashing method generally used by ale brewers. Infusion entails heating the mash in a single vessel until the starches have been converted to sugar. There is single infusion, in which the crushed malt (grist) is mixed with hot water and steeped without further heating, and step infusion, in which the mash is held for short periods at rising temperature points. Infusion mashing is simpler than decoction mashing and works well with the right types of malt. See also *decoction*.

IPA. India pale ale, a British ale style that has been almost completely co-opted by American brewers, characterized in this country by intense hop bitterness, accompanied in better examples of the style by a full-malt body. The name derives from the style's origin as a beer brewed for export to British beer drinkers in India. The beer was strong and heavily laced with hops—a natural preservative—to better endure the long sea voyage. Some British brewers claim that the beer was brewed that way in order to be diluted upon arrival in India, a kind of "beer concentrate" that saved on shipping costs.

Kräusening. The practice of carbonating beer by a second fermentation. After the main fermentation has taken place and its vigorous blowoff of carbon dioxide has been allowed to escape, a small amount of fresh wort is added to the tank. A second fermentation takes place, and the carbon dioxide is captured in solution. General opinion is that there is little sensory difference between kräusened beer and beer carbonated by injection, but some brewers hold that this more traditional method produces a "softer" beer.

Lager. The generic term for all cold-fermented beers. Lager has also been appropriated as a name for the lightly hopped pilsners that have become the world's most popular beers, such as Budweiser, Castle, Brahma, Heineken, and Asahi. Many people speak of pilsners and lagers as if they are two different styles of beer, which is incorrect. All pilsners are lagers, but not all lagers are pilsners. Some are bocks, hellesbiers, and Märzens.

Malt. Generally this refers to malted barley, although other grains can be malted and used in brewing. Barley is wetted and allowed to sprout, which causes the hard, stable starches in the grain to convert to soluble starches (and small amounts of sugars). The grains, now called malt, are kiln-dried to kill the sprouts and conserve the starches. Malt is responsible for the color of beer. The kilned malt can be roasted, which will darken its color and intensify its flavors like a French roast coffee.

Mash. A mixture of cracked grains of malt and water that has been heated. Heating causes starches in the malt to convert to sugars, which will be consumed by the yeast in fermentation. The length of time the mash is heated, temperatures, and techniques used are crucial to the character of the finished beer. Two mashing techniques are infusion and decoction.

Megabrewer. A mainstream brewer, generally producing 5 million or more barrels of American-style pilsner beer annually. Anheuser-Busch, Miller, and Coors are the best-known megabrewers.

Microbrewer. A somewhat dated term, originally defined as a brewer producing less than fifteen thousand barrels of beer in a year. Microbrewer, like craft brewer, is generally applied to any brewer producing beers other than mainstream American lagers. (See "A word about . . . Micros, Brewpubs, and Craft Brewers" on page 18.)

Original gravity. See *gravity*.

Pasteurization. A process named for its inventor, Louis Pasteur, the famed French microbiologist. Pasteurization involves heating beer to kill the microorganisms in it. This keeps beer fresh longer, but unfortunately it also changes the flavor, because the beer is essentially cooked. "Flash pasteurization" sends fresh beer through a heated pipe where most of the microorganisms are killed; here the beer is only hot for a few seconds, as opposed to the twenty to thirty minutes of regular "tunnel" pasteurization. See also *cold-filtering*.

Pilsner. The Beer That Conquered the World. Developed in 1842 in Pilsen (now Plzen, in the Czech Republic), it is a hoppy pale lager that quickly became known as *pilsner* or *pilsener*, a German word meaning simply "from Pilsen." Pilsner rapidly became the most popular beer in the world and now accounts for over 80 percent of all beer consumed worldwide. A less hoppy, more delicate version of pilsner, called budweiser, was developed in the Czech town of Budejovice, formerly known as Budweis. Anheuser-Busch's Budweiser, the world's best-selling beer, is quite a different animal.

Pitching. The technical term for adding yeast to wort.

Prohibition. The period from 1920 to 1933, when the sale, manufacture, or transportation of alcoholic beverages was illegal in the United States, thanks to the Eighteenth Amendment and the Volstead Act. Prohibition had a disastrous effect on American brewing and brought about a huge growth in organized crime and government corruption. Repeal of Prohibition came with the ratification of the Twenty-first Amendment in December 1933. Beer drinkers, however, had gotten an eight-month head start when the Volstead Act, the enforcement legislation of Prohibition, was amended to allow sales of 3.2 percent ABW beer. The amendment took effect at midnight, April 7. According to Will Anderson's *From Beer to Eternity*, over 1 million barrels of beer were consumed on April 7—2,323,000 six-packs each hour.

Quaffability. Quaff means to drink large quantities. With craft brews, this usually means a pint or more. A pale ale generally is quaffable; a doublebock generally is not. A good, truly quaffable doublebock would be dangerous, given the style's usual alcohol levels!

Real ale. See *cask-conditioned beer* and *bottle-conditioned beer*.

Real Ale Festival (RAF). An annual Chicago beer festival that celebrates "real ale." Medals are awarded to the best bottle- and cask-conditioned beers in a variety of styles. The medals from the RAF are quite prestigious and are of particular significance to brewers.

Regional brewery. Somewhere between a micro- and a megabrewer. Annual production by regional breweries ranges from 35,000 to 2 million barrels. They generally brew mainstream American lagers. However, some microbrewers—Boston Beer Company, New Belgium, and Sierra Nevada, for instance—have climbed to this production level, and some regional brewers, like Anchor, Matt's, and August Schell, have reinvented themselves and now produce craft-brewed beer. (See "A word about . . . . Micros, Brewpubs, and Craft Brewers" on page 18.)

Reinheitsgebot. The German beer purity law, which has its roots in a 1516 Bavarian statute limiting the ingredients in beer to barley malt, hops, and water. The law evolved into an inch-thick book and was the cornerstone of high-quality German brewing. It was deemed anticompetitive by the European Community courts and overturned in 1988. Most German brewers, however, continue to brew by its standards; tradition and the demands of their customers ensure it.

Ringwood. The house yeast of Peter Austin and Pugsley System breweries. A very particular yeast that requires an open fermenter, it is mostly found in the northeastern United States. Some well-known examples of Ringwood-brewed beers are Geary's, Shipyard, and Magic Hat. Ringwood beers are often easily identifiable by a certain nuttiness to their flavor. A brewer who isn't careful will find that Ringwood has created an undesirably high level of diacetyl, a compound that gives a beer a buttery or butterscotch aroma. Note that smaller amounts of diacetyl are perfectly normal and desirable in some types of beer.

Swill. A derogatory term used by beer geeks for American mainstream beers. The beers do not really deserve the name, since they are made with pure ingredients under conditions of quality control and sanitation that some micros only wish they could achieve.

Tap New York Beer Festival (TAP NY). This annual festival, held every spring, seems to have settled in at the Hunter Mountain ski resort. Originally a Hudson Valley festival, it has grown to encompass the whole state. Eight prizes are awarded in two categories: Hudson Valley beers and statewide beers. The F. X. Matt Cup is awarded to the brewery judged best in the state; the Matthew Vassar Cup goes to the best brewery in the Hudson Valley. Gold, silver, and bronze medals are awarded to the three top beers in each category. All judging is blind, and the cups are based on average point totals across the range of beers a brewery brings to the festival. It's a great time, and I intend to make it an annual event on my schedule.

Terminal gravity. See *gravity.*

Three-tier system. A holdover from before Prohibition, the three-tier system requires brewers, wholesalers, and retailers to be separate entities. The system was put in place to curtail financial abuses that were common when the three were mingled. Owning both wholesale and retail outlets gave unscrupulous brewers the power to rake off huge amounts of money, which all too often was used to finance political graft and police corruption. The three-tier system keeps the wholesaler insulated from pressure from the brewer and puts a layer of separation between brewer and retailer. Recent court rulings have put the future of the regulated three-tier system in serious doubt, however, which could spell paradise or disaster for beer drinkers.

Wort. The prebeer grain broth of sugars, proteins, hops, oils, alpha acids, and whatever else was added or developed during the mashing process. Once the yeast has been pitched and starts its jolly work, wort becomes beer.

Yeast. A miraculous fungus that, among other things, converts sugar into alcohol and carbon dioxide. The particular yeast strain used in brewing beer greatly influences the aroma and flavor of the beer. An Anheuser-Busch brewmaster recently told me that the yeast strain used there is the major factor in the flavor and aroma of Budweiser. Yeast is the sole source of the clovey, banana-rama aroma and the taste of Bavarian-style wheat beers. The original Reinheitsgebot of 1516 made no mention of yeast. It hadn't been discovered yet. Early brewing depended on a variety of sources for yeast: adding a starter from the previous batch of beer; exposing the wort to the wild yeasts carried on the open air (a method still used for Belgian lambic beers); always using the same vats for fermentation (yeast would cling to cracks and pores in the wood); or using a "magic stick" (which had the dormant yeast from the previous batch dried on its surface) to stir the beer. British brewers called the turbulent, billowing foam on fermenting beer goddesgood—"God is good"—because the foam meant that the predictable magic of the yeast was making beer. And beer, as Ben Franklin said, is proof that God loves us and wants us to be happy. Amen.

INDEX

Also by Lew Bryson

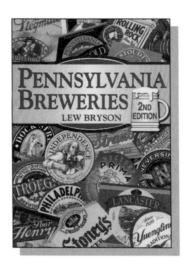

PENNSYLVANIA BREWERIES
2D EDITION

A guide to 53 breweries and brewpubs
in the Keystone state.

$16.95 • PB • 256 pages • 52 logos • 43 maps

WWW.STACKPOLEBOOKS.COM
1-800-732-3669